SRI GARIB DAS
Haryana's Saint of Humanity

SRI GARIB DAS

Haryana's Saint of Humanity

K.C. GUPTA

ADITYA PRAKASHAN
NEW DELHI

First published: August, 1976
First reprint: March, 2004

ISBN 81-7742-057-7

Published by P.K. Goel for Aditya Prakashan, F-14/65, Model Town II, Delhi – 110 009 and printed at D.K. Fine Arts Press (Pvt.) Ltd., A-6, Nimri Community Centre, Ashok Vihar Phase IV, Delhi – 110 052.

CONTENTS

INTRODUCTION

The Bhakti movement gave us a treasure house of literature. The medieval saints have made an outstanding contribution to the provincial literatures of the period. There was a remarkable development of all the provincial languages under this new inspiration. From Sheikh Farid and Namadeva down to the eighteenth century, a literary tradition was developed whose aim was the moral and spiritual regeneration of our country. To this literary tradition belonged Garib Das of Rohtak.

About fifty years ago, medieval saints were dismissed by Indian pundits as illiterate poets, whose writings were not worth studying from the point of view of literature. But the translation of Kabir's poems by Tagore and the critical study of the life and writings of medieval saints by Christian missionary scholars, suddenly aroused a deep academic interest in the writings of these saint poets. Punjabi and Hindi also acquired a very respectable status. The language and thoughts of all the great saints began to be studied minutely.

My father was a great devotee of Sant Garib Das of Rohtak. He took me a number of times to the Satsang of Garib Dasi sect where the Granth of Garib Das was read loudly. It was only when I had passed my M.A. examination in Punjabi in 1951 that my literary interest in the writings of Garib Das was aroused. I started collecting and studying all his writings, some of which were available in Gurmukhi script and others in Devnagri script. Finding that there was a great difference in the text of printed versions, I tried to search some original manuscripts. I found some and even acquired one or two manuscripts but the major part of the oldest manuscripts was in the custody of Garib Dasi sadhus. They refused even to show the manuscripts for detailed studies. A glance at some of the older manuscripts shows that the compilers have taken considerable liberty in changing the forms of the original words from Punjabi or Hariyanvi to Sanskritised Hindi. I, however, collected all the printed versions and found that the older the printed version the clearer the text.

As Hindi was declared our national language and Punjabi the official language of the Punjab, research work in these languages found a great deal of encouragement. A number of excellent books appeared on the Nirgun School of Poetry and particularly on Kabir. As Garib Das was closely associated with Kabir Panth and acknowledged Kabir as his Guru, I felt inspired to prepare a thesis on Garib Das on the lines on which work had been done on Kabir and his near contemporaries.

As soon as I started working on this thesis, I realized that Garib Das was an outstanding builder of the thought and culture of Hariyana, which has formed for centuries an important region of Eastern Punjab. He was the son of this soil, the product of this culture, who added much to the thought and literature of this region. According to the inscription of *Sarbal* Hariyana has been called "the heaven on earth" (*Desosti Hariayanakhyah prithvijana svargasannibhah*)[1]. Hariyana is also known as Bangar. The word means highland areas compared to the lowland area around Jamuna. Compared to the lowland area it was dry and forested.

Garib Das thus belonged to a region which has an eventful history and past but the permanent features of which are, the hardworking village community, the Hindu traditions, and pious people whose simple contented life has not changed for centuries. "There will be found in every house a bed for each grown up person, a corn-mill (*Chakki*), the huge pestle and mortar of wood (*Ukhal and musal*), a spinning wheel (*Charkhi*); along the wall are arranged large receptacles for grain, made of mud and called *Kothi*. A number of cooking vessels (which are of brass if in a Hindu house and of tin if in Musalman's) are scattered about the room, the commonest of which are the tray called *thali, parat, tambiya* and *tastari*, cooking pots (*bhartiya* and *patili*), the *handi* for preparing *rabri* and the *kadhaoni* for boiling milk; there will also be seen *lotahs* and

1. Janasahitya, Hariyana Lokamanas, November, 1965, p. 13

cups (*Katorah*) and the iron plate for cooking cakes (*tawa*) will be on the hearth (*Chulah*); Milk is made into curd in *Bharola* and into ghee in *balma* or *chum*."[2] Where nothing has lasted for centuries this village community with its folk-songs and folk-culture has lasted in this traditional form through all the upheavels of history. It is in such a village community that Garib Das was born and brought up. It is in such a village community that his moral and spiritual powers were fully developed. It is to such village communities that he preached his revolutionary ideas and sang his songs.

II

While the medieval saints contributed much to the social reconstruction and spiritual development of our country, they left practically no evidence of the historical role they played, nor were their contemporaries wise enough to record important events of their lives. The few historical events known about them took the form of legends. Thus to reconstruct the life stories of these saints is a very difficult task. I had to encounter the same difficulty in reconstructing the events of Garib Das' life. Fortunately, we have a little contemporary evidence from the writings of Garib Das' son, Jait Ram, who has devoted a page or two to the life of his father.

Jait Ram's historical poem about his father were helpful in clearing the confusion about Garib Das' dates of birth and death, created by later writers. He also throws considerable light on the parentage and the progeny of Garib Das. He describes briefly the character and spiritual influence of the saint.

Besides this important work of Jait Ram, no other contemporary evidence is found. Some brief historical references are found in Garib Das' own writings. We find conclusive evidence that he acknowledged Kabir as his Guru. This fact is supported by his son Jait Ram also Although Garib Das pays homage to many saints and praises them all equally, he considers Kabir the greatest and his main source of inspiration.

---

2. The Gazetteer of Rohtak District 1883-4, p. 48

This raised the question of Garib Das' relation to Kabir and Kabirpanth. The disciples of Garib Das have built a legend around the spiritual meeting between Garib Das and Kabir. This has probably been done with the clear intention of building an independent school of thought. Garib Dasis wanted to connect the saint with Kabir but they did not wish to identify themselves with Kabirpanthis. So in order to dissociate themselves from all branches of Kabirpanthis, they built a legend that the spiritual wisdom of Kabir was given to Garib Das by Kabir himself on a spiritual plane through an astral body.

But when we study the writings of Garib Das, there is no doubt left that he had studied the writings of Kabir and he tried to imitate not only the life and ideals of Kabir, but also the poetry of Kabir. Whatever may have happened on the spiritual plane, it is quite clear on the earthly plane that Garib Das imbibed and studied the writings of Kabir *quite early in life*.

We also learn from near contemporary works that the influence of Dadupanthi followers of Kabir was considerable in Hariyana and Rajasthan. Garib Das' father was also under their influence. The very scribe who wrote down the poems of Garib Das was a Dadupanthi. So we are inclined to conclude that Garib Das first came into contact with the thoughts and writings of Dadupanthi Saints. Subsequently he appears to have studied the *Adi Grantha* also.

Not much is known about the life of Garib Das. All that I have been able to get are a few anecdotes and popular tales about the life of the saint. The ordinary tales have been so badly mixed up with legends and made supernatural events that it has been quite a difficult task to separate historical events from legendry tales built up later. The only biographical notes available on the saint's life are:

(1) *Garib Acharya Ji Maharaj ka Sanskhep Jivan Charitra* by Swami Bhagat Ram.

(2) Preface of *Granth Sahib* edited by Swami Ajra Nand, 1924.

(3) *Granth Sahib arthat Sh. Jait Ram Ji Ki Bani* edited by Dulhari Dass Ji, Printed in 1955.

(4) *Garib Das Ji Ki Bani*, Belvedere Printing Works, Allahabad.

(5) *Granth Sahib*, 2nd Edition edited by Swami Chetan Das Ji, 1964.

Out of this very limited material I have reconstructed the life of the Saint into a short historical biography, which may be called the first attempt of this type. I have even recorded some of the legends in the hope that in times to come their true significance would be known.

Very little material is available on the travels of Garib Das and his relations with the rulers. Only one concrete evidence is available that he visited Mathura. Other unrecorded evidence is available on the basis of the shrines commemorating the visit of the Saint to these places. We find these shrines in Saharanpur and Paonta (Himachal Pradesh). Garib Das did not believe in going to places of pilgrimage for salvation. He speaks against them throughout his writings. He probably went to these places either on the invitation of some devotees or to keep away from political upheavals and turmoils that were taking place at Delhi which was only thirty miles from his native place.

Another unsolved historical problem of Garib Das' life is: when and where did he meet the Emperor Mohammed Shah? What was the outcome of this meeting? What trespassed between the two? Some of his biographers are not even sure which Emperor he met. If at all Garib Das met any Emperor, it was Mohammed Shah who was genial and liberal enough to do such a thing as to invite a Hindu saint. But too many legends and unbelievable stories have been added to the outcome of the meeting. It is quite possible that Garib Das asked the Emperor to be compassionate and kind to all communities, but it is hardly believable that Garib Das was so unrealistic as to suggest that if the Emperor became a vegetarian, all the ills of his state would be solved. It is true that Garib Das preached *Ahimsa* (non-violence) in a general way, but it is highly improbable that he could have suggested that the Emperor could conquer many countries through *Ahimsa.* The only credible element in the story is that Garib Das' saintliness impressed the Emperor but created a good deal of jealousy and ill-will against him in the minds of fanatic courtiers.

We, however, find that Garib Das was a true saint in the sense that he never tried to win favour of kings and rulers. He never sought the patronage of the court. Not only did he keep away from the court, but he completely kept aloof from all the great upheavals of his time. During his life time many invasions and upheavals took place. One king after another was toppled. But we do not find a single reference to events to which he was almost an eye-witness. The Saint strictly confined himself to religious activities. He did not pay any attention to the political ills of his country.

III

Was Garib Das a Hindu or did he start a sect which could claim that it was neither Hindu nor Muslim? This is the question that arises about all Saints who wrote and thought like Kabir.

There are innumerable references in Garib Das' Granth which say that he has disassociated himself from the sectarian practices of both Hindus and Muslims. Like Kabir and Guru Nanak, he tries to interpret Hindu and Muslim beliefs and practices in the light of his own experience. He rejects many basic Hindu beliefs such as the authorities of the *Vedas*, the four-fold order of society, and the four stages of life. He rejects Brahmanism and all that goes with it. He rejects some of the basic ceremonies of Hinduism like the wearing of the sacred thread and ceremonies connected with it.

But inspite of his neutral stand in the Hindu-Muslim conflict, we find that Garib Das accepts many traditions of Hinduism. He respects the Hindu *Avataras* with the same reverence as the average Hindu show for them. He accepts the morals and ideals of Hindu culture as preached through the stories of the *Ramayana* and the *Mahabharata*. Hindu heroes and heroines of the classical age are a model which he presents for imitation and emulation. The Hindu element in his thought and the terminology which he uses to express himself is so dominant that he is much more of a pious Hindu in his outlook than saints like Kabir or Ravidas. Our general conclusion is that Garib Das did not go out of the Hindu fold to the same extent as Buddhism and Sikhism did.

His followers have, however, been in a dilemma whether they should abide by Hindu ceremonies and institutions or build an independent church of their own. They have imitated Sikhism in adopting ceremonial institutions while they have imitated Hinduism in re-introducing the *Sanyasa* system and the *Mahant* order. I have no hesitation in saying that they have imitated in every respect the Nirmala Sikh sect, which was permitted to put on ochre robes to get access to the Sanskrit institutions of Benaras.

Thus we can conclude that Garib Dasis are a Kabirpanthi sect which has tried to maintain its identity and independence from other Kabirpanthi sects within the Hindu fold. The question arises: how do Garib Dasis try to maintain this position? What are the distinctive features of this sect? From our study these can be summed up as follows:

Belief in the Supreme Being. Garib Das was a staunch monist. He believed in the one Supreme God whom people called by different names. Ram and Rahim, Hari and Allah were terms applied to the same God. He is the God who neither favours Hindus nor Muslims but judges all men by their deeds. Garib Das did not believe in any other gods and goddesses. In fact he strongly denounced the worship of other gods and goddesses.

The Guru. In the life and work of Garib Das, the *Guru* takes the same place as is taken by the *Avataras* in other Hindu sects. It stands for Kabir alone in the life of Garib Das. The Garib Dasis, however, look upon Garib Das as the real *Avatara* of Kabir and they consider him to be the true Guru along with Kabir. The concept of the Guru among the Garib Dasis is almost the same as that amongst the Sikhs. The spirit of the Guru is identified with the spirit of God and is considered to be eternal. Now it is also identified with the *Bani* (Granth) of Garib Das and the Garib Dasis have started looking upon Garib Das' Granth as an embodiment of his spirit.

Worship. As the majority of the Hindu temples have idols and Garib Dasis are strongly opposed to all types of idol worship, the mode of worship of Garib Dasis has drifted away from the common Hindu mode of worship. As the Garib Dasis have given up most of the Hindu ceremonies connected with birth, wearing of sacred thread, marriage and death, their mode of worship has to be different. As a matter of fact, for over a century and a half the Garib Dasis did not have any institutions of their own except a few *mandirs* and a few copies of their Granth. The compilation of Garib Das' Granth and institution of ceremonies on the pattern of Sikh ceremonies and worship took place nearly a century and a half after Garib Das' death. In between, the followers must have adopted mainly Hindu ceremonies. This lack of institutional basis of the Garib Dasi Panth has perhaps been the one main cause of their weak influence. If they had strong, well-marked religious institutions from the time of Garib Das, Garib Dasi Panth might have been on a firmer footing. At a later stage a new idea was introduced according to which the Sri Mahant, the head of the Garib Dasi mission, should always be a celibate. Apart from being in contradiction to the fundamental tenets of Garib Das' creed, this has introduced the cult of Sadhus, who call themselves Swamis and remain unmarried. While some of the Sadhus are active missionaries and are doing good work for keeping Garib Das' creed alive, the Garib Dasi Panth is developing into a creed of Sadhus, which perhaps the founder of this faith never desired. These Sadhus are, however, to be given the credit for giving a concrete shape and form to the mode of worship and prayer of the creed, which has preserved it from relapsing into outmoded traditional Hindu forms of worship. Garib Das' Granth has now become the centre of worship of this sect. The pictures of Garib Das and other saints are respected but they are not used for worship. All prayer, and all congregations and ceremonies are held in the presence of the Granth Sahib of Garib Das. Even the readings, recitations, continuous non-stop readings (*akhanda patha*) are done exactly in the same way as the Sikhs do it.

Sacraments and formal prayers. Garib Dasis do not have any set prayers as the Sikhs or Muslims have. They do not have any morning or evening prayers corresponding to the Japji and Rahiras of the Sikhs but they have some compositions of Garib Das which are read as Arati. The *kadah prasad* and the congregational prayer has also been organised in the last few decades in imitation of the Sikhs. Some Hindu families who owe only partial loyalty to the Garib Dasi sect perform all the Samskaras of the Brahmincal order, but arrange the reading of the Granth of Garib Das in addition to it. There are a few staunch followers of Garib Das who follow the sacraments organised by Garib Dasi Sadhus.

Code of Conduct. Garib Das' religious beliefs stood for moral purity of man. Although Garib Das did not give any well formulated code of conduct, his moral influence on his followers and subsequent generations was such that they have developed a pattern of moral behaviour and formulated a code of conduct of their own. Their code of conduct can be summed up in the following principles:

1. Garib Dasis must discard all caste distinctions. All men and women are equal before God. Untouchability and casteism were completely abolished. A man of the lowest caste should be treated as equal.

2. Non-injury, *Ahimsa,* and non-killing of all animals for the sake of eating them is a very important tenet of the Garib Dasi Panth.

3. There should be no image-worship or idolatory. With complete faith in One God, man should seek the favours and the grace of God only.

4. Truthfulness, contentment, purity of mind and freedom from all hypocricy anc shams should be the practiced.

5. Fasts and going to places of pilgrimage are discouraged.
6. All superstitions are to be given up.
7. Simplicity in social life and customs is encouraged.

Despite all these liberal ideas, the religious beliefs of Garib Dasis also suffered a set-back in the face of orthodox and fanatic movements. It could never be a dominant religious movement either in Hariyana or in the Punjab, but it has existed side by side with Nath Panthis, Shaivas, Vaishnavas and Sufis. It has had its own limited sphere of influence.

IV

Garib Das did not aim at founding a new religion. He frankly admits that he is only a revivalist of the Nirguna movement upheld by Jaideva, Namdeva, Kabir, Nank, Sheikh Farid, Ramdas, Pipa and others. Out of these the influence of Kabir and Guru Nank is predominant. We have, therefore, devoted two chapters in connection with these influences. The influence of Kabir on Garib Das is by far the greatest. This is acknowledged by Garib Das and is further revealed by a closer study of Garib Das' poetry, as compared with that of Kabir's poetry.

During the time of Garib Das, Kabir Panth was divided into a number of branches, each differentiating from the other for some peculiarity. Over two centuries had elapsed since Kabir died. During these two centuries Kabirism spread under different leaders in Uttar Pradesh, Madhya Pradesh, Rajasthan and the Punjab. It must have taken different sectarian forms under different linguistic and cultural influences. Garib Das did not pay much attention to the various successors of Kabir in different provinces, though he mentions a few like Dadu and Kamal. He tried to capture the original spirit of Kabir's ideals. Out of the successors of Kabir he shows greater admiration for Dadu and Kamal than for the Madhya Pradesh branch of Kabir's followers that developed under Dharamdas. It is quite possible and also natural that Garib Das came under the influeuce of Kabir through the followers of Dadu and Kamal whose influence in this region was great. Garib Das appears to have read the writings of Dadu and Kamal.

The influence of Guru Nank, the *Adi Grantha* and Sikhism in general is also conspicuous. Garib Das mentions the name of Guru Nank, but not the name of any other Sikh Guru. Historically Guru Gobind Singh was close to him, as Garib Das was born in the year in which Guru Gobind Singh died. But he does not even mention Guru Gobind's name. Even the name of Guru Nank is mentioned along with other saints like Dadu, Namadeva and Ramanand. Garib Das does not refer to any incident in the life of Guru Nank. He completely ignores mentioning any incident of the Guru's life, though he mentions one or two incidents from the life of all other saints.

However, the influences of the *Adi Grantha* is tremendous. It is quite possible that Garib Das was in search of the most original and oldest writings of Kabir and he came across them in the *Adi Grantha* of the Sikhs. It was not essy to acquire a copy of the *Adi Grantha* in those days and they were available only in Gurmukhi script. As most of the Sikhs of Punjab went to Rohtak and Rajasthan regions when they were so cruelly persecuted that a price was fixed on the head of a Sikh, it is quite possible that some groups of Sikhs moved into the forest regions of Bangar with a few copies of the *Adi Grantha*.

Either the Saint himself studied Gurmukhi script or he had the *Adi Grantha* read to him by some Sikh devotee. We have discussed in detail the linguistic and religious influence of the *Adi Grantha* on Garib Das. When we compare them, there is no doubt left that Garib Das had studied the *Adi Grantha* closely. The influence of Sikhism in general is also quite apparent.

What Garib Das and his followers did not imbibe from Sikhism and the *Adi Grantha* was the criticism of contemporary politics and revolutionary attitude towards oppressors and tyrants The Sikhs fought against tyranny in society and on the battle-field, while Garib Das kept aloof from it. The aloofness which is maintained with regard to the tyranny and oppression of the rulers is also maintained with regard to the revolutionary movement set in motion by Guru Gobind Singh and Banda Bahadur. All those who showed the slightest (open or secret) loyalty towards the Sikh Gurus were arrested and tortured to death. That possibly explains Garib Das' complete silence about Guru Gobind Singh and Banda Bahadur who were very close to his times.

V

The language and poetry of Garib Das has many faces of its beauty and charm. Hariyana, the birth place and area of Garib Das' activities, is within three linguistic regions of Rajasthan, Punjab and Uttar Pradesh. So the language of Garib Das is representative not only of Hariyana, but also of all the neighbouring linguistic regions.

The variety of poetic forms which give expression to the poetic out-pourings of Garib Das is remarkably vast. It shows that he had a complete and wonderful grasp over this art and he was well versed in Indian prosody (*Chhanda Shastra*). His verses are light, musical and have a good amount of lyricism in them. All poems are written in order to be sung. His vast knowledge of Indian prosody is suplemented by his extensive knowledge of *Ragas* (musical modes). He has written his poems and songs in more *Ragas* than Kabir ever used, though he gives importance to those mainly used by Kabir.

His poetic style is lucid and makes his songs appealing to the learned as well as the common man. The moral and spiritual fervour of the poems is very inspiring. His *dohas, jhulnas* and *swayyas* have a special charm of their own. Although Garib Das has written in Punjabi, Western Hindi and Hariyanvi, he is at his best when he writes either in Punjabi or in Hariyanvi.

Poetry for Garib Das is a vehicle for his thoughts, feelings and experiences. When we read his verses we at once come into contact with the man behind the poetry. The man is more important than his art or style. Every verse he has written is a living image of his thoughts and experiences. His poetry tries to lift us higher from the earthly burdens of worldly life.

Garib Das puts his soul and spirit in each verse. There is a message and wisdom in all his swift-moving lines. There is repetition no doubt, but the repetition is only to emphasise the role and importance of spiritual life. He is distinguished from his contemporary poets in the eighteenth century for his superabundance. Perhaps no eighteenth century poet has written so much and with such depth and intensity.

His imagery, similies and metaphors are all homely, natural and are symbolic of the rural atmosphere and culture of Hariyana. The cow, the spinning wheel, the farmer, the shopkeeper are all seen in his poetic imagery and background scenes. His poetry is neither so abstract as to be difficult to understand nor so realistic as folk-poems are.

The linguistic contribution of Garib Das to the literature of Punjab and Hariyana is great. His mind is a rich store of words from Punjabi, Persian, Hindi, Sanskrit and Apahbramsha. When he likes, he can write in pure and chaste Punjabi. And when he likes, he can mix up Punjabi with Hindi, Persian and other dialects.

For the terminology of religious and philosophical ideas, he uses mostly Sanskrit, Prakrit and Apabhramsha words which are used throughout North India. For expression of social, cultural and personal feelings he uses Punjabi and Hariyanvi or Hindi words common to all *Sant Bhasha.* Words of Persian used by him are mainly those which had become part of the common speech or were used by Sufis and Muslim saints to express Islamic religious ideas. Most of these words were used by Punjab's Sufi poets. Punjabi and Hindi literatures were not only coming close to each other but in the Granth of Garib Das, as in *Adi Grantha,* they were wedded together without either of them losing its identity, originality and charm.

Garib Das was gifted with deep and intimate knowledge of each language which he uses in his writings. When he writes Punjabi, he writes it without betraying that he was born and brought up outside proper Punjabi areas. All the nouns, verbs, adjectives, conjunctions and declensions used by him are of pure and modern Punjabi. At times he has tried to enrich Punjabi language with words from Persian and Western Hindi and Hariyanvi. At other times he enriches Hariyanvi and *Sant Bhasha* with Punjabi. The object of the Saint perhaps is not only to synthesise the thoughts but also the languages of different regions. In this direction the contribution of Garib Das is outstanding and surpasses that of all eighteenth century poets.

The search for old copies of Garib Das' poetry and editing them in their original and pure form is an important task which may be taken up by the scholars of the future. The recent attempts to print his works without taking care to preserve the original has led to misrepresentation of his language. Many Hariyanvi and Punjabi words have been changed into Sanskritised modern Hindi, thereby making it difficult for the scholar to study all his works in their original purity.

VI

In the end, I must record my heartfelt thanks to Dr. Surinder Singh Kohli, Professor and Head of the Punjabi Department for his able guidance and supervision over the research and writing of this thesis. But for his keen interest and encouragement the completion of this task might have been difficult. I am also thankful to Dr. Hazari Prasad Dvivedi and Dr. Trilochan Singh for sparing time whenever I wished to consult them and for placing at my disposal their personal libraries for consultation, from which I benefited much.

54/3 Bharat Nagar,
Ludhiana
July, 1976

K.C. GUPTA

CHAPTER I

Origin And Development Of Bhakti Movement

The term Bhakti is derived from the Sanskrit root *bhaj* which, in one of its uses, means "to adore". It, therefore, means adoration and, in its more distinctive use, "loving devotion to God". The term has a long history.

Classical ideas about the modes of Bhakti have been expounded by Narada, Sandaliya, Prahlada and Uddhava. They unanimously describe Bhakti as the spiritual love which is directed only towards God. When a man loves God, he loves all, hates none, and feels fulfilled for ever. This love cannot be exploited for worldly purposes. It cannot be genuine if the lover shows the slightest attachment to the world. There is no room in it for jealousy or hatred because the devotee sees everything as the manifestation of God. Thus Bhakti is both the ideal of spiritual life and the means to its attainment.

In Bhakti, the mind of a devotee practises devotion unflinchingly. He remains undisturbed by the ebb and flow of life and by the sorrows and sufferings of the world. By constant practice, the mind can be made to flow uninterruptedly towards God as oil flows uninterruptedly when it is poured from one jar into another. Intense devotion for the Beloved makes this practice easy and pleasant. Such a love for the Beloved can be cultivated only by complete unselfishness, purity, compassion and truthfulness.

Love of a Bhakta is quite different from the sensuous love of worldly people. The love of a Bhakta is purged of all gross elements. He dedicates his body, mind and soul to the understanding and realization of God.

The cult of Bhakti is not a creed confined to some privileged people. It is open to people of all castes and nationalities. Even the lowliest person can attain the highest realization through devotion. Throughout Indian history, the most prominent Bhaktas have been from low caste society. By their devotion and spiritual achievements they acquired historic importance.

We give below some of the outstanding definitions and interpretations of Bhakti given by our ancient sages and scholars.

"Bhakti", says the author of *Vivekachudamani*, "is continuous meditation on one's own true form, others hold that it is the meditation on truth of one's own self."[1] Says the *Bhagvadgita* "By merely hearing about the qualities of Mine, the mind flows constantly towards Me, who am the repository of all good; this unbroken flow of mind, just like the current of Ganges emptying into the bay without a stop, is a mark of Bhakti Yoga beyond the Gunas: it is unconditioned and unthwarted love for the Supreme Person."[2] Madhvacharya defines Bhakti as "Firm love of God more than for anything else, with full consciousness of His glory and magnitude."[3]

It is from this Bhakti alone results Release. The supreme love following in the wake of previous knowledge and lasting for ever is designated as Bhakti. Bhakti should not be confused with mere emotional excitement or eroticism, as is often done; nor with fanaticism which sometime passes for religiosity and leads to all kinds of sectarian quarrels and bloodshed. Again, it is not mere credulousness or blind faith in whatever some priests may claim, or books only labelled as Shastras may be interpreted to say.

The pure love of a Bhakta is quite different from the sensuous love of the worldly people. It is always free from selfishness and egoism. It has no desire or motive behind it. It is single-minded love for the Supreme Beloved and has no thought of any other. A devotee completely forgets himself and merges his mind and soul in the Spiritual Being of the Beloved. It is a love that is completely resigned to the Will of the Beloved and dedicated to His cause.

There are different levels of Bhakti. The mental approach at the preparatory stage is different from the approach at the

1. *Vivekachaudamani*, p. 32.
2. *Bhagvadgita* III. 29. 11, 12.
3. Madhvacharya, *Mahabharata Paryanirnaya*, 1. 86.

higher stages. Summing up Sri Aurobindo's views on the subject, M.P. Pandit points out that "Bhakti may be *arta* Bhakti, which appeals for help in the hour of difficulty or it may be a deep thirst for knowledge. Whatever the nature of initial Bhakti, it should be taken as a starting point and an effort should be made to gradually cleanse its contents, purge it of its grosser motives, and turn it more and more into purer channels leading towards selfless love. In this, the seeker is helped by the very nature of Bhakti which, whatever its original motives, apparent or real, comes into its own as it grows in his being and lands him repeatedly on high points of utter gratitude, pure love and clean aspiration, all of which are doors of entry into the real Way of Love."[4]

The first stage of Bhakti is that of adoration. Usually this takes the form of some kind of external worship of the adored. The devotee tends to express his feelings of submission and reverence through physical means which is natural to a mind that normally dwells in the world of the physical senses. This worship has indeed its preparatory value. But to be truly effective in opening a way of contact and communication with the Divine who is worshipped, this outer mode of attendance must correspond to an inner feeling, a glad movement of surrender, a dependence felt within. The outer should be a means of expression, a support for the growth of an inner adoration. The inner gives life to the outer.

Swami Vivekananda considers Bhakti to be the easiest and the most natural way to reach the great Divine and in his view its great disadvantage is that, in its lower form, it often times degenerates into hideous fanaticism.[5] The fanatical people in Hinduism or Mohammedanism or Christianity, have always been almost exclusively recruited from these worshippers on the lower plane of Bhakti. The singleness of attachment (*Nishtha*) to a loved object, without which no genuine love can grow, is very often also the cause of denunciation of everything else. All the weak and undeveloped minds in every religion or country have only one way of loving their own ideal—by hating every other ideal. This is why people who are devotedly

4. M.P. Pandit, *Sadhana in Sri Aurobindo's Yoga*, Pp. 56-57.
5. Vivekananda, *Complete Works*, Vol. III, Pp. 32-33.

attached to their own ideal of God and religion, become howling fanatics in their dealings with other faiths.

According to Swami Vivekananda, this kind of instinct is somewhat like the canine instinct of guarding the master's property from intrusion; only the instinct of the dog is better than the reason of man, for the dog never mistakes its master for an enemy, in whatever dress he may come before it. But the same man who is kind, good, honest and loving to people of his own opinion, will not hesitate to do the vilest deeds, when they are directed against persons beyond the pale of his own religious brotherhood.

The Scriptures of Bhakti are very liberal and declare that the path of Divine Love is open to all. The only qualification required of a Bhakta is firm faith in the grace or mercy of God and unstinted devotion and dedication to His Will. Even illiteracy is no bar, nor a previous record of a vicious life. Says the *Bhagvadgita*, "Even a hard-baked sinner, if he comes to have an unswerving love for the Lord, must be regarded as righteous for he has decided aright. He soon becomes righteous and obtains lasting peace. I proclaim it boldly, O Arjuna, that My devotee never perishes, for those who take refuge and abide in Me—women, vaisyas, sudras, nay even those on whom their past deeds have imposed the very worst of births—attain to the highest goal."[6]

Sage Sandilya lays down: "Every one, to the lowest born, is eligible to follow the path of devotion; this is borne out by the long line of devotees; just like those virtues which for God are common to all."[7] Sri Suka salutes the Lord thus: "I bow to the Almighty Lord, by adoring whose devotees people like the Kiratas, Hunas, Andhras, Pulindas, Pulkasas, Abhiras, Kankas, Yavanas, Khasas, as well as those who are sinners, purify themselves."[8]

Untouchable saints and women saints, who have done a tremendous deal of good to the spiritual uplift of the country, bear witness to the catholicity of the path of devotion. More than any other creed or religious path, the Bhakti Movement

6. *Bhagvadgita*, IX, 30, 31 and 32.
7. *Sandilya Sutra*, 37.
8. *Srimad Bhagvata*, 11. 4. 18.

has been the greatest leveller of caste and creed differences. It not only broke the barriers between the high and the low, but also between the Hindus and the Muslims. Bhakti (Love) and Jnana (Knowledge) are not opposed to each other. Bhakti without Jnana may degenerate into fanaticism and superstitious religion. Jnana without Bhakti may not lead a man far beyond the intellect. Three things are necessary for a manbird to fly: the two wings and the tail as the rudder for steering. Jnana (Knowledge) is one wing, Bhakti (Love) is the other, and Yoga is the tail which keeps up the balance.

Sant Garib Das also says:

गरीब ऐसा सतगुरु हम मिल्या सुरत सिन्धु के नाल ।
ग्यान, जोग और भगति सब दीन्हीं नजर निहाल ॥

Garib says: In the depths of meditation, I met the Perfect Master who endowed me with Jnana, Bhakti and Yoga simultaneously and by a single act of grace.

G.G.S. p. 2.

"Sandilya feels the necessity of Yoga for concentration of mind, and cultivation of the intellect for the culture of devotion. The cultivation of the intellect for acquiring certain knowledge of Brahma should be continued till devotion is completely purified. Valid knowledge of Brahma is the end of the intellect. It cannot be brought about by voluntary action. Still, listening to the Scriptures *(sravana)*, reflection *(manana)*, and intellectual conviction *(nididhyasana)* lead to the true knowledge of God. Knowledge is absolutely necessary for the firmness and purity of devotion (*bhakti parisuddhi*). Thus the life of devotion to God need not necessarily be a purely emotional one. Sandaliya upholds the cult of devotion enlightened by reason."[9]

Thus Bhakti is not mere emotional approach to God. It is fundamentally based on knowledge and charitable actions. Bhakti is also a type of Yoga in itself. Its higher practices are a synthesis of love and spiritual union through Yoga.

The Bhakti Movement has come down to us as a distinct tradition which received inspiration from the practical life of

9. *Cultural Heritage of India*, Vol III, p. 150.

sages like Prahlada, Janaka and others. Each sage made a distinct contribution to it during the Hindu period of Indian history. During the Muslim period of Indian history, it received a new type of inspiration from the Sufi Saints and the Bhaktas tried to demolish caste and other differences among Hindus to create a unity. They also met the challenge of the iconoclastic zeal of the Muslims and asked the people to give up idolatory. This gave rise to two distinct Bhakti Movements in Indian history which we call Nirguna and Saguna Bhakti Movements.

II

Forms of Bhakti: Nirguna And Saguna Schools

The higher Bhakti Schools evolved out of lower stages of loving the Supreme and the Infinite through personāl gods and avatar-worship and reached a higher stage of strict monism. The devotees of a personal God sought divine enlightenment through either Vishnu or Siva. The former came to be known as the Vaishnava Bhaktas while the latter came to be known as the Saiva Bhaktas.

Shaivism influenced mostly the Bhakti Schools of the South and to some extent those of Kashmir. In the South, the Saiva Bhakti movement had four Schools, namely, the Das-marga, Satputra-marga, Sahamarga, Sanmarga i.e. the path of the servant, the path of the good son, the path of the friend and the true path. Each of these Schools was founded by an Acarya and each has its own long history.

Vaishnavism found its roots in *Bhagvadgita*, *Mahabharata* and the *Bhagvata*. Sir R.G. Bhandarkar, in his *Vaishnavism, Shaivism and Minor Religious Systems*, has traced the process by which the *Bhagvadgita*, with its worship of Vasudeva Krishna, developed and was modified, other cults and other philosophical conceptions mingling with or influencing it. On the mythological side, the tales of adventures of the boy Krishna with the cowherdesses, in particular Radha, had great influence on the direction of religious movements and he came to be an important object of worship. Later on, Rama came to be exalted and worshipped as God and the whole history of later Bhakti is connected with various forms that the worship of Krishna and Radha, Ram and Sita, took.

On the philosophical side, the most important fact is "the new interpretation of the ancient philosophical texts given by Ramanuja who, in the eleventh century, provided an intellectual foundation for Bhakti, which the monistic philosophy had done so much to undermine. "It was this influence which was most powerful in what has been called Hindu Reformamation, and in the four Churches of Reformation, we have evidence of the new strength and vitality which had been imparted to the spirit of Bhakti. These Churches are known respectively as (1) Sri Sampardaya of Ramanuja, (2) the Brahma Sampardaya of Madhva, (3) Rudra Sampardaya of Vishnuswami and (4) Sanakadi Sampardaya of Nimbaraka. These Churches are based on different theological foundations. The first upheld qualified monism, Vishistadvaita, the second a dualism on the lines of Samkhya-Yoga, the third pure monism, Suddhadavaita, and the fourth is a curious blend of monism, and pluralism. They held the belief in God in the same personal way "[10]

Sir R.G. Bhandarkar has well summarised what is to be said regarding the relations of various Vaishnava Systems to each other. According to him: "The points of contact between Vaishnava Systems are that their spiritual elements are essentially derived from the *Bhagvadgita*, that Vasudeva as the name of the Supreme Being stands in the background of all and that spiritual monism and world illusion are denounced by them all equally. The differences arise from the varied importance that they attach to the different spiritual doctrines; the prominence that they give to one or other of the three elements that were mingled with Vasudevism; the metaphysical theory that they set up; and the ceremonial that they impose upon their followers. The *Bhagvadgita* was supplemented in later times by the Pancaratra Samhitas and the Puranas, such as the Vishnu and the Bhagvata and other later works of that description. These occasionally elucidated some of the essential doctrines, laid down the ceremonial and brougnt together a vast mass of legendary matter to magnify the importance of their special teachings and render them attractive."[11]

10. McKenzie, *Hindu Ethics*, Pp. 166-167.

11. R.G. Bhandarkar. *Vaishavism, Shaivism and Minor Religious Systems*. p. 101.

The history of Bhakti Movement shows various complicating but inter-related trends. There are some extremely puritan movements while others have degenerated into the wildest licentiousness. "On the whole, the most attractive forms of Bhakti are those associated with Rama, and it is in connection with some of the forms of worship of Radha that some of the worst excesses have appeared. The *Bhagvadgita* and the works of Ramanuja, widely separated in time, are the great expressions of Bhakti in its most reflective manifestation. They breathe a spirit that is lofty and pure; they represent a devotion that is emotional but restrained, and a morality that is weak on the active and social side, but that contains elements in it of great worth."[12]

The *Bhaktiratanavli*, a work dating 1400 A.D. commends a purer form of Bhakti when it says: "Neither charity, nor asceticism, nor sacrifices, nor purificatory rites, nor penance and religious vows please Him. He is pleased with pure devotion. Everything else is futile, mere mockery."[13]

The *Bhaktiratanavli* lays strong emphasis on singing the praise of the Lord, bowing to Him and shampooing His feet, which are considered as means to attain an ecstatic union with the Lord. Devotion furnishes a way, indeed the only way, of escape from the fruits of karma. "Just as gold heated by fire leaves off its dross and regains its own appearance, so is the human soul cleared of its karmic impurities by the application of devotion and attains to me (by regaining the purity that is mine.)"[14]

The Muslim invasion, the rise of the reformist movements and role of the Bhaktas of low caste origin and other social and cultural needs of the times, compelled the saints of the thirteenth century or perhaps even earlier to turn away from all worship of personal gods, to give up personal piety and search for Truth and enlightenment, for the grace and pure love of the Supreme God. Some of these Bhaktas were idol worshippers in their earlier life but in their later life they gave up all idolatory and sought union with the Supreme

12. Mackenzie, *Hindu Ethics*. p. 168.
13. *Bhaktiratnanavali*, Eng. Tr., p. 26.
14. *Ibid.*, p. 38.

Being. This school of thought came to be known as Nirgun School of Bhakti. It was strongly influenced in its metaphysical outlook by the Nathapanthi Yogis, the Sufis and the Muslim saints and the Advaitists.

Dr. Pitambardas Badthwal in his *Nirgun School of Hindi Poetry* and Dr. Prabhakar Machwe in his *Hindi Aur Marathi Ka Nirgun Sant Kavya* show the strong influence of Nathapanthi Yogis on Nirgun School of poetry. Dr. Hazari Prasad Dvivedi also in his *Kabir* reveals the influence of the mystic thoughts of the Nathpanthi Yogis on Kabir. A number of mystic terms and experiences seem to have been borrowed from them.

Dr. Trilochan Singh says: "The higher spiritual and social experiences of Jaidev, Namdev and Ramananda brought a strong revolution in their minds. Their fresh experiences compelled them to break away from the purely Sargun approach to Bhakti and give up idolatory and formal ceremonies and worship connected with it. They moulded their thoughts and feelings in the Nirgun philosophy and mysticism. The early thoughts and experiences of these Bhaktas were first rays of the great Lights as radiated by the sun of Guru Nanak's philosophy. A part of the life of these early Bhaktas was spent in Sargun worship while it ended in Nirgun worship. The Sikh Gurus rejected the first part and accepted the thoughts of the Nirgun period. Then we have the Bhaktas like Kabir who were initiated into the Nirgun Bhakti alone and all their life opposed Sargun worship of God, by condemning idolatory and worship of avatars as god, which was common in Krishna and Rama cult."[15]

The main main features of Nirgun School of Bhakti are :

1. Metaphysics is subordinated to mysticism. The highest principles determined by pure reason are to be apprehended by mystic experiences.
2. God is regarded by them as real and all else is His creation and, therefore, relatively real but transitory.
3. The Nirgun Bhakti School considered the Guru or the Satguru as perfect as God Himself but not an

15. Dr. Trilochan Singh, *Bhakti and Gurmat*, *Punjabi Duniya*, 1965.

avatar of God. The Satguru is the source of all inspiration.

4. They lay much stress on the grace of God, but the grace of God depends upon moral and virtuous living.
5. They rose above all caste prejudices and even had Muslims as their disciples.
6. They completely gave up idolatory and image worship and respected the Bani of the Saints as the word of God.
7. They tried to form a cultural bridge between Hindus and Muslims, the high caste and the low caste people.

III

Impact of Islam on Bhakti Movement

The forces of Islam, one quite distinct from the other, entered India in the 13th century and proved a shocking challenge to Hindu Religion, Society and Culture. Various schools of Sufis, particularly the Chishti and the Suhrawardy, came to India with a new message of mystic faith and won innumerable converts to Islam. The simple, selfless and dedicated life of the Sufi saints attracted thousands of people to the new faith.

Caste, idolatory and esoteric obscurantism were the three baneful aspects of Hinduism that had been ruthlessly attacked by the protagonists of Islam, which itself was a non-idolatrous, simple and democratic creed that observed no distinctions of caste or race. The Bhakti reform movement was, therefore, marked by attempts at reforms in this very direction. "Firstly, by preaching and practice they denonuced the Brahmanical caste exclusiveness; secondly, though some of them inculcated Bhakti in which idols found an important place, they emphasised the unity of God and the true spirit of religion as distinguished from mere idolatory; and thirdly, they appealed to the hearts of the people by singing to them mostly in the language of the masses, as against the esoteric Sanskrit Brahminical Schools."[16] The coming of Muslims to India inaugurated a period of earnest spiritual consciousness among both Hindus

16. Shri Ram Sharma, *The Cresent in India*, p. 240.

and Muslims. Hinduism and Islam, both bound by the strict tenets of their scriptures, had no points of contact with each other. They were like the two banks of a river ever separated by the stream that flows between them. Who was to build the connecting bridge? The orthodox Hindus and the orthodox Muslims were unfit for the task, and it was left to free spirits and lovers of humanity, from both these groups, the Hindu Bhaktas and the Muslim Sufis, to devote their lives to construct this bridge.

"The main contributions of Islam to the mental make-up of the Indian Muslims," says Prof. Hamayun Kabir, "have been the insistence on a militant democracy, liberal rationalism in practical conduct, and an uncompromising monotheism that, at times, verged on iconoclasm and intolerance. In theory every religion recognises the principles of the Fatherhood of God and Brotherhood of Man. In practice, however, the Fatherhood of God often remains an article of faith divorced from the realities of life. Clash of colour and inequalities of birth, station, and wealth make the Brotherhood of Man a mere ideal unrelated to the daily activities of life. Even its worst enemies have, however, admitted that Islam broke down the barriers of colour and birth absolutely in the formal act of worship and with negligible restrictions in daily social intercourse."[17] Thus Islam has contributed greatly to the cause of removing Idolatory, superstition and caste prejudices. The intense monotheism of Islam made the people understand that all people are equal in the eyes of God.

The Muslim saints followed wherever the Muslim army led or the traders settled. In the ninth century, Abu Hafiz Rabi who was a traditionalist and an ascetic came to Sindh where he died in 106 A. H. In the 10th century, Mansur al Hallaj made a voyage to India by sea, and went back overland by way of Northern India and Turkistan. After the invasion of Mahmud, numerous Muslim men of learning and religion poured into India. It is impossible to compile a list of all of them, but some of the important ones may be mentioned here. Among them was Al Hujwiri, the author of *Kashful Mahjub* who was

17. Prof. Hamayun Kabir, *Islam in India, Cultural Heritage of India*, Vol. IV, p. 580.

a native of Ghazna and who after travelling extensively over Muslim lands came to reside in Lahore where he died in 1165 or 1169 A. D. Khwaja Muin-ud-Din Chisti came to Ajmer in 1197 A. D. and died there in 1234 A. D. Sheikh Jalal-ud-Din Tabrizi, a pupil of Shihabu-din Suhrawardi, visited Bengal.[18] Mian Mir of the Qadri order was another saint who had a strong influence on the saints of Punjab and Punjabi culture. Chisti saints like Bakhtayar Kaki, Sheikh Farid, Nizamu-din Auliya had a tremendous effect on the thought and culture of the Punjab. "There were thus men of high rank in Muslim religious biography—undoubtedly along with them a host of others of less renown who lived and laboured in India and through their personal contacts and influence spread the ideas of Islamic philosophy and mysticism through the length and breadth of India."[19]

"Indian philosophy, says Hamayun Kabir, has always emphasized the wholeness of life and brought with it an attitude of tolerance and forbearance. Indian Muslims were influenced by this spirit of catholicity of the traditions of ancient India. It is significant that the attempts at repproachment between Islam and Hinduism were as strong from the Muslim side as from that of the Hindus. Just as the teachings of Ramananda, Nanak, and Chaitanya tended to narrow the distinction between Hinduism and Islam, there were also Kabir, Chishti, and Dara Shikoh who attempted an understanding and unification of the two faiths from the side of the Muslims. Nor must it be forgotten that, though orthodoxy looked askance, one of the supreme architects of this movement for synthesis was Akbar the Great."[20]

IV

Sants (Saints) and Sant Parampara in Northern India

The word Sant now-a-days simply means a Saint. It is also used as a substitute for a Bhakta. In the *Adi Granth* and old manuscripts, saints like Kabir are called Bhaktas. Their biographies are called Bhaktamalas. Many scholars derive the

18. Dr. Tara Chand, *Influence of Islam on Indian Culture*, Pp. 46-47.
19. *Ibid.*
20. Dr. Parsuram Chaturvedi, *Uttari Bharat ki Sant Parampara*, Pp. 4-5.

word Sant from the word '*Sat.*' Dr. Trilochan Singh believes that the word is derived from the Sanskrit word "*Santri*" which means to cross over, traverse to get over, to surmount, to escape from, to be saved. In Pali writings it is used in the sense of Shanti, peace of mind. Parusram Chaturvedi thinks that it is derived from the Sanskrit word "*San*" which means sitting down, lying low, dejected.[21] It is said to be the plural of the word "San" but the objection is that the word Sant is always used as singular in both Hindi and Punjabi languages.

In the *Srimad Bhagvata*, Lord Krishna says: "Knowledge, sacrifices, repetition of mantras, going to places of pilgrimage and virtuous deeds are helpful to man, but the great help in spiritual enlightenment comes from association with saints." The Indian people believe that saints are perfect men. They are as generous as the clouds. They fulfil all aspirations of those who commit themselves to their care. They are free from greed and selfishness. Even in dire difficulty they remember God. They are softer than wax and firmer than rocks. The whole world is a home to them and they have no enemies. Enlightened saints can confer a vision on their deserving disciples. Guru Arjan writes in Sukhmani:

> In the company of the Saints,
> The mind hankereth not wildly.
> In the company of the Saints,
> The soul attaineth to happiness.
> In the company of the Saints,
> Man sees the Invisible;
> In the company of the Saints,
> He endureth the unendurable;
> In the company of the Saints,
> We reach the heights of the Spirit.
> In the company of the Saints,
> We enter the Lord's Presence;
> In the company of the Saints,
> We are aware only of God.[22]

The Saints are born in the world only to teach the people

21. Dr. Prabhakar Machwe, *Nirgun Sant Kavya*, Pp. 39-50.
22. *Sacred Writings of the Sikhs*, p. 161.

right conduct and how to establish the Kingdom of God on earth. The one purpose of a Saint's life is to protect dharma and dispel atheism. They clean the mind of the people and fill them with divine joy.

Writing on "Saints and Saintliness," Dr. Trilochan Singh says: "All the current achievements for social justice, human principles and comprehension of economic problems are in the last analysis a heritage entrusted to us by the past that was steeped in religion. We are only striving to preserve and develop the values handed down to us by the Saints of the past. The Saints were the first to proclaim humanitarian ideals, the first to fight for social justice, the first champions of the poor. They considered all nations and races equal. Their horizon was indeed global. They were the first liberators of slaves and the first to fight against the perpetuation of caste and creed. They believed in the equality of the sexes. The soul of the Saint yearns to become an instrument of God. The true Saint feels truth flowing into his soul from its fountain-head like an active force. He can no more help spreading it abroad than the sun can help diffusing its light. Only it is not by mere words that he will spread it. The love that consumes him is no longer the love of man for God. It is the love of God for all men. Through God, in the strength of God, he loves all mankind with divine love."[23] Saints have thus been the most important force in the history of India. They have brought about great social, cultural and political changes in our society.

"Deep wisdom and boundless love are the characteristics of a Saint. The Jnani sees only the unity in the diversity of the world and so feels himself one with the whole creation, and the Bhakta radiates a peace—active and exalted—which silently and gently communicates itself to others, transforming many lives and lightening hearts that are heavily laden with sorrows and cares of the world."[24] The Saints have thus built our literature and philosophy which is the pride of the land.

The Sufi mystic Rumi has rightly expressed: "One instant in the company of the Saints is better than a hundred years of

23. Trilochan Singh, *Saints and Saintliness*, *Sikh Review*, May, 1957.
24. *Cultural Heritage of India*, Vol. IV, p. 359.

prayer." In a beautiful Masnavi, Rumi describes the greatness of the Saint as follows:

> There is Water that flows down from Heaven
> To cleanse the world of sin by grace Divine;
> At last, its whole stock spent, its virtues gone,
> Dark with pollution not its own, it speeds
> Back to the fountain of all purities;
> Whence, freshly bathed, earthward it sweeps again,
> Trailing a robe of glory bright and pure.
> This Water is the Spirit of the Saints,
> Which ever sheds, until itself is beggared,
> God's balm on the sick soul; and then returns
> to Him who made the purest light of Heaven.[25]

The Saint, as we understand him here, is essentially a man or woman of heroic virtues due, we hold, to a most intimate union with God. It has been admitted not only in Indian thought but in Semitic tradition also that a Saint is a source of great inspiration. He can change and mould the mind of individuals and society. "It is not true to say that the Saint has turned his back to the world. He is the only one who has access to the depth of life, in the world. Far from vanishing like a dream, the world reveals to him the deep foundation on which it rests. For him, it reflects the face of God. For those who look on the world with physical eyes only, it means nothing. But the Saint realizes that from Him proceeds the power to greet all things with the glance of love. Because the Saint is absorbed in God, he alone is capable of seeing God and appreciating created things. Because he loves God he alone is capable of loving everybody. For the Saint, the world has no dark side, because even what seems darkest he brings into the full light of the day."[26]

Thus we conclude that in India a Saint is expected to possess the following qualities :

1. He is essentially a man of God.
2. He is devoted to Truth and service of humanity.

25. Reynolds and Nicholson, *Rumi, Poet Mystic*, p. 44.

26. Dr. Trilochan Singh, *Saints and Saintliness*, *Sikh Review*, May, 1957.

3. He is fearless and, having renounced all worldly desires, is always prepared to sacrifice his life for righteousness.
4. He aspires after complete spiritual union with God.
5. He is a true liberator of humanity. He fights for dharma in social, religious, cultural and political field.
6. His company is morally elevating and spiritually exalting.

Sant Garib Das holds the Saint in very high esteem. He sometimes identifies a Saint not only with the Satguru but also with God. For him the spirit of the Saint and the spirit of God is the same. We give below some quotations from the writings of Garib Das explaining his view of a Saint whom he also addresses as *Bhakta* and *Sadh*.

1. संत सरोवर हँस है, भक्षण करै विचार ।
पौहप वासना ज्यौं रहै, राई रिंच न भार ।।
G.G.S. p. 120

The Saints are the Swans on the lake,
They take the pearls of wisdom;
They live like fragrance in a flower,
Which is not of the slightest burden.

2. साध संगति हरि भक्ति बिन, कोई न पावै पार ।
निर्मल आदि अनादि है, गंदा सब संसार ।।
G.G.S. p. 120

No one can cross the ocean of existence
Without the aid of Saints and love of God.
They are ever and ever pure,
While the whole world is full of dirt.

3. साध साध सब को कहैं, साध समन्दर तीर ।
अवगति की गति को लखै, मिल गये नीर कबीर ।।
G.G.S. p. 120

Every one claims to be a Saint,
A real Saint is like a sea-shore;
He loses himself in the Infinite,
As Kabir merged in the Divine.

4. साध कहावन कठिन है, मग पर धरै न पांव ।
सौंहगी संगति है नहीं, चढ़ो नाम की नांव ।।
G.G.S. p. 120

It is difficult to become a Saint,
It is better not to set foot on this path;
A Saint is not easily accessible,
Ride the boat of God's Name.

5. सांई सरीखे संत हैं, यामैं मीन न मेख ।
पड़दा अंग अनादि है, बाहर भीतर एक ॥

G.G.S. p. 119

The Saints are like unto God,
Let there be no doubt about it;
Within and without they are the same,
The veil separating the two is very thin.

6. महिमा कीजे संत की, तन मन धन सब देह ।
शिर मांगै टाला नही, मोरध्वज लखि लेह ॥

G.G.S. p. 119

Always praise the Saints and serve them,
With your body, mind and wealth.
If the Saint wants your head, do not hesitate to give it;
Follow the example of Moradhvaja.

Thus according to Garib Das, the Saint is a treasure of wisdom. He is one with the spirit of God. Service of the Saint is the service of God

V

Jaideva, Ramananda and Namdeva

The Nirgun Sant tradition to which Garib Das belongs can be traced to Jaideva, Ramananda and Namdeva. These are the great names in the writings of Kabir and the Sikh Gurus. They are also mentioned in the writings of Garib Das. They are generally associated with the Vaishnavism of the 13th and 14th centuries.

जैदेव नामा बीप सुदामा तिनको कृपा भई है अपार ।

Jaideva and Namdeva, so also Sudama have received boundless grace from the Lord.[27]

धन्ने सेव्या बाल बुध, तिरलोचन गुरु मिल भए सीध ।
बानी को गुरु किया प्रकास, रे मन तू भी हो जा दास ॥
जैदेव त्याग्यो अहम्मेव, नाई उधरेउ सन्त सेव ।

27. *Adi Granth, Rag Bhilawal*, p. 856

कबीर ध्यायो एक रंग, नामदेव हरजीउ बसे संग ।।
रविदास ध्याए प्रभ अनूप ।
गुरु नानक गोविन्द रूप ।।

Guru Arjan, Rag Basant, Adi Granth.

Dhanna served God with the innocence of a child;
Trilochan became perfect after meeting the Guru;
The Guru spread the light of His word,
O mind, you should also follow him.
Jaideva gave up all egoism,
The barber was also saved by serving the Saints.
Kabir worshipped with single-minded devotion,
Namdeva lived in union with the Lord;
Ravidas worshipped the Ineffable One,
Guru Nanak is Govind Incarnate.

There are three stages in the development of the Nirgun movement : (1) Those Bhaktas who in their early life believed in idolatory and image worship but, in the light of later experiences, gave up all Sagun Bhakti and strictly preached the ideas of Nirgun Bhakti. We may place Jaideva, Ramananda, Namdeva and Dhanna in this category. (2) Those Bhaktas who were initiated into Nirgun Bhakti from the very early period and devoted all their lives to Nirgun Bhakti. In this category we can place Kabir and other disciples of Ramananda, disciples of Namdeva like Trilochan and later Kabir Panthis like Dadu and others. (3) The Sikh Movement which had social and political foundations also.

Ramananda, the founder of this great movement in North India, was fifth in descent from Ramanuja. He was born at Prayag in a Brahmin family. He was not a founder in the sense that he started the movement; the work had already begun before he was born. But from his time onward, we can trace an uninterrupted flow of this stream of thought throughout the Indian middle ages. His unique contribution to Indian spiritual life was the spirit of synthesis observed in his teachings; he accepted all that was true and of permanent value in our spiritual heritage—the philosophy of meditation (Yoga) and knowledge from the North and absolute surrender (Prapatti) of the Bhakti cult from the South—and rejected all that was untrue, ephemeral or rigidly sectarian. There is a popular verse to this effect:

Bhakti arose in the Dravida land; Ramananda brought it to the North; and Kabir carried it to the seven Continents and nine Divisions of the world.[28]

Ramananda borrowed ideas from all important religious schools and vitalised them with the love and devotion of his heart and founded a new spiritual path of spiritual realisation. We do not come across many of his sayings but the radiant personality of his disciples, the men he created, constitutes his living message. We come across only one song of his, incorporated in the *Adi Granth*, but this single poem is a sufficient indication of his philosophy.[29]

> Whither need I go to seek holiness?
> I am happy here within myself at home.
> My heart is no longer a pilgrim,
> It has become tied down to itself.
> Restlessly, one day I did want to go,
> I prepared sandalwood paste,
> Distilled aloe wood and many perfumes;
> I set out towards a temple to worship,
> Then my Guru showed me God in my heart.
> Whatever holy places I seek as a pilgrim,
> All I find is worship of water and stones;
> But Thou Lord, equally pervadeth all things.
> I have studied all Vedas and Puranas,
> There or elsewhere Thou sayest, seek God.[30]

"Thus Ramananda was the bridge between the Bhakti Movement of the South and North. Ramananda's teachings gave rise to two schools of thought, one conservative and the other radical. The first remained true to ancient beliefs and allowed only slight changes in doctrine and rites; the other struck out a more independent path and attempted to create a religion acceptable to men of different creeds, especially Hindus and Muslims. The greatest name in the first school is that of Tulsidass and in the second that of Kabir."[31]

28. Khiti Mohan Sen, *Medieval Mystics of North India, Cultural Heritage of India*, Vol. III, p. 378.

29. *Ibid.*, p. 379.

30. *Sacred Writings of the Sikhs*, p. 233.

31. Dr. Tara Chand, *Influence of Islam on Indian Culture*, p. 143, 145.

Namdeva was born at Narsi Bamni in 1269 A.D. and was a near contemporary of Ramananda. A tailor by profession, he turned to religious life when still quite young. He had close associations with the famous ascetic scholar, Gyan Deva, and the poetess Janabai. He was imprisoned by Sultan Mohammed Tughlaq but refused to give up his faith. He was set free when the Sultan was convinced of his spiritual greatness. Namdeva spent about ten years in the Punjab. He died at Pandharpur. There are 60 hymns of Namdeva in the *Adi Granth* and innumerable Ahhangas in Marathi, many of which are autobiographical.

If I should bring milk
And cook rice in it
To feed the idol,
The calf has already
Made the milk impure
By tasting of it.

Why to His image
Need I offer milk?
God is with us here
God is beyond us there,
In no place is God not,
Nama bows to the Omnipresent
Who filleth the whole earth.[32]

The above hymn of Namdeva shows that he had completely given up idolatory and image worship, though in his early life he worshipped the idol of Vithal.

In the poetry of Garib Das of Rohtak we find references to Jaideva, Ramananda and Namdeva showing thereby that he associated himself ideologically with these great saints of the Nirgun school. Referring to the story of how Jaideva forgave the thugs who had cheated him, Garib Das writes:

जयदेव कूं आदर किया, ठग बैठाये पास ।
करे अधीनी बन्दगी, वै ठग भये उदास ।।
राजा सें जयदेव कह्या, ये दो मित्र हमार ।
इनकी पूजा कीजिये, ले अपना जन्म सुधार ।।

32. *Sacred Writings of the Sikhs*. p. 224

Jaideva showed great respect to the thugs and seated
them by his side. He showed great humility
which made the thugs sad.
He introduced the thugs as his friends
and asked the Raja to show them the respect
due to Saints.

G.G.S. p. 259

Refering to Ramanada, Garib Das writes:

रामानन्द से इष्ट गुरु, तरे शीश के भाइ ।
चेलों की गिनती नहीं, पद में रहे समाइ ।।

Guru Ramanada initiated so many disciples and created so many Gurus that they cannot be counted. They all were devoted to his feet.

Garib Das also refers to Namdeva and other disciples of Ramananda at various places in his Granth.

VI

Kabir and Kabir Panthis

But the one Saint to whom Garib Das owed much and whom he acknowledges as his Guru is the famous Saint Kabir. Legend surrounds his early life and struggle. As we are dealing with the impact of Kabir on Garib Das in a separate chapter, it is sufficient to say here that "the mission of Kabir was to preach a religion of love which would unite all castes and creeds. He rejected those features of Hinduism and Islam which were against this spirit, and which were of no importance for the real spiritual welfare of the individual. He selected from both religions their common and philosophical ideas, their dogmas and rituals. He used both Sanskrit and Persian terms and both forms of the vernacular, Rekhta and Hindi Bhasha. He placed the greatest value upon the inwardness of religion and impartially condemned the external formalism of both. He deliberately abandoned the division between the two faiths and taught a middle path. A great religious reformer, the founder of a sect to which millions of northern Hindus still belong, it is only as a mystic poet that Kabir lives for us. His fate has been that of many revealers of Reality. A hater of religious exclusivism and seeking, above all things, to initiate men into liberty of the children of God, his followers have honoured his memory by re-erecting in a a new place the barriers which he laboured to cast down. But his wonderful songs survive, the spontaneous expressions of his vision and his love; and it is by these, not by the didactic teachings associated with his name, that he makes his immortal appeal to the heart. In these poems a wide range of mystic emotion is brought into play; from the loftiest abstractions, the most other-worldly passions for the infinite, to the most intimate and personal realisation of God, expressed in homely metaphors and religious symbols drawn indifferently from Hindu and Mohammedan belief. He is, as he himself says, at once a child of Allah and Ram. The Supreme Spirit, whom he knew and adored and to whose joyous friendship he sought to induct the souls of other men, transcended whilst He included all metaphysical categories, all credal definitions; yet each contributed something to the description of that infinite and simple Totality who revealed Himself, according to their measure, to the faithful lovers of all creeds."[33]

About his own initiation by Ramananda, he says:

> He became suddenly revealed in Benares and Ramananda illumined me;
>
> I brought with me the thirst for the Infinite and I have come for the meeting with him.
>
> In simplicity will I unite with the Simple One; my love will surge up.

And then again he makes clear his fundamental approach to religion (which strongly influenced Garib Das) by saying :

> If God be within the mosque, then to whom does this world belong?
>
> If Ram be within the image, which you find upon your pilgrimage, then who is there to know what happens without.
>
> Hari is in the East ; Allah is in the West: Look within your heart, for there you will find both Karim and Ram.
>
> All the men and women of the world are His living forms.
>
> Kabir is the child of Allah and of Ram: He is my Guru, He is my Pir.[34]

33. Rabindranath Tagore, ***Poems of Kabir*****, Pp. viii-ix.**
34. ***Ibid*****, p 72.**

And rightly does Evelyn Underhill remark: "Last, the warmly human and direct apprehension of God as the supreme object of love, the soul's comrade, teacher and bridegroom which is so passionately and frequently expressed in Kabir's poems, balances and controls these abstract tendencies which are inherent in the metaphysical side of his vision of Reality; and prevents it from degenerating into the sterile worship of intellectual formulae which became the curse of the Vedantist school."[35]

Kabir's was the first attempt to reconcile Hinduism and Islam. He was the first to come forward boldly to proclaim a religion of the centre, the middle path, and his cry was taken up all over India and was re-echoed from a hundred places. He had numerous Hindu and Muslim disciples and today his sect numbers a million.[36] Garib Das has made innumerable references to the life and spiritual greatness of Kabir which we will discuss in the chapter dealing with Kabir's influence on Garib Das.

There is sufficient historical evidence to show that the influence of Kabir came to inspire Garib Das through the Dadupanthi disciples of Kabir. Dadu was born in Ahmedabad and died at Naraina in Rajasthan where his followers have made their chief centre. "The great dream of his life was to unite all the divergent faiths in a bond of love and comradeship, and he founded the Brahma or the Parabrahma Sampradaya, to give effect to this great ideal. His sayings possess great depth and liberality and show clear traces of the influence of Kabir. Dadu believed not in the authority of the Scriptures, but in the value of self-realisation. To attain realization, we must divest ourselves of all sense of the ego and surrender our lives entirely to God. All men and women are brothers and sisters in the presence of God. He resides within the hearts of men, and it is there that we must meditate on him. Union with God is possible only through love and devotion and it is deepened not by prayers but by joining in service of the universe. We are united with God when, shedding all sins and impurities, we sincerely surrender ourselves to

35. *Ibid.*, Pp xxix-xxx.

36. Dr. Tara Chand, *Influence of Islam on Indian Culture*, p. 165.

the divine will."[37] Referring to Dadu and Guru Nanak Garib Das says:

नानक दादू अगम अगाधू, तिरी जहाज केवट सही।
सुखसागर के हंस आए, भक्त हिरम्बर उरधरी ॥

Infinite and profound were Nanak and Dadu. They got across the Ocean of Existence because the ship of their lives was captained by a Perfect Pilot. The love of His devotees drove Him to leave the World of Bliss and descend on earth.

VII

Sikh Gurus and their Influence

Garib Das was a near contemporary of the Sikh Gurus. The Sikh Gurus not only preached Bhakti but applied it actively to social, cultural and political forces in the field. They used it not only to teach the love of God but also to win social and political freedom of the country and combine religion with a practical approach to all human problems.

"The mission of Nanak was the unification of the Hindus and the Muslims. He realised that in order to heal the wounds of society it was essential to end the conflict of religions. He regarded himself as a prophet of God, who had come from the divine court and received from His door-step the signs (Aayats), the chapters (Surahs) and the traditions (Hadith) of the Prophet. He taught that there is one God in the world and no other and that Nanak and the Caliph (or son) of God speaks the truth."[38]

"The Sikh," says Duncon Greenlees, "is not a Hindu nor a Muslim; he is the disciple of the one Eternal Guru of the world and all who learn of Him are truely Sikhs and must not corrupt His teachings with confused utterances of men who live among them and around. Sikhism is not a disguised Hindu sect, but an independent revelation of the Truth of all sects; it is no variant of Muslim teachings save in that it too proclaims the love of God and the need for men to hold Him always in their heart. It too is a distinct religion like the other great religions of the world."[39]

37. Kshiti Mohan Sen, *Medieval Mystics of North India*, *Cultural Heritage of India*, Vol. III, p. 384.
38. Khazan Singh, *History of Sikh Philosophy*, Vol. II, p. 348.
39. Duncan Greenless, *The Gospal of the Guru Granth*, p. 260.

Prof. Toynbee says: "The Indian and Judaic religions are notoriously different in spirit and where they have met, they have sometimes behaved like oil and vinegar. Their principal meeting ground has been India, where Islam has impinged on Hinduism violently. On the whole, the story of the relations between these two great religions on Indian ground has been an unhappy tale of mutual misunderstanding and hostility. Yet on both sides of this religious barrier, there has been a minority of discerning spirits who have seen that at the bottom, Hinduism and Islam are an expression of the same fundamental truth and that these two expressions are, therefore, reconciliable with each other and are of supreme value when brought in harmony. The Sikh Religion might be described, as a vision of this Hindu-Muslim common ground. To have discovered and embraced the deep harmony underlying the historic Hindu-Muslim discord has been a noble spiritual triumph; and the Sikhs may well be proud of their religious ethos and origin."[40]

Thus we note that the Sikh Gurus tried to place themselves outside the field of Hinduism and Islam as a result of which their writings exercised great influence on the Hindu Bhaktas and Muslim Sufis of the Punjab. While we are devoting a complete chapter to the study of the influence of Sikhism on Garib Das, the following factors are notable:

1. Like the Sikh Gurus, Garib Das led a house-holder's life.
2. Like them, he criticised the formalism and dogmatism of both Hindus and Muslims.
3. Like them, he tried to synthesise Hinduism and Islam.
4. The influence of the *Adi Granth* and of Punjabi language on him is quite marked.

We shall see in subsequent chapters that the lives, the language, the thoughts and religious institutions of the sikhs had a tremendous influence on Garib Das.

VIII

Place of Garib Das in Sant Parampara

Garib Das of Rohtak belonged to the Nirgun school of

40. Arnold Toynbee, *Foreword to Sacred Writings of Sikhs*, p.10.

religious idealists, who discarded idolatory and formal Hindu practices almost completely. Although his disciples claim him to be an Avatar of Kabir, he did not go to the extent of saying, as Kabir and Guru Nanak did, that he was neither a Hindu nor a Muslim. He maintained a contact with the Hindu traditions and practices of non-violence, vegetarianism, cow-worship and a few other practices common to progressive Vaishnavas. But Garib Das did maintain that Hindus and Muslims were equal in the eyes of God.

Garib Das treated all castes and creeds as equal but he did not oppose Brahmanism so vehemently as did Kabir or Guru Nanak. Garib Das had some Muslim followers also, but they were more admirers than actual initiated disciples.

Like the saints of Nirgun school, Garib Das did not believe in avatar worship or the worship of God manifest in the form of Rama or Krishna. He appears to have accepted the ethical influence of the *Ramayana*, the *Bhagvata* and the *Mahabharata* but not the cults around Rama and Krishna. In his writings he shows respect for all leading saints of the Nirgun school of thought but rarely mentions others. He consciously deemed it his mission to be the torch bearer of the Bhakti movement started by saints of the Sant Parampara. Garib Das showed the following prominent qualities for which he was universally respected and loved:

(1) Like Kabir and Guru Nanak, he emphasised sincere practice as the essence of true religion. He hated and condemned hypocricy of all types.

(2) Like all medieval saints, he preached in the language of the people and his vast collection of poetry is in the simplest language which can be easily understood in Punjab, Rajasthan, Uttar Pradesh and Bihar.

(3) He gave up idolatory, image worship, going on pilgrimages as means of salvation. He also gave up all formal worship of avatars as the manifestations of God Himself.

(4) He was fully aware of the moral degradation of the times. His sensitive soul reacted to it in the same way as that of any other saint. He did not run away from society. He lived in the heart of society like other householders and

had sons and daughters. He propagated the love of God and Truth among the masses.

(5) Like the enlightened medieval saints, he shunned riches and people of the upper strata. He identified himself with the humblest peasant of Haryana and led a very simple and examplary holy life. He always tried to impress by precept and example that the chief aim of a saint's life should be to love and instil affection in the hearts of the people.

(6) Like the Saint Poets of Medieval India, Garib Das enriched the religious literature of his country produced in the regional language of the land of his birth. The thoughts and culture of Haryana Prant as well as the rest of India are fully reflected in the language and thoughts of this saint.

CHAPTER II

The Life and Works of Garib Das

In the history of Bhakti literature, there are two well known personalities known by the name of Garib Das. The first in chronological order is Garib Das, the son of Sant Dadu Dayal, who succeeded him after his father's death. He was born in the year 1632 B.S. or 1575 A.D. and succeeded his father Dadu Dayal at the age of 28.[1] He was the elder of the twin sons of the saint. He was so deeply absorbed in his religious practices that he unconsciously neglected the great task of consolidating the followers of Dadu, the unity of whose Panth was breaking under the stress and strain of strong personalities. On the advice of Rajjab, he abdicated the *gaddi* in favour of his younger brother, Maskin Das, after some years. He was a prolific poet and wrote innumerable works out of which only four are available in print: Anbhai Prabodh, Sakhi, Chaubole, and Padas.[2]

The second Garib Das is generally known in the history of literature as Garib Das of Rohtak or Garib Das of Chhudani. He was born in the year 1717 A.D. and died in 1774 A.D. His writings and sayings resemble those of the Garib Das of Dadu Panth which has sometimes caused a confusion between them. But Garib Das of Rohtak, though strongly influenced by Dadu and Dadupanthi Saints, tried to connect himself so closely with the spirit of Kabir and adapted his thought and work so well to the conditions of the time and the place he lived in, that he emerged as the greatest single force in Haryana in the 18th and the 19th centuries.

Kshitimohan Sen says: "There were many mystics bearing the name of Garib Das. The earliest one was the son of Dadu. The second Garib Das was born in a Jat family in the village Chhurani in the Rohtak district in A.D. 1717 and died in 1778 A.D. It is said that he was given spiritual initiation by Kabir in a dream. This Garib Das was a householder and the heads

1. Parsuram Chaturvedi, *Uttari Bharat ki Sant Parampara*, p. 432.
2. *Ibid.*, p. 455.

of his religious organisation are also householders. He worshipped God under the different names of Ram, Hari and Allah. He also preached that all external forms and observances of religion were unreal and that the only true path was the path of love and devotion. His prayers are extremely touching. There was a third Garib Das in the Punjab, who tried his best to bring about a synthesis of the Hindu and the Mohammedan religious practices."[3]

We do not know much about the history of this third Garib Das nor do we know whether he left any written work. Kshitimohan Sen also does not throw any further light on him beyond stating that he belonged to Punjab. Dr. Shaym Sunder Shukla mentions four Saints by the name of Garib Das: (1) Garib Das of Rohtak (18th Century), (2) Garib Das Dadupanthi (17th Century), (3) Garib Das Babripanthi, a Gurubhai of Bhikha Sahib and (4) Garib Das Satnami, grandson of Swami Jagjivan Ram.

Garib Das of Rohtak is such an outstanding personality that Dr. Mohan Singh says: "Garib Das (1774-1780 A.D?) of the Rohtak District, founder of the Garib Dasi Sect of Dadu Panthis, may be considered as the last of the Hindu Raja Yogi and Bhakta Poets who has as great a mastery of popular poetic language and style as Ghulam Farid had, but whose knowledge of other Indian languages was greater than that of any other Indian poet of medieval India, the only poet who comes near to him being Shah Qayam Din Chisti of Kari Gaon in Bombay, a descendant of Baba Farid and successor to his Gaddi in the 16th Century."[4]

II

The Land And The People

Haryana, the land of the sturdy Jats of the Rohtak area, is the cultural meeting ground of the three neighbouring cultures of Punjab, Rajasthan and Uttar Pradesh. The people of this area are the product of the land. The inhabitants of this dry and arid area are too busy struggling against the adverse

3. Kshiti Mohan Sen, *Mydieval Mystics of North India, Cultural Heritage of India*, Vol. III, p. 391.

4. Dr. Mohan Singh, *An Introduction to Punjabi Literature*, p. 152.

forces of nature. They live in small villages and all have to work hard to maintain themselves, from the village head-man down to the servants and sweepers. The only wealthy class is composed of the bankers *(shahs)*, who conduct most of the trade, finance the crops and frequently own a large part of land. As a result of this struggle for existence, certain qualities are developed in the people which stand them in good stead. They have become self-reliant, courageous, fearless, freedom loving and democratic, both in their attitude towards women and towards each other. Living so close to the soil and leading such active pastoral and farming lives, they have developed certain physical and moral qualities, quite their own, resembling partly the qualities of the Punjabis and partly that of the people of Rajasthan.

To no tract in North India, do the words of Sir C. Metcalfe quoted below, apply more aptly than to the Rohtak district: "Village communities seem to last where nothing else lasts. Dynasty after dynasty changes, revolution succeeds revolution, Hindu, Pathan Mughal, Mahretta, Sikh, English are all masters in turn, but the village community remains the same."[5]

Jait Ram, son of Garib Das, has given us a vivid picture of the Haryana of his times which does not differ from the Haryana of today.

1. बिन अस्नान न भोजन पावें, सहज मतै सुखदाई ।
   गंगा जमना भाव पिछानें, लोहागर पोहकर को जाई ।।
2. गया पराग पिंड भरावें, पितरौं कारन जाई ।
   गंगा जमना फूल जो डारें, गरड़ बचावैं आई ।।
3. कथा कीरतन गावन ध्यावन, गीता पाठ कराहीं ।
   श्रवन सुनें भागवत सब लीला, राम राम मुख गाहीं ।।
4. ऐसी चाल देश की कहिए हरियाना मन मान्या ।
   अती जाजुल करम नहीं कोई करें सो बहु पछिताना ।।
5. तातें करम कोई जन करिहैं और कहै क्यों कीन्हा ।
   जाकूं सब मिलकर समझावें फिर संकल्प भर दीन्हा ।।
6. अपने अपने हीले माहीं करम लिख्या सो पावै ।
   खेती बनज करै मन मान्या कहीं न भटका खावै ।।

5. *The Gazetteer of Rohtak District*, 1883-4.

7. दूध दही मन मान्या होई कोई जन बिरला खाली ।
अती सुन्दर नीकी नर काया सबकै मुख पर लाली ।।
8. कुटचलनी तिरिया कोइ नाहीं मरजाद रूप व्योहारा ।
जैतराम ऐसा हरियाना सब देसां सें न्यारा ।।[6]

In this beautiful patriotic poem, Jait Ram, gives a vivid though brief picture of the life and culture of the Haryana of his times. According to him the people of Haryana had very simple, refined and noble habits. No one took his meals without taking his bath. They all lived a contented and happy life accepting things as children of nature. They deemed the Ganga and the Jamuna as sacred rivers and and went on pilgrimage to Pushkar. They went to holy places like Gaya and Prayag; they honoured their dead according to Hindu custom. They performed Kirtan, singing of divine songs; they listened to the *katha* and interpretations of the *Gita* They listened to Krishan Lila as described in the *Bhagvata;* they also listened to *Ramayana* and sang the glory and the name of Rama. Haryana thus preserved the best of religious traditions If any one committed a crime or a sin, he repented bitterly over it. So, very few people indulged in evil acts. If any one committed an evil act, the people of the village gathered together and tried to correct him. They succeeded in changing his mind so well that he did not commit that act again. Thus the Pachayat system prevailing in the society had a strong moral and spiritual influence over the people there. The Karma theory had a strong influence on the minds of the people. They believed that whatever one sowed, he had to reap. The main professions adopted in the rural society were farming and trade. They did not hanker after money in far off towns and places. There was plenty of milk and butter in Haryana and there was hardly any one who could not afford to drink milk and take curd as his daily food. The people of Haryana were very handsome. The face of every one had a red glow of robust health. You could not find a single evil minded woman in Haryana. They were all homely, well disciplined and maintained the high moral traditions of ancient Hindu women. Such is Haryana, the most outstanding country.

6. *Jait Ram Ki Bani*, p. 365.

III

Life and Works

Forty six miles to the west of Delhi there is a small village named Karontha, where lived towards the close of the seventeenth century a Kshatriya Jat named Hardev Singh and his pious wife, Dayali Devi. They had a son named Balram Singh. About sixteen miles from Karontha, in Chhudani, there lived a rich farmer, Shiv Lal, who offered the hand of his only daughter, Rani, to Balram Singh. Having no one to look after his vast property he asked his son-in-law to come to Chhudani and stay there. The whole family thereafter shifted to Chhudani.

For nearly twelve years after his marriage, Balram Singh did not have any child, which worried both his father and father-in-law. They prayed to God for the gift of a son and sought the blessings of many saints. There came to Chhudani a Siddha Yogi, who camped in a small hut near a pond outside the village. Hearing about the remarkable spiritual powers of the Siddha Yogi, Balram Singh's father-in-law met him, made offerings of food and clothes and begged him to bless Rani and pray for the birth of a son in her house. The story goes that the Siddha said: "Your daughter and son-in-law are not ordinary people. In their last birth they performed great *tapasya*, as a result of which a great soul will be born in their house. He shall be the living image of Kabir."

It is said that about ten months after this incident a son was born to Rani, on the Purnima of Baisakh in the year 1774 B.S. (1717 A.D.).*

There was great rejoicing in the house. According to local custom, food and clothes were given to the poor and sweets were distributed. Legend says that the child began to play as soon as he was born which surprised the father and the mother. Then the child disappeared for some time and when they

* Almost all authors are unanimous about the date of birth, though there is some difference about the date of death.

The following writers give this date of birth :

Bhakt Ram, *Jiwan Charitar of Garib Das;* Kahan Singh, *Mahan Kosh;* Parshuram Chaturvedi, *Uttari Bharat ki Sant Parampara;* Dr. Mohan Singh, *Introduction to Punjabi Literature;* Dr. S.S. Kohli, *Panjabi Sahit da Itihas!*

We have established his date of Death as 1778 A.D.

prayed he again appeared as a natural child. They realised that what they saw was some vision, the significance of which they could not understand.

The child was loved and pampered by everyone. His mother always tried to protect her son from the evil eye of the people who admired his charming ways. Another legend says that three months before the birth of this child, when one day Rani was going to the well to fetch some water, two Saints came near her and touched her feet. When out of great surprise she asked them why they had treated her like that, the Saints said that they had actually paid homage to the great soul who was to be born in her house.

The child was named Garib Das after performing the Hindu rites according to Sanatana Dharma. When he grew up his playmates and parents addressed him simply as Gariba. He loved to play with the children such games as showed the religious tendencies of the child from the early years. At times he would sit on a raised platform like a Guru and deliver a sermon, preaching: "Do not steel, do not abuse; speak the truth; respect your parents."

At the age of five, while he was playing with boys, a playmate's little finger was seriously injured by a stone edge flung towards him by Garib Das. The finger began to bleed and the boy began to cry. Garib Das caught hold of his finger and asked the boy to look towards the sky. In another minute he assured the boy that a star from the sky will come down and start shining in his hand. Hoping for such a miracle the boy looked at the sky while Garib Das bandaged him. It is said that the wound was healed as soon as bleeding stopped and legend has added a miracle to the story saying that a star was constantly shining in the boy's hand.

Chhudani was at this time suffering from an extreme scarcity of water. There was no well in the village from where sweet drinking water could be acquired. For getting drinking water people had to go to a place one-and-half mile away to a well built by the Nathpanthis. Garib Das' father was now determined to solve the problem of scarcity of water. He decided to dig a well for drinking water no matter what the cost. At the time of the inauguration of the well-digging ceremony, which was accompanied by many religious rites, Garib Das told his father that the well should not be dug in the place selected for the purpose. If he wanted sweet water he should dig a well about twenty yards away from that place. When the digging of the well was complete they found that the water that came out of it was sour. So another well had to be dug for sweet water in the place chosen by Garib Das. The watcr of this well turned out to be sweet. Ever since then his father and the villagers started taking the utterances of Gariba seriously. The same year he is said to have predicted an earthquake. He gave the exact time and day of the earthquake and it proved to be a blessing in disguise. The well sunk for the second time was a little crooked. It became straight after the earthquake.

Rajasthan and Haryana were the resort of Bairagi Sadhus, Nathpanthi Yogis und Kabirpanthi Saints. Kabir's message to this area was spread by Dadupanthi Saints. They exercised a tremendous influence on the people. Garib Das' family was a devotee of Kabirpanthi and Dadupanthi Saints who were constant visitors to Chhudani. From his earliest days of childhood Garib Das sought the company of Saints. He kept away from home for long hours of the day and at times even showed signs of renouncing the world.[7]

There were some Ramanandi Bairagis residing in Chhudani. Their huts caught fire and it was feared that the fire would spread throughout the village. Garib Das jumped into the hut that was half burnt. Everyone thought that he would be consumed by fire. But soon the fire died down and the village was saved from being destroyed. Garib Das came out safe and sound from the hut.

Haryana is the land of cows and cowherds. The cow is the life-line of the people of this land. It gives them milk, butter, curd, manure and is so useful that people almost worship it. The influence of Vaishnavism and the teachings of *Bhagvatpurana* also had a great influence in inculcating cow-worship. Everybody of that period took pride in grazing herds of cows in the field. The service of the cow was considered to be the service of god. Once the cows of Garib Das

7. Khan Singh, *Mahan Kosh*, p. 299.

strayed into the barley fields of a farmer and destroyed the crops. The farmer reported to the Nawab but when it was checked up it was found that the barley field was intact. This story, probably lifted from the life of Gura Nanak, is found in some of his later biographies to show the miraculous powers of the Saint during his early years.

Once, while Garib Das was grazing cows in the forest, a tiger appeared on the scene. The cows were frightened. Garib Das stood there fearlessly and encouraged by the fearlessness of their Master, the cows grouped themselves in a circle and stood ready to fight the tiger with their horns pointed towards the tiger. The tiger moved away and a later legend says that when Garib Das commanded the tiger to go to some other forest the tiger went away leaving the cows unmolested.

During his boyhood he was fond of memorising religious songs of the Saints like Kabir, Guru Nanak and Dadu and sang them in a very melodious strain. He even learnt about music and musical instruments from wandering singers. One Yogi is said to have given him a Sarangi as a gift and taught him some Ragas. Garib Das sang such melodious songs on that Sarangi that the people were charmed just as snakes are charmed by the snake-charmer.

Garib Das was hardly ten or twelve when he went to meet his aunt (Rani's sister) at Khedanagar. His cousin, named Asanand took him to a Ramanandi Saint named Baudhidas. Baudhidas asked Garib Das whether he had been initiated into spiritual teachings by any Guru. Garib Das said that he had not adopted any one as his Guru. Baudhi Das' disciple Yogidas then urged Garib Das to accept his Master as his Guru and wear the *tilak* and *kanthi*. He also spoke about *thakur-puja* and going to pilgrimages and encouraged those ideas in the name of Ramananda which the great saint had given up during his own life-time.[8] Garib Das' mind had already come too strongly under the influence of Kabir and Dadu. He revolted against Karmkanda saying:

करम काण्ड उरले ब्योहारा ।
नाम लेय सो गुरू हमारा ।।

8. Bhagat Ram, *Garib Acharyaji Maharaj ka Sankshipt Jiwan Charitra.*

Rituals are lower practices,
I will adopt him as Guru who
is absorbed in the Name of God.

Early in life he also revolted against idolarory. He refused to pay any homage to any idol of the Hindu tamples even in a formal way. He also did not believe that going on pilgrimages was a means of salvation.

We do not know much about the early education of Garib Das. A small village like Chhudani probably could not afford to give him much of a formal education. But by association with saints, fakirs, Yogis and Dadupanthi priests and perhaps even Sikh priests he appears to have learnt much about the religious literature of the Bhaktas of the medieval times. In his writings he acknowledges the influence of Kabir, Guru Nanak, Pipa, Ravidas and others. He also shows considerable knowledge of the *Bhagvatapurana* and the *Ramayana*. The *kathas* of these religious classics was generally performed in Chhudani and Garib Das must have learnt much from them.

It is not exactly known who initiated him into the Kabirpanthi ideals so deeply and profoundly that he identified himself completely with the spirit of Kabir. In his writings Garib Das mentions Kabir as his Satguru and as his ideal. So deeply was he attached to Kabir's ideas that he refers to Kabir and his life at many places.

गरीब अलल पंख अनुराग है, शून्य मण्डल रहै थीर ।
दास गरीब उधारिया, सतगुरु मिले कबीर ।।

Garib's soul is a bird which soars into Sunya Mandal;
Garib has met Kabir, the Satguru, who has liberated him.[9]

गरीब ऐसा सतगुरु हम मिल्या, सुरति सिन्धु के तीर ।
सब संतन सिरताज है, सतगुरु अदल कबीर ।।

Such a true Guru have I met on the shore of Surati,
As is supreme among Saints. His name is Kabir;[10]

His writings leave no doubt that he acknowledges no other Guru except Kabir and there is a historical legend that Kabir

9. G.G.S., *Gurdev ka Ang*, p. 6.
10. *Ibid.*, p. 2.

met him in a vision and initiated him. In this vision he experienced the highest ecstasy. He attained oneness with Kabir, which has been recorded by his son Jait Ram also. It is this spiritual unity and affinity which Garib Das had with Kabir that made subsequent writers on him build up the theory that he was an avatar of Kabir. We will compare the writings and thoughts of Kabir and Garib Das in a separate Chapter.

Marriage and Household Life

In due time Garib Das was engaged to Mohini, daughter of Chowdhary Nyadar Singh of Barona, a village 30 miles away from Chhudani on the road going from Rohtak to Sonipat. Mohini was a devoted wife who exercised a great influence by her piety and nobility on both her husband and her children. She gave birth to four sons and two daughters. The names of the four sons were: (1) Jait Ram, (2) Turti Ram, (3) Angad Rai (4) Asa Ram. The names of his two daughters were (1) Dil Kaur and (2) Gyan Kaur. Jait Ram and Turti Ram were twin brothers and as Jait Ram was born first, he was always treated as the elder of the two.[11] Like his Master, Kabir, Garib Das led a very contented and ideal householder's life in which his responsibilities as a householder did not disturb his religious life. His devotion and Bhakti continued to be intense and sustained. His sons and daughters also were all very religious and did not upset his mission as a religious teacher.

Travels and Missionary Journeys

Although Garib Das did not believe in visiting holy places for salvation and pilgrimage, he did undertake some missionary journeys to various places. We have some historical evidence of his visit to Mathura. During this journey he must have visited Vrindavan, Banaras and Allahabad. He shows such close knowledge of Kabir's shrine in Banaras that he most probably visited the place. We also have some historical

11. Jait Ram, his son, writes :

तुरती राम और अंगद राय,
तीजे आसाराम कहाय ।
चौथा जैतराम है भाई,
सतगुरु चरणां सुरती लाइ ।

Sri Jait Ram ji Maharaj ki Bani, p. 35.

evidence of his travels to Delhi and Saharanpur. During his visit to Saharanpur, he might have visited Hardwar also. Perhaps during an extremely disturbed period of Nadir Shah's invasion he visited Himachal and stayed at a place called Haripur, only three miles from Paonta Sahib.[12] The historical temple in this place is still known as Garib Nath's Mandir. There is no truth in the legend stated in his biography by Bhagat Ram that the Nahan State was established by the blessing of Garib Das. Nahan State has existed from time immemorial and long before Garib Das went there, Guru Govind Singh visited the place as the guest of Nahan Maharaja.[13]

Anecdotes and Legendry Stories

Mansa Ram a disciple of Kabir was performing *tapasya* in the hills near Almora. He told his disciple, Handi Bhadhanga, that Kabir was born as Garib Das in a small village named Chhudani. Handi came to the village to find out the truth about it. He stayed near Garib Das for some days and after many discourses, some of which are recorded by subsequent writers, reached the conclusion that Garib Das was really the avatar of Kabir.

According to another anecdote, two famous disciples of Kabir, Arjan and Surjan, lived upto the time of Garib Das. Kabir had told them that they would be liberated when he came to the earth again as Garib Das. They came on a bullock cart to Chhudani and on meeting Garib Das gave up their bodies. They felt blessed after meeting their Master again.

A Hindu under the influence of Muslims killed a cow and committeed a sin which no Hindu could forgive. To make him repent for his sin of killing the cow, Garib Das asked him to go and bathe in the Ganges. This legend which gives importance to bathing in the Ganges contradicts another legend about the sacred river. When his mother Mata Rani wanted to go and bathe in the Ganges he assured her that the Ganges would come to Chhudani for her sake. It so happened that the

12. There are shrines commemorating the visit of Garib Das at Saharanpur and Paonta Sahib.

13. 1. Kartar Singh, *Life of Guru Govind Singh*, p. 61.
    2. Dr. Trilochan Singh, *A Brief Life Sketch of Guru Govind Singh* p. 13.

same evening every one saw a vision or in reality that the Ganges was flowing through Chhudani and they bathed to their heart's content.

Kanh Ram, a rich merchant of Asauda village, had a young son who showed ascetic tendencies at a very early age. Being rich and having only one son he was anxious that his son Santosh Das should get married. The father arranged to engage his son to Lakshmi Bai, daughter of a Seth. But the son ran away from home and took refuge in the holy presence of Garib Das. No one could persuade him to go back and marry. Kanh Ram thought that Garib Das had spoiled his son, but when he went to Chhudani he found that the Saint was a householder. So he begged Garib Das to persuade his son to marry. Garib Das cxpressed his intention to see the girl. When Lakshmi Bai came to his presence, she assured him that she would not interfere in the religious life of her husband. On this condition Santosh Das agreed to marry. It is said that Garib Das frequently went to his house and stayed with him. A cot is still preserved there which was used exclusively by Garib Das.

During his stay in Asauda village, a Pundit who had completed *katha* of the *Bhagvata* performed the last day's closing ceremony hoping that the people would make considerable offerings for his months of labour. This Pandit Mani Ram made eleborate ceremonial preparations for the occasion. On the same day, a courtesan who was dancing also attracted crowds. Pandit Mani Ram got only thirty rupees for his *katha*, while the dancer got thousands. Mani Ram was greatly upset. Sant Garib Das asked him not to judge the fruits of his labour by the money offered to him. Evil attracts more attention in the Kali age, he told the Pandit.

A peasant who later on came to be known as Bankhandi Das was very much impressed by the life of Santosh Das. He wanted to renounce life and perform *tapasya*. Santosh Das sent him to Garib Das who gave him spiritual instructions and advised him not to go to the forests for performing *tapasya* but meditate at home. He lived in his house and meditated so deeply that he achieved realization of God. Another legend says that the Nine Nathas or the Nine Yogeswaras came from the celestial spheres to meet Sant Garib Das and after having a spiritual discourse with the Sant went away. On parting, they begged for a piece of cloth used by the Sant. Garib Das, gave them his *dupatta*.

There is a village called Basiar near Sunam. The Chowdhary of the place named Ram Rai was a religious minded man. One day he saw a Sadhu coming to the village. After taking his bath the Sadhu began to sing melodious songs of Sant Garib Das. Ram Rai came to know from the Sadhu that Garib Das was still living. He became so eager to meet the Sant that he at once made preparations and left for Chhudani. As soon as he entered Chhudani he met a saintly looking man who guided him to the place of Garib Das. Later on he came to know that the person who had guided him was Garib Das himself. There is a similar story in Guru Nanak's life also. When Angad came to him for the first time he met Guru Nanak in the fields. Guru Nanak led his horse to his residence and only on reaching the residence Angad came to know that it was Guru Nanak who was leading him. Thus when Ram Rai met Sant Garib Das, he was overwhelmed by his humility and spiritual greatness. After receiving spiritual initiation from Garib Das, he became a great devotee of the Saint.

Atkali Das, a Vaishnav, who had gained great importance for his learning and orthodoxy came to Chhudani to test the spiritual greatness of Sant Garib Das. As soon as he reached Chhudani, he found to his surprise that Sant Garib Das had already made arrangements for feeding of all his companions. After taking his meals, he had a long discussion with Garib Das. Atkali Das tried to explain that idol worship and devotion to Lord Krishna, real Avatar of God, was the only way to salvation. Garib Das gave very convincing arguments against idolatory and convinced him that the worship of God alone could give true enlightenment. He condemned idolatory in very strong words.

Thandi Ram was a devoted disciple of Sant Garib Das who obeyed the Master most conscientiously. One day the Master asked him to go and look after the fields of barley. Thandi Ram sat there obeying the command of his Guru and did not come back till the Master sent for him on the third day. Sant Garib Das blessed him and declared that Thandi Ram had a very pure soul. Wherever he went he worked wonders with his spiritual powers. So he asked Thandi Ram to go in whichever direction he wished to go and establish a centre of his own. It is said that Thandi Ram established a religious centre at Bodagram near Meerut and he is still remembered there for his spiritual powers.

Chowdhary Ram Sahai of village Badli once made up his mind to see Sant Garib Das about whom people talked so much. He was proud of his position and he wanted to show off to the Saint that he was also a very important person. When he met Garib Das, the Saint requested him to sit on the cot while he himself sat on the floor. Touched by the humility of the Saint, the Chowdhary began to feel very uneasy about the seat. He then apologised for his audacity and sat on the floor with the Saint and thereafter became his humble devotee. During his visit to Jhapdoda village near Bhadurgarh, Sant Garib Das initiated Hari Das and his brother and they both became his great disciples. Kashi Das, another person who pretended to be a Siddha capable of reaching the "*dasam dvar*," also found his hypocricy exposed when he met Garib Das. The saint admonished him for leading people to darkness. He was given spiritual instructions and ever since then he became a disciple of the Master and sincerely devoted himself to the love and service of God.

Emperor Mohammad Shah Invites Garib Das

After the death of Bahadur Shah in 1712, it is said, "no member of the house of Timure remained in India, who was fit to take the helm of the ship of the State, which soon drifted on to the rocks. The degraded wretches that polluted the throne of Akbar deserve only a passing notice, the rest of our history is filled with the tragedy of disruption of the splendid edifice reared and fostered by the great Mughals."[11]

Farrukhsiyar was deposed, imprisoned, blinded and ultimately killed in an ignominious manner in April, 1719. Muhammed Shah, the eighteen year old grandson of Aurangzeb was put on the throne in September, 1719. According

14. Sri Ram Sharma, *The Cresent in India*, p. 697.

to Sir Jadunath Sarkar, though Muhammed Shah "was a mere cypher in respect of public duties, there were some redeeming traits in his private character. Naturally timid and wavering, he was also free from insolent pride, caprice and love of wanton cruelty. He never gave consent to shedding blood or doing harm to God's creatures. During his reign, the people passed their lives in ease and the empire outwardly retained its dignity and prestige. The foundations of Delhi monarchy were really rotten, but Muhammed Shah by his cleverness kept them standing."[15]

This Emperior heard of the immense popularity of Garib Das and sent one of his Hindu ministers to invite the Saint to the court. When the Emperor's envoy met Sant Garib Das, he said: "Only two types of people go to the court. One are those who commit crimes and seek the pardon of the king. Others are those who seek power and position through flattery. I do not belong to either of the two classes." So saying, Garib Das refused to go to the court of the Mughal Emperor.

When the Emperor came to know about it, he wrote a polite letter requesting Sant Garib Das to oblige him just by one visit. Garib Das agreed. He went to Delhi and stayed with Sant Charan Das who not only entertained him but offered him an *Angarkha* as a gift which is still preserved at Chhudani.

When Garib Das met the Emperor, the Mughal ruler was very much impressed by the Saint's simplicity and nobility. The sermon which Sant Garib Das delivered had great effect on him. The Emperor then sought the blessings of the Saint and begged him to pray for the stability of his kingdom. Sant Garib Das assured him that his rule would spread far and wide if he agreed to the following three conditions:

1. He must ban cow-slaughter.
2. He must keep only his legal wives and release all other women from the bondage of the harem.
3. He should not levy any tax on foodgrains.

Muhammed Shah might have agreed to one or two conditions, but the Saint did not know that the Emperor's rule was

15. *Ibid*, p. 698.

completely controlled by the courtiers. The Qazis were enraged at the thought of a ban on cow-slaughter. Fearing that Garib Das may not influence the Emperor in the wrong direction, they persuaded Muhammed Shah to sign orders for his imprisonment. Sant Garib Das is said to have cursed the throne and the rule of the Mughal Emperor and escaped miraculously from the prison. A year later Nadir Shah invaded and the rule of Muhammed Shah collapsed. A famine is said to have raged in the country. There was great scarcity of food. Once his disciple Santosh Das sent with the Saint a bullock cart full of barley for the people of Chhudani, but some robbers waylaid it. The leader of the robbers imprisoned Garib Das. His disciples came and secured his release. Five days after this incident some unknown assailants attacked this leader of the robbers and cut off his hands. He came to Sant Garib Das for forgiveness. The Saint forgave him and gave him spiritual instructions.

IV

The Writings of Garib Das

At Chhudani Sant Garib Das used to sit under a tree and dictate religious hymns and songs. These were recorded by the Dadupanthi scribe named Gopal Das.[16] Innumerable small compositions were written. People copied them and thus his writings spread from hand to hand. Various Sadhus and many centres devoted to Sant Garib Das had copies of these works. His *padas* according to Dr. Ram Kumar Verma exceeded 17000.

The tree under which he composed these works is called Jand Sahib. It is opposite the Samadhi now called Chhatri Sahib.

According to Swami Chetan Das the total number of *padas* is about 18500. But different manuscripts have different numbers, of *padas*; some exceeding 18500, some less than this.

16. There was a Mahatma named Gopal Das belonging to Dadupanth. He was well versed in *Santabani* and a great scholar and saint. On hearing about the fame of Garib Das in Rajasthan he came to meet him. On being impressed by the utterances of Garib Das, he said, "Master, if you permit me I would like to record your *bani*." Then Gopal Das recorded the *bani*.

Swami Chetan Das, *Granth Sahib*, Second edition, p. 54.

Manuscripts are found in various places. We have been able to examine the undermentioned at the following places.

(1) Shri Garib Dasi Yoga Ashrama, Barh Shah Bulla, Delhi, 4 Manuscripts: The total number of *padas* in the three larger ones are 18770, 18591 and 18542 respectively.

(2) Mahant Ganga Sagar, Chhudani, 4 Manscripts.

(3) Garib Dasi Kutia, Ludhiana, 1 Manuscript.

(4) Ayali, 1 Manuscript.

(5) Swami Chetan Das, 1 Manuscript.

(6) Swami Bhagat Ram, 1 Manuscript.

The custodians of these Manuscripts are reluctant to permit detailed examination.

Garib's Granth was first printed as Sri Ratan Sagar by Madhavanand in Gurmukhi script in 1899 A.D. and was printed by Punjab Economical Press, Lahore.

One of his disciples named Ajranand felt the need of compiling all these works into one volume just as the writings of the Sikh Gurus were compiled by Guru Arjan into *Adi Guru Granth Sahib.* After preparing a volume of 673 pages he named it *Granth Sahib.* To distinguish it from *Adi Guru Granth Sahib* of the Sikhs we will call it *Garib Das' Granth Sahib* or simply *G.G.S.* It was first published in 1924 A.D. The practice of reading it and worshipping it was also introduced. Some decades ago Mahant Ram Kishan Dass invited Sikh Granthis from Delhi who performed the Akhand Path (continuous reading) of the *Adi Guru Granth.* Along with it Garib Das' *Granth* was read in the same manner at Chudani Sahib. The Granth has been given a second title also, *Satgura Sri Garib Das ji Maharaj ki Bani.* It was published by Arya Sudharak Press, Baroda on September 15, 1924. The second edition has been printed in 1964 as edited by Swami Chetan Das and Dr. Shyam Sunder Das.

The Grantha Sahib of Garib Das has the following chapters and verses on pages numbered as per the Baroda edition:

132. राग दीप	56	514—515
133. राग कल्याण	72	515—518
134. राग केदारा	25	519—521
135. राग हेली	61	521—523
136. राग परज	34	523—525
137. राग जैजैवन्ती	115	525—529
138. राग बिहाग	41	529—531
139. राग सोरठ	153	531—535
140. राग मलार	118	535—540
141. राग मारू	85	540—544
142. राग मंगल	222	544—552
143. राग चौरी	247	552—558
144. राग विनोद	63	558—561
145. शब्द चौरी	20	561—561
146. राग बिजोग	9	561—562
147. राग सिंध	19	562—562
148. राग बरवे	40	563—564
149. राग बिहंगम बरवे	167	564—569
150. राग सरबंग	34	569—570
151. राग बधावना	20	570—571
152. राग सेहरा	7	571—571
153. राग डोरी	14	571—572
154. राग केहरा	49	572—574
155. राग जोंगडा	88	574—579
156. राग बंगला	65	579—583
157. राग छन्द बंगाली	65	583—586
158. राग नेहपाल	21	586—587
159. राग भैरों	8	587—587
160. राग रामकली	53	587—589
161. राग प्रभाती	86	589—593
162. राग बिलावल	269	593—603
163. राग आशावरी	660	603—632
164. राग सारंग	29	632—633
165. राग नट	28	633—634

166. राग बसंत	92	634—639
167. राग धमार	106	639—643
168. राग होरी	190	643—653
169. राग काफी	68	653—669
170. राग धनासरी	21	669—669
171. राग हिंडोलना	8	669—670
172. राग टोडी	33	670—671
173. राग शब्द	46	671—672
174. राग चौरी	19	672—673
175. राग धून	16	673—673

At the end of the Granth there are 431 hymns of Bhakta Kabir also, covering 20 pages.

Jait Ram and Turti Ram

Jait Ram was the elder of his twin sons. He was saintly and of an ascetic temperament. The people of Karontha begged Bhakta Garib Das to come to the ancestral village and preach there. Sant Garib Das sent his son, Jait Ram, who built a very important centre at Karontha. He was also a saint and poet and has left his own Granth.

When Sant Garib Das was about to bestow his *Gaddi* on his son Jait Ram, his wife Mohini requested him to give it ro Turti Ram. She probably feared that if it was bestowed on Jait Ram, he might shift the Seat of Guruship from Chhudani to Karontha. So she persuaded Jait Ram to abdicate in favour of his brother.

Different dates of his death are given by different authors,[17] but the correct dats is that given by his son Jait Ram who says:

संबत अठारहसो पैंतीसा, परलोक सिधारे हैं जगदीसा ।
मास भादवा दूज कहावै, पखवारा सुकल पक्ष आवै ॥

Jait Ram ki Bani, p. 140

So Garib Das died in the year 1835 B.S. (1778 A.D.) on the second of the moonlit half of Bhadon. The District Gazetteer

17. Dr. Mohan Singh 1780 A.D., Kahan Singh 1825 B.S.

of Rohtak also says: "He died in Sambat 1835 and over his remains a handsome Samadhi was erected."

The line of his spiritual successors is as follows:

1. Garib Das
2. Turti Ram
3. Dani Ram
4. Sheelwant Ram
5. Shiv Dayal
6. Ram Krishna Das
7. Ganga Sagar

The Head of the Garib Dasi Panth is called the Shri Mahant. The main centre is still at Chhudani which is run by a Trust. Although there is no particular ban on the celebration of general Hindu festivals, Garib Dasis celebrate two anniversaries connected with the birth and death of Sant Garib Das. For three days they gather together in the month of Phalgun (March) and then they again get together in the month of Bhadon (August-September). Their greetings when they meet each other is '*Sat Sahib*.

Deras and *Kutias* of Garib Das Panth

I District Rohtak (Haryana)

1. Chhudani Sahib (छुडानी साहिब). This is the Headquarters of the Panth. Here we have the *Samadhi* of Garib Das called *Chhatri Sahib* (छतरी साहिब) and a tree called *Jand Sahib* (जांड साहिब) under which the Saint had meditated and sung his songs. The following articles used by the Saint in his lifetime are preserved in Chhatri Sahib: (a) *Angarakhas* or Robes, (b) *Dhotis*, (c) *Topi* or Cap, (d) *Pagari* or Turban, (e) *Patka* or Wrap, (f) A Pair of Shoes, (g) *Lota* or Waterpot, (h) *Katora* or Cup, (i) *Palang* or Cot, (j) *Chadar* or Bedsheet, (k) *Takia* or Pillow and (l) *Dori* or Rope for drawing water from the well. These articles are exhibited on anniversary days.

2. Madana Kalan (मदाना कलां)
3. Sampla (सांपला)
4. Karontha (करौंथा)
5. Samaila (स्मायला)
6. Deegal (डीगल)
7. Bahadurgarh (बहादुरगढ़)

8. Asauda (आसौदा)
9. Bhainswal (भैंसवाल)
10. Bhalawar (भलावड़)
11. Ahir Majra (अहिर माजरा)
12. Gopalpur (गोपालपुर)
13. Beri (बेरी)
14. Mandauthi (मण्डौठी)
15. Chhara (छारा)
16. Kanonda (कणोंदा)
17. Gauchhi (गोछी)
18. Balagarhi (बालागढ़ी)
19. Khanpur (खानपुर)
20. Sukhi (सूखी)
21. Rasulpur (रसूलपुर)
22. Bakheta (बखेटा)
23. Kalhawar (कल्हावड़)
24. Juan (जुआँ)

II District Jind (Haryana)

1. Khatkar (खटकड़)
2. Chhan (छान)
3. Baroda (बडोदा)

III District Karnal (Haryana)

1. Ugra Kheri (उगरा खेड़ी)
2. Kurad (कुराड़)
3. Naguran (नागुरन)
4. Kailana (कैलाना)
5. Bhusle (भूसले)
6. Jaru Ki Khedi (जरू की खेड़ी)
7. Aara Ki Khedi (आरा की खेड़ी)

IV District Ambala (Haryana)

1. Kalahati (कलाहटी)
2. Balana (बलानाँ)
3. Kunjapura (कुंजपुरा)
4. Malaud (मलौड)
5. Rampur (रामपुर)
6. Batrohan (बटरोहण)
7. Sajadpur (सजादपुर)

V District Patiala (Punjab)

1. Patiala (पटियाला)
2. Nabha (नाभा)
3. Bhadsan (भादसाँ)

4. Machhrai (मछराय)
5. Ladpur (लाडपुर)

VI District Sangrur (Punjab)

1. Sunam (सुनाम)
2. Batariyana (बटरियाणा)
3. Basiark (बसियार्क)
4. Kanhgarh (कान्हगढ़)
5. Kapial (कपियाल)
6. Bhawi (भवी)
7. Jalur (जलूर). Here we have the *Samadhi* of Swami Brahmasagar Bhuriwale Maharaj, a great Garib Dasi saint, whose death anniversary is celeberated here in the month of Magh (January) every year.
8. Barnala (बरनाला)
9. Dhuri (धुरी)
10. Chanda (चाँदा)
11. Jainpur (जैनपुर)

VII District Ludhiana (Punjab)

1. Ludhiana (लुधियाना). There are three *Deras* and one *Dharamsala* in this town. Birth anniversary of Bhuriwale Maharaj is celeberated here in the month of Bhadon (August) every year.
2. Dulma (दुलमा)
3. Jhaner (झनेर)
4. Sandaur (संदोड़)
5. Ram Talai (रामतलाई)
6. Chhapar (छपार)
7. Brahmi (ब्रह्मी)
8. Rakba (रकबा)
9. Mandiani (मंडियानी)
10. Talwandi Chhoti (छोटी तलवंडी)
11. Talwandi Barhi (बड़ी तलवंडी)
12. Kailpur (कैलपुर)
13. Bhatian (भाटियाँ)
14. Vasian (वासियाँ)
15. Ayali (ग्रयाली)
16. Sarawa (सरावा)

VIII District Jullundur (Punjab)

1. Nur Mahal (नूरमहल)
2. Mahatpur (महतपुर)

3. Jandiala (जंडियाला)
4. Tagran (तगड़ां)

IX District Hoshiarpur (Punjab)

1. Baddon (बड्डों)
2. Matabpur (मताबपुर)
3. Rampur Poswala (रामपुर पोसवाल). This is the blrthplace of Bhuriwale Maharaj.
4. Ratewal (रतेवाल)
5. Aduwana (अड्डुवाना)

X District Ferozepur (Punjab)

1. Ferozepur (फीरोजपुर)
2. Moga (मोगा)
3. Talwandi (तलवंडी)

XI District Amritsar (Punjab)

1. Amritsar (अमृतसर)
2. Balehar (बलेहर)
3. Kairon (कैरों)
4. Manihala (मनिहाला)
5. Dasuwal (दासूवाल)
6. Kalar (कलार)
7. Gularhwal (गुल्हडवाल)

XII District Ganganagar (Rajasthan)

1. Sri Vijaynagar (श्री विजयनगर)

XIII District Jaipur (Rajasthan)

1. Alwar (अलवर)
2. Harsaura (हरसौरा)
3 Paonta)वप.टा)
4. Kisangarh (किसनगढ़)

XIV Union Territory of Delhi

1. Delhi (दिल्ली)
2. Ispur (ईसपुर)
3. Bajidpur (बाजीदपुर)

XV District Ahmedabad (Gujrat)

1. Petlad (पटलाद)
2. Shantipur (शान्तिपुर)

XVI Uttar Pradesh

1. Saharanpur (सहारनपुर)
2. Rampur (रामपुर)
3. Uttarkashi (उत्तरकाशी)
4. Haridwar (हरिद्वार)
5. Rishikesh (ऋषिकेश)
6. Varanasi (वाराणसी)

CHAPTER III

Political, Social and Religious Conditions

Apart from the Sikh Gurus and, for a short period, the Satnamis, very few medieval Saints took part in political movements of the time. They accepted Muslim Rule and its despotism as an individual accepts fate. They no doubt did a lot to bring moral and spiritual awakening among the people, but for fear of being persecuted as political rebels, they did not criticise or condemn the evil acts of the rulers.

As Wilbur. S. Deming puts it, "the Hindus had become demoralised and to a certain extent denationalised. In the narrow sense it is possible that Bhakti poets taught many religious themes that had little to do with the political regeneration of the country, themes which seemed to oppose such regeneration like that of renunciation and turning away from the things of the world."[1]

No doubt there were great political and social upheavals throughout the 18th Century, but it is a tragic fact that most of the Hindu saints of India did not utter a word of protest against the despotism and cruelty that prevailed during their times.

Sant Garib Das lived all his life only about 30 miles away from Delhi. We have to see what the political conditions were at different stages of his life and whether he reacted towards them or not. We will also study whether the political situation of a particular period warranted any comments or reactions from a religious and social reformer. We will base our comments and conclusions on Garib Das' political thinking on these findings.

Bahadur Shah (Shah Alam I) died in 1712, a few years before the birth of Garib Das. "After him," says S.R. Sharma, "came the nightfall of the Empire, and the rule of 'her sister chaos.' Shah Alam's rule was marked by a sanity and liberalism not unworthy of a descendent of the great Akbar. His successors

1. W.S. Deming, *Ramdas and Ramdasis*, p 16.

were definitely cast in an inferior mould and were undoubtedly of poor clay."[2]

The following were the Emperors who ruled in Delhi during the lifetime of Garib Das (1717-1774 A.D.)

1. Farrukhsiyar 1713-19 A.D.
2. Rafiud-Darajat and Rafiud-Daula 1719 A.D.
3. Muhammed Shah and Shah Jahan Sani 1719-48 A.D.
4. Ahmad Shah 1748-54 A.D.
5. Alamgir II 1754-59 A.D.
6. Shah Alam 1759-1806 A.D.[3]

Two Sayyid brothers, Husain Ali and Abdulla, were the real King Makers and dictators for some decades. The treatment that Farrukhsiyar received from the Sayyids was in no way more harsh than what he had meted out to his possible rivals. His worthlessness, intrigues and ingratitude made his removal almost necessary for his ministers.[4]

The King was imprisoned, blinded and killed in an ignominous manner. Garib Das was quite young at that time and we should not expect him to have taken note of the political events of this period.

Muhammad Shah became the Emperor in 1719 A.D. "Although a mere cypher in respect of his public duties", says J.N. Sarkar, "there were some redeeming traits in his private character. Naturally timid and wavering, he was also free from insolent pride, caprice and love of wanton cruelty. He never gave consent to shedding of blood or doing harm to God's creatures. In his reign the people passed their lives in ease, and the empire outwardly retained its dignity and prestige. The foundations of Delhi Monarchy were really rotten but Muhammed Shah by his cleverness kept them standing."[5]

We find some references to Muhammed Shah[6] and his reign

2. S.R. Sharma, *The Crescent in India*, pp. 687-88.
3. R.C. Majumdar and others, *The Advanced History of India*, p. 629.
4. S.R. Sharma, *The Crescent in India*, p. 698
5. J.N. Sarkar quoted by S.R. Sharma, *The Crescent in India*, p. 698.
6. Garib Das sermonises to a Shah (Emperor) in his writings who his biographers believe was Mohammed Shah, whom he is said to have met. Swami Yogendrananda writes:

"देहली दरबार में मुहम्मद शाह की बीसियों प्रार्थना पर आप पधारे ! आपके उपदेशों का पूर्ण प्रभाव बादशाह पर पड़ा था।"

Introduction to *G.G.S.* (1965), p. 17.

in the writtings of Sant Garib Das. He did not believe in hobnobbing with kings and courtiers or going to the royal courts for favours and patronage. He says in his writings: "One should not go to the royal courts as it disturbs the contemplative life of a Saint and whatever alms are received from the court are like drinking blood."[7] Again: "It is a grievous sin to go to the royal courts. The religious life of the Saint is poisoned just as the human body suffers from snake-bite."[8]

When Garib Das received a pressing invitation, he met the Emperor and the meeting was quite cordial. The historical description of the meeting shows that the Emperor showed great respect for the Saint and the Saint fearlessly asked the Emperor to be genial and tolerant towards the Hindus. But the Emperor was a mere puppet in the hands of his bigoted ministers who were even thinking of reimposing *jazia*.[9]

So, although the meeting between the Saint and the Emperor was very cordial, the overbearing ministers tried to harass the Saint who was saved from molestation by the intervention of the Emperor. The legend, however, attributes it to a miracle performed by the Saint.

In the writings of Garib Das there is a vague reference to Delhi as a den of sin. There are also vague references to the inevitable fall of the despotic empire and the ultimate victory of Good over Evil.[10]

7. गरीब राजद्वार ना जाइए, सुन चेला यह सीख ।
   खात भजन में भंग हो, रक्त सरूपी भीख ।।

   G.G.S., p. 143.

8. राजद्वार न जाइए, लागै मोटा पाप ।
   खात भजन में भंग हो, ज्यों डंक मारा सांप ।।

   Ibid.

9. दिल्ली मण्डल पाप की भूमाँ, धरती नाल जगाऊं सूमाँ ।
   हस्ती घोड़ा कटक सिघारौं, दिसटि परै असुरों दल मारौं ।।

   Ibid., p. 490

10. दिल्ली के तखत छत्र फिर भी फिरायसी ।
    खेलत गुफ्तार सैंन, भजन सब फोकट फैन,
    महियल राजा बाला पुरुष, सतगुरु दिखलायसी ।।
    आवैगा दखिन सैं दिवाना, काबुल का काल,

There are, however, no direct references to or vivid descriptions of the terrible state of affairs that prevailed throughout the country. The whole of the Punjab was in revolt. The Marathas were at the gates of Delhi. The economic and political conditions were deplorable. "Public business was dealt with as if it were a child's toy; revenue business was disposed of by the heads of the army, and night watchmen decided cases instead of the Qazi. The Emperor was immersed in pleasure, the nobles drank with envy and the servants of the state were starving."[11]

The Hindus probably felt that nemesis was overtaking the Mughal Empire, and the events leading to its fall probably would bring a more tolerant government. But then came two disasterous invasions—the invasion of Nadir Shah and the repeated inroads of Ahmad Shah Abdali. These two political upheavals shook the whole of the empire from its very foundations. But our Saint makes no reference to them. Staying only thirty miles away from Delhi, Garib Das was almost an eyewitness to these events.

Like most of the medieval Saints, Garib Das showed almost complete indifference to the political oppression, misery and degradation of the times. The horrors perpeterated by the King Makers and the invasions of Nadir Shah and Ahmad Shah Abdali did not invoke any direct comments from Garib Das. He seems to have confined himself and his activities only to the religious sphere and as men around him were unarmed, weak, poor and destitute, the Saint perhaps considered silence and fatalistic acceptance of the happenings to be the best attitude.

किलि किलयं, गलि है तुरकाना,
किलि किलयं, अवतार कला,
जीतन जग झुझमला ऐसा पुरुष भ्राया ।
कहता है गरीब दास, दिल्ली मण्डल होय विलास,
निहकलंक राया ।।

Ibid, p. 491.

The above quotation shows that Garib Das like most Hindus was a fururist expecting the great Kalki Avatar to be born. He hopes that a time will come when the Great Reformer Avatar will be born and he will destroy root and branch the evil forces that were dominant at Delhi.

11. S. R. Sharma, *The Crescent over India*, p. 724.

The Hindu idea of a Saint, fundamentally, was of one who had renounced the world and worldly desires. From this spirit of escapist renunciation stemmed the apathy of the Hindu Saints towards all political and economic upheavals in the country. It is because of this outlook that apart from the Sikh Gurus in the north and Swami Ram Das (Shivaji's Guru) in the south, very few Saints were able to give a lead to the people.

Following this tradition of saintliness, Garib Das maintained an unconcerned and indifferent attitude towards the political situation in his country during his lifetime. There is not a word of condemnation of the atrocities perpeterated by the rulers and the misery heaped upon his countrymen by the inhuman cruelty of the invaders. There is only an implied reference to Kali Yuga, the dark age, in which, the poet says, there is utter demoralisation. He writes: "The Pandits have become wild beasts and swallow raw meat. The Brahmin brews wine and drinks it with roasted mutton. The Hindus and Muslims drink wine from the same cup and have lost their distinction while participating in evil. Women have become dissolute and are not loyal to their husbands. No one mourns the dead. The neighbours make merry while there is sorow in the next house."[12]

II

Social Conditions as Reflected in Garib Das

Garib Das lived in the Hindu Society of Eighteenth Century Haryana. The age old Brahmanical structure of Hindu Society, which might have proved useful in the past, had become the cause of an immense setback in the face of Islam. Nevertheless, the general structure of Hindu Society in the times of Garib Das was the same and was traditionally based on Smrities. The four-fold order of Society, the *Varnashrama*, was still prevalent.

12. पण्डित व्याघ्र होहिं, काचा ही गोस्त खावैं ॥
बम्मन के घर भाठी, दारू बकरे तलिए ।
हिन्दू तुर्क न भिन्न, निवाले प्याले रलिए ॥
पंच भरतारी नारी, पतिव्रता नहीं कोई ।
मुवे पुरुष नही शोक, डिगे घर ग्रानन्द होई ॥

Ratan Sagar, p. 127.

Brahmanism still dominated and was the object of severe attacks from Saints of the Nirgun School. Garib Das wrote :

If you, O Barhmin, claim to be of highest birth,
Why did you not come out by a different path.
You wear the sacred thread on your body,
You have forgotten the real path.
Every one is made of the same flesh and bones,
Be it a Brahmin or a Sudra.[13]

The social life of the people as reflected in Garib Das' poetry was built around the village where there was a clearly defined system of organisation, each member of the communitty contributing his or her share to the well-being of the group. The joint family system prevailed and the family bond was a strong one, the sons bringing the bride home to live under the paternal roof and every member of the family being surrounded by social and religious obligations which followed him or her from birth to death. The women performed practically all the manual work in connection with the household and shared in disciplining and training the children. Muslim influence was far less predominant in villages as compared to towns.

The impact of militant Islam and the gentle influence of Sufism was strongly felt by the Hindu Society and its leaders of this period. Garib Das' writings show the existence of both, the orthodox Hindu views and the liberal trends which tried to liberate the Hindu mind from the shackles of a closed and static society.

The Hindus and Muslims know not the true values,
They keep fasts which are without conviction.
Both religions havs no real faith in God,
The Hinus bow to the East and the Muslims to the West.
Forgetting these creeds, I looked north and south,
And, for sure, I found God in all directions.[14]

13. जै तू ब्रह्मन ब्रह्मनी जाया, तो श्रान बाट क्यों न श्राया ।
तैं घाल्या कंध जनेऊ, तू भूल्या बाट बटेऊ ।।
है सब हाड मांस मल गूदा, यामै को ब्राह्मण को सूदा ।

G.G.S., p. 644

14. हिन्दू तुरक कदर नहीं जानैं, रोजा ग्यास करैं धिगतानैं ।
दोनूं दीन यकीन न श्रासा, वे पूरब वे पछिम निवासा ।।

Although caste system prevailed in the old traditional manner, its hold on the mind of the masses was loosening. Each caste was still performing the function accorded to it, but the Bhakti movement had given the lower castes an equal opportunity to pray and worship. The saints of the Bhakti Movement created new scriptures, new temples and new prayers and congregations, the study and use of which was open to all castes and creeds.

> God's realm is a wonderful place,
> It is a place for the liberated souls;
> It is a congregation of the intoxicated ones,
> There are no differences of caste and creed.[15]

Although Kabir, Guru Nanak and later on, Garib Das tried their best to bridge the religious differences between the Hindus and the Muslims, they were not able to do much in that direction except that they set up some schools of thought which continued to stand in between the two commnities as integrating forces. Dr. R.C. Majumdar says : "It is noteworthy that neither the Hindus nor Muslims imbibed, even to the least degree, the chief characteristic features of the other's culture which may be regarded as their greatest contribution to human civilization. The ultra-democratic social ideas of the Muslims, though strictly confined to their own religious community, were an object-lesson in equality and fraternity which Europe, and through her the world, learnt at a great cost only in the nineteehth century. The liberal spirit of toleration and reverence for all religions, preached and practised by the Hindus, is still an ideal and despair of the civilized mankind. The Hindus, even with the living example of the Muslim community before their very eyes, did not relax in the least their social rigidity and inequality of men exemplified in the caste system and untouchability. Nor did the Muslims moderate their zeal to destory ruthlessly the Hindu temples and images of gods, and their

---

दोउं दीन का छाड्या लेखा, उत्तर दक्खिन में हम देखा ।
गरीब दास हम निश्चय जाना, चारों कूंट दसौं दिस ध्याना ॥

Ratan Sagar, p. 289

15. अजब खूब खालिक जहाँ, मुक्ति मुहला मोख ।
मजलिस मतवाले महलि, जाति पाँति नही दोख ॥

G.G.S., p. 28

attitude in this respect remained unchanged, from the day when Muhammed bin Qasim set foot on the soil of India till the eighteenth century A.D., when they lost all politicat power. The Hindus combined catholicity in religious outlook with bigotry in social ethics, while the Muslims displayed an equal bigotry in religious ideas with catholicity in social behaviour."[16]

While the political status of the Hindus was not such as to inspire love and goodwill towards the Muslims, the social and religious differences were so acute and fundamental that they raised a Chinese wall between the two communities. Religion which formed the very basis of culture and the keynote of life both among the Muslims and the Hindus, kept them apart like two poles in the cultural sphere. The movement started by Ramananda, Kabir and Guru Nanak to bridge the gap was carried further by Garib Das in a number of ways. He, being a staunch Kabirpanthi, carried the mission of his Master as far as the times and the society in which he lived allowed. He deplored the artificial difierences created by Hindu and Muslim fanatics and pointed out that both worshipped the same God and aspired after the same spiritual Truth.

What of the Hindus and what of the Muslims,
All were born in the same way,
What of the Brahmin and what of the Sudra,
They are all made of the same flesh and blood.[17]

Garib Das broke down even the linguistic barriers between the Hindus and Muslims. He frequently used Persian, Hindi, Rajasthanl, Punjabi and mingled Sanskrit and Sufi religious terminology to remove all narrow sancity attached to any language. He came out strongly against language fanaticism which has cropped up again in free India today in an equally ugly from. The spoken langauges had, by now, become as important as the classical and court languages. People could now read the writings of the Saints in popular languages and

16. R.C. Majumdar and others : *The History and Culturre of the Indian People*, Vol VI, p. 616-17.

17. कैसे हिन्दू तुरक कहाँ, सबही एकै द्वारै आया ।
कैसे ब्राह्मण कैसे सूदा, एकै हाड चाम तन गूदा ।।
G.G.S., p. 494

enter religious life without the aid of priests and Pandits. It is his grand mastery of the modern languages that led Dr. Mohan Singh to say that Garib Das' knowledge of other Indian languages was greater than that of any other Indian poet of medieval India, the only poet who comes near to him being Shah Qayam Din Chisti.[18]

The medieval Saints were making a searching criticism of both Hinduism and Islam. They were imbibing the best that was in both. They were trying to synthesise the social structures of Hinduism and Islam into a well integerated Indian Culture that we are still trying hard to achieve. The path of righteousness, love of God and spirituality was the common meeting ground for both the Societies. Garib Das pointed out the errors of both Hindus and Muslims. He wrote : "A child in the mother's womb is neither Hindu nor Muslim. The two creeds quarrel in vain because their Maker is one and the same.[19]

Garib Das' writings show that idolatory and image worship were still rampant in north India and like his predecessors he tried his best to fight it. His intense monism inspired him to preach vehemently against idolatory and image worship. People were responding to these healthy ideals with great enthusiasm.

Leaving the Supreme God, they worship stones,
They turn their back to the Living Spirit,
And worship dead Matter.
They love the dead stone
and turn away from the Living God.
They will go straight to Hell,
And never attain salvation.
They worship a stone as God,
Utterly blind is this world.
They serve not the True Lord,
Where will this worship lead them?
I am sorry for them.

18 Dr. Mohan Sing, *Introduction to Punjabi Literature*, p. 152.

19. गरीबदास गति गर्भ की, कछु लखै न माता ।
दोहुं दीन भिड़-भिड़ मरैं, वोह एक विधाता ।।
G.G.S., p. 601.

How can iron be transformed,
without contacting the Philosper's Stone?[20]

Socially, the Hindu were demoralised and down-trodden. J.N. Sarkar says, "The only life that the Hindus could lead was a life deprived of the consolations of religion, deprived of social union and public rejoicing, of wealth and confidence that is begotten by the free exercise of natural activities and use of opportunities, in short, a life exposed to constant public humiliation and political disabilities. Heaven and earth alike were closed to him as long as he remained a Hindu. Apart from the restrictions about food, differences of religious doctrines and rituals, rules forbidding inter-marriages etc., this polar difference in their outlook upon life made a fusion between Hindus and Muslims impossible. In addition to these the Quranic polity made life intolerable for the Hindus under orthodox Muhammaden rule."[21]

Under these conditions, Saints like Garib Das were trying to break down the social barriers and build a spiritual unity between the Hindus and the Muslims. They deemed the two, Hindus and Muslims, alike in the eyes of God. They also pointed out that cultural differences between the two were the artificial creation of different religious orders. Garib Das advised Hindus and Muslims to respect each other's sentiments about the cow and the swine. The Saint perhaps did not realise that the cow was worshipped by the Hindus while the swine was hated by the Muslims.

Garib Das says Hindus eat the hog,

20. गरीब पारब्रह्म को छांड़ि कर पूजें आन अनीत ।
चेतन सेती श्रोलने, जड़ सेती है प्रीत ।।
गरीब पाहन सेती प्रीतड़ी, चेतन सेती दोष ।
दोजख धारै जाँहिगे, कदे न पावैं मोख ।।
गरीब पत्थर परमेश्वर कहैं, योह जग अंधा घोर ।
साहब पर सेवा नहीं, पौंहचेंगे किस ठौर ।।
पत्थर परमेश्वर कहैं, बड़ा अंदेशा मोहि ।
पारस सैं भेट्या नहीं, कैसे पलटै लोह ।।
G.G.S., p. 88.

21. J.N. Sarkar : *Auragnzeb*, p. 444.

Muslims devour the cow.
Both of them indulge in slaughter,
The Devil has gripped them both,
Both are headed towards Hell.[22]

Thus we see that in the 18th Century Indian society there was a mighty effort on the part of Hindu and Muslim saints to understand each other's culture. The medieval Saints emphasised that the true ideals of both Islam and Hinduism were the same, namely, the worship of one Supreme Being, abstinence from earthly joys and mercy towards all creatures. The fanatics on both sides created a great barrier between the two. The Muslims abused the Hindus as *kafirs* while Hindus denounced the Muslims as *mlechhas.* But under the influence of Saints like Garib Das people were trying to understand these swear words differently. Garib Das has given a remarkable exposition of the word *kafir* as follows:

Listen to my dissertation on *kaflr*,
In the name of Ram and Khuda.
kafir is one who gives no charity,
*kafir*is one who quarrels with the Saints.
kafir is one who disobeys his father,
Such a *kafir* goes to hell.
He is a *kafir* who kills his daughtar,
He is a *kafir* who sets a forest on fire,
He is a *kafir* who sacrifices animals,
He is a *kafir* who worships idols,
He is a *kafir* who steals crops
He is a *kafir* who kills the peacock,
kafir is one who takes intoxicants,
kafir is one who smokes tobacco.[23]

22. गरीब सूर गऊ कू खात हैं, विसमल करैं हमेश ।
दोहुं दीन दोजख गए, जम कूँ पकरे केश ।

Ratan Sagar, p. 66.

23. काफिर बोध सुनो रे भाई, दोहूं दीन बीच राम खुदाई ।
काफिर दान यज्ञ नहीं करहीं, काफिर साध संत से भ्ररहीं ।
काफिर पिता वचन उलटाहीं- इतने काफिर दोजख जाहीं ।
वै काफिर जो कन्या मारैं, वै काफिर जो वनखंड जारैं ।

So a heretic (kafir or mlechha) was to be judged by his deeds and not by race, caste or creed. A heretic was one who was devoid of moral and spiritual qualities and indulged in vice. Thus there were *kafirs* and *mlechhas* among Hindus as well as among Muslims. There were saintly and holy persons amongst both, and these great men were universally respected.

Garib Das did not travel much. His contacts and influence were confined to Haryana, Punjab, Rajasthan and a part of Uttar Pradesh. His writings portary the social and cultural conditions mainly of Haryana and the neighbouring regions. They are replete with the rural social culture of this region. The cow and the spinning wheel, the two main props of Indian economy, have dominated the minds of Indian thinkers from the ancient times to the modern. The word spinning wheel occurs frequently in Garib Das' poetry.

Garib Das refers to a famine which took place during his life time. Mughal history has recorded some famines upto the time of Aurangzeb. This famine possibly occured either after the invasion of Nadir Shah or after the invasion of Abdali. The exact date is not known. The Saint showed considerable concern about it. He says : "The princes and the nobles of Delhi who lived on *nan* and *pulao* go about begging, but they do not get a loaf now."[24]

Tobacco was introduced in India during the time of Jahangir. As the habit of smoking was spreading fast, Jahangir, Shah Jahan and Aurangzeb issued edicts prohibiting smoking. But this evil kept on growing. Guru Gobind Singh made smoking a taboo for the Sikhs. He thought of nipping this evil in the bud. The use of other intoxicants was also common. Garib Das wrote very strongly against smoking and taking intoxicants.

वै काफिर जो श्रंतर काती, वै काफिर जो देवल जाती ।
वै काफिर जो खेती चोरं, वै काफिर जो मारैं मोरं ।
काफिर भंग भसौडी भरही, काफिर हुक्के कूं सर करही ।
G.G.S., p. 397

24. सहजादे मांगत फिरैं, दिल्ली के उमराव ।
एक रोटी पाई नहीं, खाते नान पुलाव ॥
G.G.S., p. 189

He writes :

Those who drink wine and eat meat
And commit adultery; their head is cut off
Seventy times in different births,
God is my witness.[25]

Again :

Tobacco invites death, my man;
Characterless people smoke *hukka*.[26]

He points out that people, particularly Sadhus, were in the habit of taking tobacco and other intoxicants and indulged in adultery. Thus there was a strong feeling against drinking wine and smoking tobacco, although these habits had unfortunately been on the increase and had even been made attractive by commercial firms trading in tobacco and wine.

Women were highly respected in society. A faithful wife became the symbol of a faithful devotee or Bhakta. Women also played a great part in helping men in the fields and in their manual labour. The cottage industry of spinning or preparing other household necessities was maintained mainly by women. Sita and Savitri formed their ideal which sustained family ties so strongly that there were no divorces. Pious women went to the temples regularly and led an extremely religious life at home and in public. They shared the joys and sorrows of life with men. Garib Das highly praised these women. At the same time, he condemned women who used ornaments and toilet only to look smart and attract people and mislead them.

Religious Conditions

Sant Garib Das was primarily a religious teacher. We get a vivid picture of the religious conditions of his times from his writings. One of the most striking features of the religious condition of the times is that inspite of the bigoted policy of Aurangzeb and some of his successors resulting in forced con-

25. सुरापान मद मांसाहारी, गमव करैं भोगैं पर नारी ।
सत्तर जनम कटत हैं सीसं, साक्षी है साहिव जगदीशं ।।
Ratan Sagar, p. 210

26 तमाखू तलबदार जम का जमान,
हुक्का हुकम नेश पीबैं हिवान ।
G.G.S., p. 462

versions on a large scale, Garib Das' homeland, so close to Delhi, preserved its ancient Hindu piety, traditions and faith almost unmolested.

As it appears from the writings of Garib Das, people were still inspired and guided by the ideals potrayed in the *Mahabharta*, *Ramayana* and *Bhagvata Purana*. The Vaishnava piety preached by the *Bhagvata* and the ascetic ideals practised by *Sadhus* and mendicants were still popular. The Saint makes strong comments about them. He says :

> The *Udasi* (ascetic) wanders from one home to another begging for simple food. Why should a saint beg for his food, if his mind is fixed on God?[27]

Saiva Sidhanta and Nathpanthi Yoga still prevailed in their medieval pattern. The influence of Yoga was still quite strong. To attend to the emotional needs of these schools of thought Garib Das has written *Krishna Stotra*, *Shiva Stotra* and has referred frequently to the stories from the *Mahabharata*. For him, God alone was Krishna as well as Shiva.

The formal worship of various gods and goddesses was still prevalent. The priests and pandits and mullas dominated the village society. The reformist leaders had, however, introduced new forms of worship in which Hindu dieties and priests had no share. The musical services like *bhajan*, *katha* and *kirtan* and open air sermons were popular in which people could engage in prayer and worship of God without the aid of idols or priests. "A *bhajan* is a choral service in which all those who are present, have a share. A *kirtan* is a service in which a leading singer expounds a theme and invites a group of attendants or the audience to join in a refrain. A *katha* is interpreted in two ways. In the Punjab, *katha* simply means the interpretation or explanation of scriptures. In Maharashtra and some other provinces, *katha* seeks to arouse patriotic and religious fervour by the musical narration of the exploits of heroes and gods".[28]

The writings of Garib Das show that the influence of Mullas,

27. रूखा-सूखा भिक्खा माँगै, घर-घर फिरै उदासी ।
सो भिक्खा को माँगन जावै, जिनकी वृत्ति प्रकासी ॥
G.G.S., p. 265

28. W.S. Deming : *Ram Das and Ramdasis*, p. 10

Qazis and Brahmins was on the wane. There was a strong reaction against Brahminical sacerdotalism and an effort was being made to lift religion from formal and outward piety to an inward discipline. Garib Das, like Guru Nanak, also attacked the outer forms of religion.

> "Those who worship *Saligram* waste their time in offering milk to a lifeless stone. Ravidas was dearer to God than those Brahmins who wore the sacred thread. Wearing the sacred thread is useless. It will be burnt with the body. It lasts only a few months. Of what use is then the sacred thread?"[29]

The Yoga of the Nathpanthis and all the hypocricy that prevailed with it is vividly brought out in the criticism levelled against it by Garib Das.

> "These people have put on a religious garb and left their homes. But their mind is not in their control. They have put on ashes on their bodies and make many pretentions. They know not their real home while they mislead people by various formal practices. They have split their ears and have become Yogis. They appear to be happy from outside but at heart they are suffering and in sorrow. They themselves are alive but they worship an idol which is utterly lifeless. They know not the Anhad Sabad, Celestial Music. The idol which they worship is made by the potter or the sculptor. He chisels the face with his hammer. Worship of such stone gods is a life in darkness."[30]
>
> *G.G.S.*, p. 482

29. जिन शालिग शिला बुलाई, जड़ पाहन दूध पिलाई ।
जाकै कनक जनेऊ बाना, रैदास विप्र हम जाना ।।
गल सूत जनेऊ धागा, सो देही संग जरि जागा ।
योह चालत है षटमासा, इस धागे की क्या आसा ।।

G.G.S., p. 535

30. भेख बनाइ दई है टीकी, इन्द्री, मन, मनसा नहीं जीती ।
बहु विधि भांति किए आचारा, कहा भया तन लाई छारा ।।
जूट रखाय भद्र भए भाई, निज घर की कोई खबर न पाई ।
कान चिराय भए है जोगी, बहरमुखी है रिधि के भोगी ।।

Notwithstanding a more realistic and practical apporach to religion introduced by the Nirgun school of Bhakti the spiritual hunger of the common people still maintained the traditional forms of worship. The emotional expression of religion continued to manifest itself among them, chiefly in the form of poetry and legend. The epic stories and the legends of the *Mahabharata*, the *Ramayana* and the popular *Puranas*, like the stories of Prahlada, Draupadi, Harishchandra, Sita and Rama, Krishna and the Gopis, still fascinated the minds of the people and we find Garib Das refering to them frequently.[31]

Dr. Farquhar in his *Outline of Religious Literature of India* points out that there were three distinct stages in the theistic movement which had Vishnu as its centre. The first stage was represented by the original heroic poems called the *Mahabharata* and the *Ramayana* which narrated historical legends without any attempt at transformation or enlargement. In this stage, there was no attempt to gloss over the faults of the heroes. In the second stage, the, two of these heroes, Rama and Krishna, were identified with Vishnu. In the final stage, the *Bhagvad Gita* carried the process a step further when it identified Krishna, the hero of the epic, not merely with Vishnu but also with Paramabrahma of the *Upanisads*. Krishna here becomes the Absolute, the one without a second, the source of all things and all beings. In the poetry of Saint Garib Das we find indications of the prevalence of all these types of Krishna and Rama worship side by side, although Garib Das himself accepted these heroes only as historical figures and not as manifestations of God. For him, God was all in all. In Him he saw Krishna, Rama and Siva.[32]

It appears from the writings of Garib Das that the Bhakti practised in Haryana under the influence of Kabirpanthi and Dadupanthi Saints was wholesome and restrained. It was neither

---

चेतन मूरत जड़कू पूजें, अनहद शब्द न मूरख बूझें।
याह जड़ मूरत घडी ढठेरे, माथा फोरैं भारि अंधेरे ॥

G.G.S., p. 48

31. See his पांडों की कथा, अम्बरीषकी कथा, हरिश्चन्द्र की कथा etc.

32. See his कृष्ण स्तोत्र and शिव स्तोत्र etc.

as hysterically emotional as the Bhakti of Sri Chaitanya in Bengal nor so deeply intellectual as the Bhakti of Jnanadeva in Maharashtra. The Nirguna Bhakti tradition repeatedly mentioned in the Grantha of Garib Das shows that it had taken quite deep roots in Haryana.[33]

Inspite of the fact that Garib Das preached against asceticism and self-mortification, ascetic tendencies were still quite strong in Haryana. Garib Das' own son become a sanyasi. The Yogis and Sadhus frequented Haryana and are repeatedly mentioned in the songs of Garib Das. The Shakta Cult, notorious for its degenerate practices known as *Vamacara* (left-hand practices), is also severly criticised by Garib Das. "Association with a Shakta is like association with Ravana, Kamsa and Hiranyakahsyapa."[34] Yet the basic philosophy of Saiva Sidhanta, the Tantra Cult, was present in a new and adapted form in Garib Das' Bhakti and mysticism also. We shall discus it in detail in the next chapter. (The terms *Sabda*, *Shiva*, *Shakti* etc. occur frequently in the writings of Garib Das.)

A very healthy feature of the religious situation of this period was that there was an attempt to synthesise Saivism and Vaisnavism and abridge the ideological gap between them. The synthesis of Hinduism and Islam was also accompanied by a synthesis of the divergent school of Hindu sects and creeds. A unity of spirit was developed in a diversity of expression. An attempt was made to bind the Hindus in the spiritual bond of a Universal Religion.

Garib Das was primarily a mystic poet and not a historian. As a Saint of the Nirguna School he was keenly interested in the Saints of the past and his writings throw a good deal of light on the life of Jayadeva, Namadeva, Kabir, Sadhna and others. He also refers to Guru Nanak, Gorakh Nath and some legendry figures of Mahabharata times. Garib Das has written a *Bhaktamal* of his own. We find the following accounts of medieval Saints.

33. See भक्तमाल in *G.G.S.* and in *Ratan Sagar*.
34. साकट सेती साख क्या, रावण कंसा बूझ ।
हिरणाकुश और बालि से मारें परगट गूंज ।।
G.G.S., p. 89

Gorakh Nath

Gorakh Nath has been considered a historical figure by some writers but has been treated as a mythological figure by many others. Dr. Sukumar Sen says : "Historicity can be safely postulated for almost all the early Natha Siddhas except Gorakh Natha, the most important figure of them all." Dr. Mohan Singh treats him as a mythological figure in his *Gorakh Nath and Medieval Mystics* but in his later writings, viz., his *History of Punjabi Literature*, he treats him as a historical figure. Garib Das considers him a historical figure like Dattatreya and Jalandhar Nath. Gopi Chand and Bhartrihari are also mentioned by him in the context of Gorakh Nath. These great Yogis are mentioned with great respect though their creed, particularly its formalism, is not accepted.

Jayadeva

Jayadeva is the next Saint mentioned with great admiration as one who achieved perfection and the grace of God. "Jayadeva was once entertained by a King who honoured him for his saintliness and scholarship. When he took leave of him after a year, he met a group of thugs on the way who robbed him of every thing, cut off his hands and threw him into a well. There came a caravan of traders who rescued him from the well and took him to the next big city. The ruler of the state came to meet him and honoured him by making him his minister. After twelve years there was a great famine and the same thugs came to Jayadeva disguised as Sadhus. Jayadev recognised them but did not disclose their identity to anyone else. He entertained them as his friends for a whole year. The king also honoured them and knowing them to be Jayadeva's friends, he gave them a good load of wealth and two men to guard them on their way through the forest. On the way, the king's men asked them how the friendship developed between them and Jayadeva. They told a lie and said that Jayadev was a gangster who had committed many crimes and that he had bribed them lest they revealed his true story. Immediately a big meteor fell from the sky and the thugs were buried under it. The matter was reported to Jayadev who felt extremely sorry for them and rubbed together the stumps of his hands which immediately beame whole.[35]

Guru Nanak

The name of Guru Nanak is mentioned with utmost respect throughout the *Granth* of Garib Das. His name occurs along with Dadu and Kabir. In one place he says that Guru Nanak was an *avatar* of Janak.[36] This theory was first introduced by Meharban, nephew of Guru Arjan, and was very much resented and criticised by the Guru. Guru Arjan describes Guru Nanak as *Gobindrupa,* Embodiment of the Supreme Spirit. Bhai Gurdas also calls him Nirankari. In Bhai Mani Singh's *Sikhandi Bhaktamala*, a story is told that some Sikhs asked Guru Arjan whether Guru Nanak was really an *avatar* of Janak. Guru Arjan severely criticised this theory.[37]

Namadeva

Some of the stories of Namadeva which we fiind also in the autobiographical hymns of the Saint in the *Adi Granth*, are recorded by Garib Das in his *Bhaktamal.* The name of Namadeva occurs in many places. The followings story about Namadeva is told in the *Bhaktamal* of Garib Das. It is said that one day Namadeva's father asked him to offer milk to the family God. Namadeva took this duty seriously and begged and prayed to the God to drink the milk. Moved by the innocent prayers of Namadeva the Divine Spirit appeared in the form of the deity and drank the milk.[38]

Kabir

A few stories of the life of Kabir are also given. Kabir being the Guru of Garib Das received his attention to a considerable extent. Two interesting anecdotes are, (1) the suffering

35. *G.G.S.*, p. 259
36. अंस औतार सैं जनक नानक भए।

    G.G.S., p. 579
37. Bhai Mani Singh : *Sikhan di Bhaktmala,* p. 89
38. *G.G.S.*, p. 312

of Kabir at the hands of Sikandar Lodhi and (2) his talks with Sikandar Lodhi when the Emperor was impressed by the spiritual greatness of the Saint.

It is related that when the Mullas and Qazis raised a hue and cry against Kabir, the Saint was arrested and thrown before an elephant. The elephant would not move and harm the Saint who sat in Samadhi. When the elephant refused to harm the Saint, the Emperor fell at the Saint's feet. There is an autobiographical hymn of Kabir in the *Adi Granth* and Garib Das appears to have taken the historical element from it. But in Kabir's hymn the name of the Emperor is not given. Garib Das clearly gives it as Sikandar Lodhi.[39]

For want of adequate historical evidence many scholars doubt it. As Garib Das lived only about two hundred years after Kabir, his evidence should be taken as conclusive because he had access to much material which is lost today.

Another interesting story is that one day both Kabir and Ravi Das took some holy water of the Ganges in a bottle of wine and paraded the streets as if they were drunk. This shocked the whole city. The Saints wanted to test their followers. Only a few faithful ones had full confidence that Kabir and Ravidas could never drink wine. They refused to talk ill of the Masters.[40]

There is a controversy amongst scholars, who have specialised on the life and writings of Kabir, about the place of Shah Taqoi in the Saint's life. "Great interest attaches to the mention of Sheikh Taqi," says G.H. Westcott in his *Kabir and Kabir Panth.* According to the Hindu legends Sheikh Taqi was a rival and opponent of Kabir, while Muhammedans regarded him as a Pir (Guru).[41] From the writings of Garib Das it is clear that he was a rival who was probably jealous of Kabir.[42] Garib Das also makes it clear that Kabir was initiated into spiritual life by Ramananda at the age of five. This is a fact mentioned by very few historians. The meeting is vividly

39. *G.G.S.*, p. 313
40. *G.G.S.*, p. 313
41. G.H. Westcott : *Kabir and Kabir Panth*, p. 23
42. *G.G.S.*, p. 448

described by Garib Das.[43] There is a popular saying attributed to Ramananda that Bhakti arose in the Dravida land, Ramananda brought it to the North and Kabir spread it to the seven continents and nine divisions of the world. There is a poem of Garib Das which says exactly the same thing about Ramananda. He says :

> There was Bhakti only in Dravad Land,
> There was not the slightest Bhakti left here,
> There was worship of evil here and a lot of hypocricy.
> Ramananda came from Dravid land
> and stayed at Benares.[44]

Thus Garib Das believes that Ramananda, a great mystic, came from the South and settled at Banaras. He had about fourteen hundred disciples.[45]

The other saints mentioned by Garib Das are Trilochan of Maharashtra who became very popular for his piety and saintliness;[46] Bajid and Shaikh Farid, the well known Sufi Saints, the latter of whom was noted for his ascetic temperament; Tukaram who maintained his faith in God all through trials and tribulations.;[47] Sadhna the butcher who, though bricked alive, died fearlessly.;[48] Ravidas and Rani Jhali, who was probably Mira Bai, and Narsi Mehta; Rabiya and Mansur, the great Muslim mystics. There are many other references to lesser known Saints like Tursi and Tapiya.

Mythological References in Garib Das

Mythology, which with its wonders and marvels admits of equally marvellous explanations of them, is the key to Hindusim.

43. *G.G.S.*, p. 197
44. भक्ति द्राविड़ देश की, इहां नहीं एक रंच ।
    ऊत भूत की ध्यावना, पाखंड और प्रपंच ।
    रामानंद आनंद में, काशी नगर मंझार ।
    देश द्राविड़ छांड़ि करि, आए पुरी विचार ।।
    G.G.S., p. 197
45. *Ibid.*
46. *G.G.S.*, p. 269
47. *G.G.S.*, p. 270
48. *G.G.S.*, p. 310

No Indian writer and no Indian Saint upto this day has been able to completely do without it. Garib Das refers to a number of well-known mythological stories which we will describe here briefly.

Urvasi : She is a celestial nymph known for her beauty and charms. A sight of her beauty is said to have caused the birth, in a peculiar way, of the sages Agastya and Vasishtha by Mitra and Varuna. She roused the wrath of these two gods and incurred their curse, as a result of which she came to live upon earth and became the wife of Pururava.[49]

Hidimb : A powerful demon and cannibal who had yellow eyes and a horrible aspect dwelt in the forest to which the Pandavas retired after the burning of their house. He had a sister named Hidamba, whom he sent to lure the Pandavas to him. But on meeting with Bhima she fell in love with him, and offered to carry him away to safety on her back. Bhima refused and while they were parleying, Hidimb, her brother, came up and a terrible fight ensued in which Bhima killed the monster. Hidimba was as first much terrified and fled, but she returned and claimed Bhima for her husband. By his mother's permission. Bhima married her and had a son by her mamed Ghatotkachha,

Harischandra : He was the twenty-eighth King of the solar race and son of Trisanku. He was cleberated for his piety and justice. There are several legends about him. He once incurred the anger of Visvamitra who demanded the sacrificial gift due to him as a Brahmin, and the King offered him whatever he might choose. Viswamitra stripped him of his wealth and kingdom, leaving him nothing but a garment of bark and his wife and son. In a state of destitution he left the kingdom.[50]

Ahilya : She was the beautiful wife of Rishi Gautama. In the *Ramayana* it is stated that she was the first woman made by Brahma, and that he gave her to Gautama. She was seduced by Indra. It is said Indra assumed the from of her husband and deceived her. Another story is that Indra secured the help of Moon, who assumed the from of a cock and crowed at midnight. This roused Gautama to his morning devotions

49. *G.G.S.*, p. 75
50. *Ratan Sagar*, Pp. 123-125

when Indra went in and took his place. Gautama expelled Ahilya from his harmitage and cursed her and made her invisible. She was restored to her natural state by Rama and reconciled to her husband. According to the *Mahabharata*, Gautama's curse impressed upon Indra a thousand marks resembling the female organ. So he was called *Sahasrayoni*. But these marks were later on changed to eyes and he was called *Sahasranetra*.[51]

Moradhvaja : He was a King known for his charity and virtues. His son was Tamradhvaja. One day god Visvambhara came to him along with a tiger. He asked the king to arrange food for his tiger. He also told the king that his tiger would eat either the flesh of the king or of his son or of his queen. When Moradhvaja actually offered the flesh of his son Tamradhvaja, the god was plased and blessed the king. Garib Das has written the whole story to illustrate his idea of self-sacrifice.[51]

Ganika and Ajamil : The story of Ganika and Ajamil is repeatedly told in Bhakti literature. Ganika was a prostitute who was completely changed when a sadhu visited her and asked her to utter the name of God. The sadhu left a parrot with her to remind her of the truth.[52] Ajamil was a great sinner who had a son named Narayana which is also the name of God. When Ajamil was about to die he called out "Narayan" and thus began to think of God. It is believed that because he remembered God at the time of his death he was saved. All Bhaktas believe that if a man remembers God at the time of his death he is saved.[53]

Durvasa : He was a rishi, a son of Atri and Anusuya According to some authorities he was an emanation of Siva. He was noted for his irascible temper and many a one fell under his curse. It was he who cursed Sakuntala for keeping him waiting at the door, and so caused the separation between her

51. *Ratan Sagar*, p. 111—13
52. छान छिवाई, गऊ जिवाई, गनिका चढ़ी विमान मैं।
    सदना बकरे कूं मत मारै, पहुंचे श्रान निदान में।
    Ratan Sagar, p. 143
53. श्रजामेल से श्रधम उधारे, पतित पावन बिरद तास के।
    Ibid.

and King Dushyanta. But it was he who blessed Kunti, so that she became the mother of five sons. Garib Das relates the story of Durvasa and Ambarish so often told in the *Puranas*. He also sings the story of Durvasa and Draupadi and Krishna told in the *Mahabharata*.[54]

54. *G.G.S.*, p. 253

CHAPTER IV

Philosophy and Religion of Garib Das

Garib Das was not a philosopher in the technical sense of the term. As a matter of fact, like all medieval saints, he discouraged all philosophy which confined itself only to the sphere of the intellect (buddhi). They depended for their higher experiences and knowledge on intuition and they were of the opinion that intellect was only an instrument of human understanding. It could go only to a certain limit beyond which intuition alone reveals Reality.

Although we find no distinct or independent philosophical theories in the monumental religious writings on Garib Das, they give us immense material on the nature of the Ultimate Reality, the Soul and the World. We will discuss the Philosophy of Garib Das under the following heads: (i) Metaphysics, (ii) Ethics, (iii) Mysticism, (iv) Social Philosophy. Next, we will discuss the Religious Idealism of Garib Das along with its institutions.

Metaphysics

In the writings of Garib Das, "metaphysics is subordinated to mysticism". The highest principles apprehended by pure reason are to be apprehended in mystic experiences.

God is the Ultimate Reality. He is formless and hence all anthropomorphism is condemned. God is One and Absolute. All creatures and creation depend on the One God. He is the Lord of heaven and earth. He begets not nor is He ever begotten. None can be compared to Him. In the entire Universe there is but One Eternal Lord. All things arise from the power of His action under the influence of His creative Will. Infinite are His names and endless are His universes of wondrous workmanship. At the time of Creation, there was only the one Absolute God. And all will dissolve into Him, at the time of dissolution.

"He is One, Infinite", says Garib Das, "He is Unseen, Unfathomable, without support, Ocean of Mercy, Compassionate,

Creator and Omnipresent. He is merciful and kind to the poor and humble. He can be seen within the heart. He is the Lord. He is the immortal Being and the all pervading spirit. From the Unmanifest comes the Manifest and in the Manifest is the Unmanifest and millions are His manifestations. The Supreme and Merciful Creator is seen in His creation. He is Unborn, Transcendent and without any form. The Creator is ever in His creation and the creation is the living Form of the Creator. He is on the earth. He is in heavens. He is everywhere. The Unfathomable One is everywhere."[1]

Sant Garib Das does not see God as an abstract nothing. To him God is Light (*Nur*). His light is like the blazing splendour of the sun. It is the light that shines in all souls and pervades everywhere. It is the light the vision of which alone dispels all inner darkness. The light of God is revealed in the Saints. The spiritual experiences of the Saints are an evidence of the revelation of His light. His light is beyond the comprehension of ordinary mortals.

Says Garib Das: "Contemplate on the Divine Light which is the true breaker of bonds. The Inscrutable is a self-existent Light, which mysteriously pervades the earth, the waters and the sky. In this and other worlds there is but one light of God.

1. अलफ, अपार, अलील, अगोचर, निरबानी, निरधारं ।
कृपासिंधु करीम पुरुष तूं, है हाजिर कर्तारं ।।
दीन दयाल दया के सागर, दिल अंदर दीदारं ।
बेचगून, चिंतामणि साहिब, है सो वार न पारं ।।
अकल, करीम, पुरुष अविनाशी, रमता राम कहावै ।
बाहर भीतर, भीतर बाहर, खेलत है निरदावै ।।
मालिक, मीरां, मौला साहिब, मुरशिद पीर हमारा ।
सरगुण, निर्गुण, निर्गुण सरगुण, अनंत कोटि अवतारा ।।
अलफ, इलाम, करीमा, कादिर, है कुदरत कै मांही ।
स्थावर जंगम जूनि जिहाना, सब घट व्यापक साँई ।।
निरजूनी, निर्लेप, निरंजन, मंजन मूर्ति मीतं ।
खालिक खलक, खलक मैं खालिक, सोहं शब्द अतीतं ।।
अरस कुरस में व्यापक देवा, पूर रह्या जगदीशं ।
दृष्टि मुष्टि सैं अगम अगोचर, देख्या बिसवे बीसं ।।

G.G.S., 378

Make Faith thy telescope and see His light in your own heart and in your own spiritual experience. The heart is the Temple of God which is light. God is self-absorbed in His light. He can be seen in the transcendent state. Fools in their ignorance cannot see His light. He has been realized by the Saints in the spirit of true Yoga. In the Sunya (Transcendent State), He can be realized."[2]

According to Garib Das this transcendent state of God, in which His light is revealed, is a higher spiritual state which was not achieved even by Gorakh and Dattatreya. "There the *dhyana* of Gorakh and Dattatreya does not reach. There only the supreme light of God prevails."[3] Garib Das further calls it *Nur Nagar*, the City of Light. It is a state of Nirvana, a state which can be attained through the Satguru.[4] This Formless Light is Perfect, Ineffable, above all *gunas*, beyond knowledge (*Jnana*) and contemplation (*dhyana*). His mystery has not been known by any of the great Sages like Narada, Sanaka, Sanandana, or even by the Sheshnaga. The object of our worship should be His light and not any gods or goddesses.

2. बंदीछोड साहिब का ध्यान धारौ, निरालंब निजनूर निज नेक है जी ।
जल थल मैं थीर गंभीर गैबी, देखो लोक परलोक मैं एक है जी ।।
धरि ध्यान दुरबीनि अकीन कीजै, दिल देहरै पैंठि करि परखि भाई ।
कुरबांन कर्तार के सेहरे परि, जहां सुरति और निरति दोहूं निरखि आई ।।
अलहनूर मौले मगन आप हैं जी, गलतांन सुभांन सही देखि लीजै ।
बैठे अरश के तखत परि आप सांईं, दीदार कै वासतै शीश दीजै ।।
जोती जगमगैं जोग बिजोग बांनी, जाकी पलक मैं खलक जिहांन है जी ।
नहीं दीखाता मुगध की दृष्टि आवै, संतौं खोजि लीया कलधूत है जी ।।
शून्य सैल करि सिध मैं सुरति पैठी, जहां आप अविगति अनभूत है जी ।।
G.G.S., p. 435

3. जहां दत्त गोरख नहीं ध्यान ध्यानी, अचल नूर ही नूर देखौ तमासा ।
अरश कुरश के बाग मैं कौन माली, जहां नूर जहूर के कंद हैं जी ।
कहै दास गरीब संभालि भईया, देखौ चाखते नहीं जो अंध हैं जी ।।
G.G.S., p. 437

4. नूर नगर बेगम पुरा, परपट्टन थानं ।
सतगुरू सैन लखाईयां, जो पद निरबानं ।।
G.G.S., p. 594

We should sing of the Divine Light. We should praise the Divine Light. We should perform the *Arati* of and worship only the Divine Light.[5] Thus Garib Das concentrates on strict monism in his metaphysical thought and expression.

Garib Das accepts the age-old belief of the Upanishads that all is He, manifested as the many, so that He may enjoy the bliss of reuniting all in the One eternal. God carries the four-fold function of creation, preservation and destruction and bestowal of grace. Souls in their essential nature are the same as God. The Nirguna and the Saguna is represented by such Upanishadic thoughts : "There is One without a second. All this is Brahman."[6] There is the same relation between the

5. अविगत गति कुछ समझ पड़ै नहिं, क्यों पूछै मति मेरी ।
निरंकार, निर्लेप, निरंजन, गुण अतीत तेहु देवा ।
ज्ञान ध्यान से रहै निराला, जानी जाय न सेवा ॥
सनक, सनन्दन, नारद मुनिजन, शेष पार नहिं पावै ।
शंकर ध्यान धरै निस बासर अजहूं ताहु भुलावै ॥
नर की आरति नूर कै झाजै, नूर के ताल पखावज बाजै ।
नूर के ज्ञान नूर कूं गावै, नूर सुनन ते बहुर न आवै ।
नूर की बानी बोले नूर, झिलमिल नूर रह्या भरपूर ।
नूर कबीरा नूर ही भावै, नूर कै कहइ परम पद पावै ॥
G.G.S., p. 278

6. देव ही नहीं तो सेव किसकी करूं, किसे पूजूं कोई नाहीं दूजा ।
दूजा कर्ता ही नहीं तो कीरति किसकी करूं, पिण्ड ब्रह्मण्ड मैं एक सूझा ॥
G.G.S., p. 429

निरगुण सरगुण दुहूं सै न्यारा, गगन मंडल गलतानं,
निरगुण कहूं तो गुण किन्ह कीन्हे, सरगुण कहूं तो हानं ।
निरगुण सरगुण सैं है न्यारा, शब्द अतीत अमोलं ।
G.G.S., p. 330

रूपो न रेखो न धूपो न छाया । थांनो न मानो न ज्ञानो न ध्यानो ।
लिखता न बकता न रखता न बेदो पुरानो ॥
तालो न ख्यालो न मालो न मेला । उपजै न विनसै न गुरुवा न चेला ॥
काया न छाया न माला न मूलं । शाखा न वृक्षो न पतरो न फूलं ॥
वृद्धो न बाला विशाला न पीतं । निहचल निराकार रहता प्रीतम ॥
G.G.S. p. 340

The same ideas are expressed in the following Upanisads:
Chandogdya Upanisad, III. I4 : 1 and VI. 2 : 1
Manduka Upanisad, II. 2: 11

Transcendent and the Immanent Spirit as between milk and ghee or between water and the ocean. Garib Das says: "Just as a bubble swells out of the ocean and merges back into the ocean, so also the soul of man comes out of and ultimately merges into the Infinite Being. Only the Saints realize this. Just as there is fire in the wood and can be taken out with some effort, just as there is oil in sesame and can be taken out by pressing, just as there is butter in milk and can be taken out by churing, so also there is the spark of God in man and he can ignite it by meditation. He who realizes this is a Saint."[7]

Hidden in the soul of every man, God sees all and knows all. He watches all the game that he has himself started, and knows everything that is going on everywhere. Being one with each soul, He knows the needs of everyone and he hears the prayers of everyone. He shares everyone's feelings. He takes part in the joy and suffering of everyone.[8] He protects the Saints and punishes the evil doers.

God alone is Truth. Truth is the antithesis of falsehood. The Eternal Spirit of God is Truth, the world is false. In the beginning and in the middle and in the end, there was, there has been and there shall be Truth. Where there is Truth, there is no falsehood. Those who love Truth have no fear or delusion

7. जैसें पानी के बीच मैं बुद-बुदा होत हैं,
फिरि पानी के बीच पानी समाया।
ऐसै ब्रह्म दरियाव बिचि बुदबुदा ख्याल है,
किसी पारखी संत की दृष्टि आया ॥
जैसे तिली मैं तेल है काष्ट मैं आगि है,
दूध मैं घृत मथि काढ़ि लीया।
सोई नर साध अगाध निहचल भये,
नूर प्याला जिन्हौं जांनि पीया ॥
G.G.S. p. 422

8. जांनैं जांननहार सकल की जानता।
घटघट मैं अविनासी पूरण प्राण था ॥
अविगति भिन्न अभिन्न मंहल मैं महल है।
हाजरि नाजरि देखि कहो क्या गहल है ॥
G.G.S., p. 447

but those who live in falsehood and ignorance live in fear and delusion.[9]

Soul of Man and the World

Apart from saying that the world is made of five elements and twenty five Tattvas, Garib Das is silent about the mode of Creation. He did not apply his mind like earlier metaphysicians to cosmological reflections on Creation and the Creator. He has given only the traditional view which stems from mystical experiences. He takes two aspects of existence—the Unmanifest God (*Nirguna*) and the Manifest Universe (*Saguna*). The *Saguna* being His play is transient. All that is manifest is *maya* which will not last.

Says Garib Das : "So fascinating is *maya* that humanity is caught in its charms. The whole world play is *maya*. The Light of the Guru alone can show man the way out of it. One who is fascinated by *maya* cannot discriminate between friend and foe. Such a man cares only for eating, drinking and being merry. *Maya* invokes deep earthly attachment. It poisons the mind and the soul.[10]

"All created things are *maya*. Even Brahma, Vishnu and Siva are *maya*. All fulfilments of desires are due to *maya*. Kings and paupers are victims of the snare of *maya*. All

9. सोचे का सेवन करूं, झूठे को ल्यूं लूटि ।
सोच शब्द सैं यौं डरै, ज्यों स्याने की मूठि ।
सोचे कूं सिरदा करूं, झूठे झलकै मांहि ।
त्रिगुण अगनि जलत है, झूठे बह बह जांहि ॥
G.G.S., p. 107

10. ऐसी माया मोहिनी, ब्रह्म सरीखा खेल ।
सतगुरु शरणें ऊबरे, जाकी बंकी हेल ॥
ऐसी माया मोहिनी, मोह्या सकल जिहान ।
इस माया की लहर मैं, आए चतुर सुजान ॥
ऐसी माया मोहिनी, दुश्मन गिने न मीत ।
आन अटक मानें नहीं, खाने ही सै प्रीत ॥
ऐसी माया मोहिनी, मोहे मोर चकोर ।
पशु पक्षी छाँड़े नहीं, बाँधे बिस की डोर ॥
G.G.S., p. 84

creatures subject to birth and death are slaves of *maya*. Only Saints like Kabir have conquered *maya* and also birth and death.[11]

"*Maya* is the very matrix of creation. *Maya* is the be all and end of the World. *Maya* spreads in various spheres of creation.[12] Those who say that they have renounced *maya* still live in *maya*, as the whole world, whether cities or forests, is *maya*. There is a *maya* which is the cause of sarrow and there is also a *maya* which is the dispeller of sorrow.[13]

"The body of man is the temple of God. Within it resides the Supreme Being. Man should renounce all promiscuity and such living as may corrupt him.[14] Made from material elements, Man is a being who carries the Light of God in his soul. Within him resides the Perfect Being. Man should not search Him outside his own Self. He is within him.[15] The body should not be mistaken for the real Self. The real Self is immortal while the body is transient."

Garib Das at times identified the Mind with the Soul, because the wisdom of the Soul is reflected through the Mind. Mind has a divine as well as an earthly aspect. The divine aspect is the source of supreme wisdom and leads to enlightenment, while the earthly aspect leads to egoism and abandonment to the lower Self. The Mind has fallen from its heavenly

11. माया ब्रह्मा विष्णु है. माया शंकर शेष ।
पांच तत्व गुण तीन लग, माया ही परवेश ।
माया ही के रंग हैं, माया ही के रूप ।
माया ही के रंक हैं , माया ही के भूप ।। *G.G.S.*, p. 85

12. माया की बाजी रची, माया ही के फूल ।
माया आदि अरु अंत है, लखिए माया मूल ।। *G.G.S.*, p. 86

13. एक माया दुख भंजनी, एक माया दुख मूल ।
एक माया तो गंध है, एक माया है फूल ।। *G.G.S.*, p. 88

14. काया खोजि ले रे, तौ मैं रहता पुरुष अलेख ।
बिबचारनि का संग छांड़ि दे, क्या दिखलावै भेष ।। *G.G.S.*, p. 583

15, जल बूंद सैं जिनि साज साज्या, लहम दरिया नूर वे ।
है सकल सरबंग साहिब, देखि निकट न दूर वे ।। *G.G.S.*, p. 454

abode. It is like a precious gem which once it has been shattered can never be restored to its original shape.[16] The Mind is the creator, the Mind is the reborn. The Mind plays with Good and Evil.[17]

Garib Das calls the divine aspect of Mind *Nuri* (born from Light) and he calls the earthly aspect of Mind *khaki* (earthly). The earthly mind is absored in the lower desires. The divine mind leads to the path of God.[18] Garib Das advises man to conquer the earthly mind with the divine mind, to overpower the weak, unstable and wandering earthly mind and live in the love and protection of the divine mind. He who conquers the mind conquers the world.[19] The mind is absorbed in the delusion of the three *gunas*; the same mind freed from all earthly ties and attractions attains contentment, peace and joy. The mind stands in the way of our spiritual journey and it is the mind that helps us to attain our goal.[20]

16. योह मन गिरा आकाश तें, फूट्या लाल रतन।
    फिर उल्टा मिलता नहीं, कीजै कोटि जतन ॥ *G.G.S.*, p. 72
17. योह मन करता आप है, योह मन नव अवतार।
    सुर असुरों में खेलता, हरदम बारम्बार ॥ *G.G.S.*, p. 73
18. काया मांही दोय दिल, इनमें कौन हमार।
    को अमरापुरि जात है, को भरमै संसार ॥
    नूरी सेती मिलि रहो, खाकी खारिज कीन।
    ज्ञान शब्द से मारिये पांच पचीसौं तीन ॥
    नूरी मन से मिलि रहो, खाकी बड़ा बखील।
    सतगुरु हेला देत हैं, क्यू कीजै शिष ढील ॥ *G.G.S.*, p. 76
19. मन की माया मेर है, मन त्यागे नहि रिंच।
    मन जीते सतगुरू मिलैं, छांड़ सकल परपंच ॥
    मन की माया मेर है, मन जीते जग जीत।
    मन ही मुक्ता हो गया, मन ही पड़दा भीत ॥ *G.G.S.*, p. 79
20. मन ही मारग में खड़ा, मन ही निश्चित धाम।
    मन संसारी में रम्या, योह तिरगुण मन काम ॥
    शील संतोष विवेक कूं, मन ही धरै चलाय।
    मन ही अस्थिर हो रह्या, मन ही ज्ञान सुनाय ॥
    G.G.S., p. 79

Man is the meeting point of Nirguna and Saguna. He has the qualities of both. He has been created out of the Trinity—Brahma, Vishnu, Siva. In the earthly body of man, there are the nine doors of the senses and the Divine Spirit resides in the tenth door, the *Dasam Dwar*, which will be further discussed under mysticism. Man has to struggle through his lower self to his higher self with the help of the Guru.

Ethics of Garib Das

In Indian philosophical thought, ethics has rarely been studied as a separate and distinct subject. It has always been embeddedin the main body of religious and speculative thought. We have therefore to extricate the ethical element from the general religious and philosophical setting.

The Brahmanical morality was based on the authority of the Scriptures. The Brahmins made people do certain things in the name of morality because the Vedas and Shastras commanded them to do so. Garib Das, like many other medieval Saints, rejected this approach. He laid stress on the universal elements of morality.

The most remarkable feature of the ethics of Garib Das is its wide scope. He has subscribed to an ethics which covers nearly all progressive movements of the times such as Sikhism, Vaishnavism and Sufism. He laid the greatest stress on universal moral and spiritual principles. He set very high ethical standards for his followers. Although no ethical code is to be found which sums up his moral discipline, yet the main features of his ethical outlook can be deduced from his writings.

The ethics of Garib Das is individualistic and practical. We will analyse the various virtues which are essential for the attainment of highest knowledge. Ethics is, as we shall note, only preparatory to mystic realization. The divine and demonic heritages are distinguished from each other and identified with knowledge and ignorance. The divine heritage consists of virtues while the demonic heritage consists of vices. We will consider the virtues first.

Purity

Both by precept and example, Garib Das insisted on pure living in thought, speech and deeds. Purity in thought and life was to be maintained at all levels. He has devoted a whole chapter to Purity called *Paknama*. Purity is service, purity is worship and purity is the idol. Purity is the sandalwood, purity is the offering and purity is the highest attainment. Purity is the seat of the worshipper as well as of the object of worship. In purity should men bow to God. It is by being pure that one can see the Pure one.[21]

Because of his stress on purity, Garib Das condemned hypocricy in all forms and in all phases of life. "The hypocrite", says Garib Das, "neither likes the path of Bhakti nor of Mukti; in falsehood he wanders imitating the ways of the Saints."[22] He condemns the hypocricy of Yogis, Bairagis, Sanyyasis. "Thou wearest *kanthi* and *mala* to become a *vairagi*; thereby you only court death by hypocricy. Do not put on the garb of holiness like a hypocrite. You cannot become a Bhakta in this way."[23] Purity in thoughts and actions can be attained by the mind, without any show of piety through holy garbs. If the mind is kept pure and unsullied, then moral behaviour can become above reproach. Garib Das demanded a well disciplined life based on devotion to God with a pure mind. The way to keep

21. पाख सेवा पाख पूजा, पाख शालिगराम वे ।
पाख चन्दन पाख अरपन, पाख है औह धाम वे ।।
पाख सिज्या पाख आसन, पाख है औह तखत वे ।
पाखे पुजारी पूजता, जौ पाख है सब बखत वे ।।
पाख बानी पाख प्रानी, पाख बोलनहार वे ।
गरीबदास पाख हो करि, पाख कर दीदार वे ।।
G.G.S., p. 457.

22. कपटी कूं भावै नहीं, भक्ति मुक्ति की रीति ।
झूठा लंगर फिरत है, साधौ टोहत सीत ।।
G.G.S., p. 108.

23. कण्ठी माल। तिलक जनेऊ । जम किंकर करि हैं बहनेऊ ।।
तन पाखण्ड करौ मति भाई । भक्ति पुरातम तुम नहिं पाई ।।
G.G.S., p. 501.

the mind and the conduct pure was to centre one's entire thought upon God and to associate with real saints. Sinful thoughts came to those who turned their mind to lower desires and wordly pursuits in the name of religion.

Truthfulness

Purity is possible only if the mind cleaves to truthfulness, because truth is eternal. Man must eschew that which is false and misleading. Man must cling to truth and give up that which is unreal. God and everything leading to God is truth, while the world and everything worldly is false. Man must contemplate Truth. He must pray for imbibing Truth. The false and evil minded will go to hell because God is Truth. The Saints of God are the messengers of Truth.[24]

Men should give up falsehood in every form. Mere lip service to holy living is of no avail. It is only good deeds that matter. Merely preaching virtue is no use. The heart of the matter is to practise it. He is a Yogi who practises true living and not merely talks abouts it.[25]

Patience and Forbearance

Garib Das lays a great stress on patience, endurance and forbearance. He has devoted a whole chapter entitled *Jarna ka Anga* to this ethical subject. Life is full of suffering and temptations. A man can get through it safely and without being molested by evil passions. "A man should have such patience

24. साच शक्ति नरहरि रची, झूठा रच्या जिहान ।
झूठा सब संसार है, साचे साधू जान ।।
सत्य सुकृत की बंदगी, सति सुकृत का जाप ।
झूठा दोजख दीजिये, सांचा आपै आप ।।
साहिब सेती दोस्ती, सन्तों सेती प्यार ।
जिन कूं शंका है नहीं, धर्मराय दरबार ।।
G.G.S., p. 108.

25. कथनी से क्या होत है, करनी कारण मूल ।
करनी कर जरना जरै, लगे पान फल फूल ।।
G.G.S., p. 37.

and powers of endurance'' says Garib Das, "as the earth itself. The more you dig it the more it surprises you with its patient silence. Man should have the endurance of fire among the elements. It seeks not the evil of others. Man should have the sympathy and tolerance of rain which falls equally on the good and the bad and does not discriminate between the high and the low. Such a man sees evil and overlooks it (*dithi anadithi kare*) He takes the the sufferings of others on his own head and shows unbounded compassion. Man should have the endurance and tolerance of sandalwood, which has fragrance although enveloped by snakes on the outside. He who lives in patient tolerance, leads an eternal life. He is a true Yogi and is free from the cycle of birth and death. He who endures and lives in such great patience is an embodiment of God Himself."[26]

Discrimination, Calmness and Contentment

Garib Das strongly emphasises the virtues of contentment (*santosh*) and peace of mind (*sila*), both of which are always associated with discrimination (*viveka*). Without the wisdom to discriminate betwen true and false happiness and without the

26. ऐसी जरना चाहिये, ज्यूं पृथ्वी तन थीर ।
खोदे से कसके नहीं, ऐसा वज्र शरीर ।।
ऐसी जरना चाहिये, ज्यूं अग्नि तत में होई ।
जो कुछ परे सो सब जरे, बुरा न बांचे कोई ।।
ऐसी जरना चाहिये, ज्यूं घनहर जल मेह ।
सब ही ऊपर बरषता, ना दिल द्वेष सनेह ।।
दीठी अनदीठी करें, सब अपनें शिर लेय ।
संग से कदे न बीछरूँ, जो मुझ सरबस देय ।।
ऐसी जरना चाहिये, ज्यूं चन्दन के अंग ।
मुख से कुछ न कहत है, तन कू खात भुजंग ।।
जरै सो अविचल रहे, जरें सो प्रलों मांहि ।
जरना जोगी ना मरै, आवागमन न जाहिं ।।
जरै सो निर्गुण नूर है, जरै सो निर्गुण तन्त ।
जरै सो सत साहेब है, जरै सो सत भगवन्त ।।

G G.S., **Pp. 35-37.**

ability to judge the nature of God's will and purpose, there can be no true contentment. "Entertain calmness and contentment through discrimination" says Garib Das, "and acquire true knowldge of the Divine. If you entertain compassion and fore-giveness, you will be like God Himself. Such a man indeed attains the Eternal and union with the Fearless Beloved."[27]

He who understands the Will of God is contented with what God gives him. He does not hanker after any material gain. He has only one thirst, that is, to attain the grace and love of God. While he entertains a deep longing for the Beloved, he remains contented with what God gives him. He accepts suffer-ing with calmness. According to the Buddha, this is the principle that is responsible for the purification of one's mind and thoughts. *Sila* is compared to a golden ship to cross the ocean of *Samsara*. As the virtuous person is caused to be born with every handsomeness, birth after birth, *Sila* is compared to the artist's brush that would paint all beautiful appearences.[28]

Charity, Humility and Forgiveness

Dana literally means charity. A Bhakta who is a house-holder must give charity. A monk knows no charity because he has to beg for his own food. Garib Das places charity far above *Japa* (meditation), *Tapa* (penance), *yajna* (sacrifices) and *tirtha* (pilgrimages). It is one of the highest virtues. He who gives, deserves to get the grace of God. Charity is not to give with the hope of getting in return. Real charity is that which is given without any thought or desire to get something out of it. It is called desireless charity (*nehkami dana*). In the religious

27. शील सन्तोष बिबेक दे और ज्ञान बिज्ञाना ।
दया दुलीचै बैठ करि होइ ब्रह्म समाना ॥
क्षमा छत्र जाकै ढुरत, है तामस नहीं तेज ।
सो नर परसे जानिये, अबगति की सेज ॥
G.G.S., p. 595.

शील सन्तोष बिवेक दे, क्षमा दया एक तार ।
भाव भक्ति वैराग-दे, नाम निरालम्ब सार ॥
G.G.S., p. 379.

28. Gunaratna Thera, *The Dhamma*, p. 97.

history of India those who gave the largest in charity have been the greatest people.[29]

Charity is generally associated with unselfishnesss and the will to share one's earnings with others. Self-sacrifice and benevolence alone inspire a man to be truely charitable. A selfish man cannot be charitable.

Humility and Forgiveness are the two other great virtues on which Garib Das lays great stress. Vanity and egoism only bring sorrow and suffering to man. He who sees the light of God in every human soul alone is capable of true forgiveness. Humility and forgiveness are extolled by Garib Das in a number of his songs. They form the corner-stone of his ethics. "Compassion is the source of all virtues and it is based mainly on forgiveness."A man looks on the whole world with equal mindedness and consciousness of human frailties. So he foregives easily. Humility is called *dasabhava* by Garib Das. Thus he associates humility with the spirit of service. "He who lives in humility loses the stain of countless sins of past *karma*. He is liberated from the wheel of birth and death. All *japa* (meditations), all *tapas* (austerities) and all virtuous deeds are useless without humility. Humility gives man the greatest spiritual blessings. Without humility, the proud and vain Ravana lost his Lanka. He who has doubts and delusion in his mind cannot know what humility is. Humility is as precious as the philosopher's stone (*paras*). There is nothing like it in the three

29. जप तप तीरथ थोथरे, जाकी क्या आशा ।
कोटि यज्ञ पुन दान से, जम कटै न फांसा ।।
यहां देन वहां लेन है, योह मिटै न झगरा ।
वाह बिना पंथ की बाट है, पावै को दगरा ।।
बिन इच्छा जो देत हैं, सो दान कहावै ।
फल बांचै नहीं तासका, अमरापुर जावै ।।
सकल द्वीप नौ खंड के, क्षत्री जिन जीते ।
सो तो पदमैं ना मिले, विद्या गुण चीते ।।
कोटि उनंचा पृथ्वी, जिन दीन्ही नाना ।
परशुराम अवतार कूं, कीन्हीं कुरबाना ।।
G.G.S., p. 598.

regions."[30]

Humility is always accompained by forgiveness. He who forgives others is always forgiven by God. No human being is perfect. Every one is trying to perfect himself through the grace of the Guru. So God alone is the true judge of our inner character. We should forgive even our enemies.

Ahimsa (Non-Violence)

Garib Das lays great stress on *ahimsa* (Non-injury to all living creatures). Life as we see it exists in all creatures and every life is precious. The ideal which Garib Das preaches is the avoidance of injury to all forms of life. He does not go so far as the Jain saints do, but he goes further than his Guru Kabir and many other medieval Saints. This theory of *ahimsa* or non-injury to all living creatures is a logical outcome of the metaphysical theory of the potential equality of all souls and recognition of the principle of reciprocity, i e., we would do to others as we would be done by them. "It is unfair to think that *ahimsa* is the remanant of the savage's primitive awe for life, as some critics have thought. If every soul, however lowly, can become as great as any other soul, then one should recognise the value and the claim of every life, as his own. Respect for life wherever found becomes then an irresistable duty."[31]

30. कोटि कर्म जो तन लिपटाई, दासातन बिन कटें न भाई।
दासातन जो जीव कै आवै, जूनी जनम न देह धरावै ॥
जप तप करनी कीरति करहीं, दास भाव बिन सभ पर हरहीं।
दास भाव है अगम अगाहा, दासभाव सा और न लाहा ॥
दास भाव करिहैं रघुनाथा, दास भाव सा और न नाता।
दास भाव करिहैं आदि सांईं, दास भाव सैं दुनी रचाहीं ॥
दास भाव बिन लंका खोई, राज रसातल कुलहिं बिगोई।
दास भाव बिन हार्‌या जनमा, आशा तृष्णा रह गई धनमा ॥
सकल मनोरथ पूरण काम, समरथ साहिब राजा राम।
जाके दिल में है दुचताई, दासातन आवै नहिं भाई ॥
R.S., Pp. 208-209.

31. Chatterjee and Dutta : *An Introduction to Indian Philosophy*, p. 109.

Those who kill living creatures, says Garib Das, commit a grievous sin. They will be victims of the cycle of birth and death as lower animals. One must respect life in all creatures. This is the greatest *dharma*, greater than *asvamedha yajna*.[32] From this deeply ingrained feeling of *ahimsa*, similar to that of orthodox Vaishnavas, stems Garib Das' strong feeling against eating of meat which will be discussed when we deal with his religious doctrines.

The Five Passions

Great hinderance to religious and spiritual life is caused by the five lower passions—*Kama* (lust), *krodha* (anger), *lobha* (greed), *moha* (attachment) and *ahamkara* (egoism). These lower passions are our real enemies. He who conquers them conquers and realises his true self. "These five are your enemies, O man," says Garib Das, "the *Atma* is like an orphan when surrounded by them. Only a great spiritual effort can free a man from these enemies."[33]

Anger is the devil (*Chandala*). It is so powerful that it drowns a man in troubled waters in no time. It is like a mad elephant which can be controlled only by the iron spike of Forgiveness. Greed inflames the desires of man so much that he wishes to possess all the three worlds. It can be controlled only by contentment (*santosha*). *Moha* also makes a man selfish and mean. It brings self-intoxication. This

32. जी हिंसा जो करत है, या आगै क्या पाप ।
कंटक जून जहान में, भेड़िया सिंह अरु सांप ।।
आतम प्राण उधारहिं, ऐसा धरम न और ।
कोट यज्ञ असमेध फल, सबद समाना भौर ।।
G.G.S., p. 270.

33. काम क्रोध लोभ मोह, शत्रु हैं तुम्हारे ।
हरष शोक राग द्वेष, पकरि क्यों न मारे ।।
तीनि चीन्हि पांच मारि, पकरौ मठ धारी ।
पुत्र तौ पचीस संगि, सैना है अपारी ।।
G.G.S., p. 587.

can be controlled only by discrimination (*viveka*).[34]

All egoism is caused by desire and sense of possession. This desire to have more and more wealth is the ruin of the world. Desire is the servant of death. Where there is greed and desire, there is death.[35] *Ahamkara* is the greatest hindrance to spiritual progress. The greatest yogis and ascetics have fallen because of this weakness, which they could not overcome. There is a constant battle within man between forces of evil and good. This battle is the one in which man must co-operate with the forces of good and not be misled by the temptations of evil. The fight is tough but it is not difficult to overcome the evil forces.[36]

34. क्रोध बली चंडाल है, बल रापति द्वादस सहंस ।
ता सिर अंकुश शील का, तोरत गज के दंत ।।
ता सिर अंकुश क्षमा का, मारै तुस तुस बीन ।
त्रिलोकी सें काढि दै, जै कोय साधु प्रबीन ।।
लोभ सदा लहर्या रहै, त्रिलोकी मैं अंछ ।
बलरापति बीस सहस्त्र हैं, पलक पलक प्रपंच ।।
ता अंकुश संतोष है, त्रिलोकी सें काढि ।
काटै कोटि कटक दल, संतोष तेग बड बाड ।।
मोह मुवासी मस्त है, बलरापति तीस सहंस ।
त्रिलोकी परिवार है, जहां उपजै तहां वंश ।।
सिर अंकुश बिवेक है, पूरण करैं मुराद ।
त्रिलोकी की बासना, लै बिवेक सब साधि ।।
G.G.S., p. 227.

35. इच्छा सब जग लूटिया, इच्छा किनैं न लूट ।
बखतर तोडैं भरम के, ज्ञान शब्द की मूठ ।।
इच्छा दासी जम की, खड़ी रहै दरबार ।
पाप पुण्य दो वीर हैं, याह सत खसमी नार ।।
G.G.S., p. 143.

36. शील संतोष बिवेक से, जाकैं दरवाना ।
काम क्रोध भागे जवैं, गढ देख्या सामां ।।
लोभ मोह मारे परे, सैना सब भागी ।
सतगुरु कै प्रताप सें, जब आतम जागी ।।
G.G.S., p. 242.

Garib Das also throws some light on the well known group of four values—*dharma* (virtue), *artha* (wealth), *kama* (pleasure) and *moksa* (self-realization). These values are not to be the end of our life. They are only instrumental values. They are also inter-related, so long as we do not make one of them the sole end. The main aim of ethical effort should be *atma-guna*, virtues of the soul, like kindness, purity and truthfulness.

Social Philosophy

Social philosophy as reflected in the writings of Garib Das has alread been discussed. We may briefly sum it up as prograssive Hinduism aiming at integrating all conflicting religious forces prevalent during that period.

Hindus and Muslims are one

One of the greatest difficulties of those times was to reconcile Hindus and Muslims. Garib Das pointed out that Hindus and Muslims were children of the same God. The differences between the two creeds were artificial. He had abandoned the sectarian outlook of both the creeds.

All castes and creeds are equal in the eyes of God

Garib Das was strongly against the caste system. He felt that Brahmanism had done untold damage to Hindu Society and the social oppression of the Hindus had tempted many low caste Hindus to accept Islam. Garib Das strongly criticised the oppressive attitude of the Brahmins to low caste people.

The rich and poor are equal

Wealth does not deprive a man of the right to equality in the eyes of God. The status of human beings should be judged not by their possessions or power but by their deeds.

> God sees everyone with equal mindedness,
> He is in every heart and soul;
> There is no difference between the high and the low;
> He is a supereme saintly man,
> Who meditates, practices *tapasya* and virtues;

He, who guides the misguided,
Is a worthy human being.[37]

Against Renunciation

Garib Das was a strong advocate of houshold life and disapproved of renouncing the world as the Yogis and Sanaysis did. He himself was a householder and spent all his life in using his moral and spiritual influence to change the society around him.

Why go to the moutains?
And why give up the city dwellings?
God is the same in the forests and the cities
For those in whose heart resides His name.[38]
From where will a man eat if he does not work?
It does not befit a farmer that
He should go to beg at the door of others.[39]

Religious Doctrines of Garib Das

Like his Guru, Kabir, Garib Das placed his creed as a middle path between Hinduism and Islam. Although the influence of Hindu orthodox traditions and beliefs was quite strong on him, yet he did not completely identify himself either with Hinduism, as it existed, or with Islam.

37. एकै नजर निरंजना, सभही घट देखै ।
ऊंच नीच अन्तर नहीं, सब एकै पेखै ॥
सोई साध सिरोमनी, जप तप उपकारी ।
भूले कूं उपदेश दे, दुर्लभ संसारी ॥
R.S., p. 358.

38. पर्वत डूंगर क्यूं चढौ, बस्ती तजो न गाम ।
बन बसती मैं एकसा, जाकै हिरदै राम ॥
G.G.S., p. 138.

39. जा घर तो करनी नहीं, काहे खट्या खाहिं ।
कीरत नहीं किसान की, पर घर मांगन जाहिं ॥
G.G.S., p. 95.

He preaches to his disciples to give up the path of the Vedas as well as of the Koran. He believes in the path of truth and Light.[40] He compares the four Vedas and the eighteen Puranas with a deep but dried-up well which can slake no one's thirst.[41]

God is to be worshipped within the heart He should not be confined to any place. Garib Das says that the belief of the Hindus that God can be found only in the Dehra (*mandir*) or He can be found only in the Mosque (*masjid*) is wrong. Both Hindus and Muslims live in delusion. They have closed their eyes to the real light of God. Both Hindus and Muslims are absorbed in a wrong type of worship. Neither of them can attian the presence of God in this way. Both of them are devoid of true contemplation without which all religious life is ignorance and leads to death. They pay more attention to the worship of tombs and idols and not to the Light of God.[42]

Like the Upanishads, Garib Das points out that the path of pure devotion to God is as sharp as the sword. It is an extremely narrow and difficult path to tread. He who is wide swake and careful can move on it; all others are likely to lose balance.[43]

40. वेद कुरान कूं छाड़ दे बावरे, नूर ही नूर कर ले जुहारा ॥
R.S., p. 222.

41. चारि बेद और पुरान अठारा, यौह एक ऊजड भेरा है ॥
G.G.S., p. 565.

42. हिन्दू हदीरे पूजहीं, मुसलम पूजें गोर ।
दोऊ दीन धोखे पड़े, पापी कठिन कठोर ॥
हिन्दू तो देवल बंधे, मुसलम बंधे मसीत ।
साहिब दर पौंहचें नहीं, चिणी भरम की भीत ॥
षट दल दोनूं दीन की, भली बिगूती बात ।
मैं मेरी के कारनैं, खाई जम की लात ॥
षट दल दोनूं दीन की, दरगह मैं नहीं साख ।
बिना बंदगी भूत हैं, क्या कौडी धज लाख ॥
G.G.S., p. 144.

43. सूक्षम मारग सोधि ले, झीना पंथ अपार ।
गवन कौन विधि कीजिये, खांडे जेही धार ॥

The whole path of Bhakti is subtle and mysterious and free from formalism. That is why Garib Das again and again gives his own definition of Bhakti.

The life of man becomes futile, if he does not devote it to the love of God. The body, the mind and the soul and all the earthly comforts were given to man only to enable him to realise his higher self. This love of God should be sought in the company of Saints.[47]

The True Teacher (*Satguru*)

The Guru or the Divine Teacher is the source of all divine knowledge and inspiration. "Unaided man cannot come to God. He needs the awakening word of the real teacher sent to him by God Himself. Such a teacher has to be himself a saint wholly devoted to the Lord, sincere, kindly and of good repute. The Guide must be detached fram worldliness in order to be able to save others from the world and bring them safely to infinite bliss."[45]

Without a Guru's teaching and without the aid of scriptures, the self cannot be realized; only by means of this combination can the knowledge of one's own self shine out bright. By bringing together the Guru, the scriptures, and the willing pupil, a man comes to engage in good conduct and in self knowledge.[46] So bring out the eradication of ego by the Guru's power, the aid of scriptures and the devoted control of your self.[47]

It is hard to give up sense-objects, hard to see the truth, hard to be in the Natural State without the guidance of the Guru. The syllable *gu* means darkness, while the syllable

धार अकारं दीखती, औह् तो पंथ अदेख ।
ये कौन मंडल को जाहिगे, नांनां वाणी भेष ॥
G.G.S., p. 81.

44. भक्ति हेत गृह बाँधिया, घण नामी घट माँहि ।
साधूजन सेवे बिना, सांई पावै नाँहि ॥
G.G.S., p. 69.

45. Duncan Greenless, *Gospel of the Guru Granth*, p. 86.
46. *Yogavasishta*, 30; 130-141; 31-34.
47. *Mandukya Upanisad:* 4-27.

ru means dispeller, Thus Guru means dispeller of darkness.

Garib Das says : "I have met a Satguru, who is an embodiment of the Supreme Spirit. His Light has been revealed to me in every pore of my heart ever since he has given me the Divine Name which I repeat continuosly without effort (*ajapa-japa*). The True Guru has intoxicated me with Divine Love. He has given me the cup of divine love to drink and awakened my consciousness. My mind is absorbed in the sea of his spirit. The hard veil is broken and I have attained the difficult path to God. This Satguru is no other than the Great Kabir who is my Saviour.[48]

"By the grace of the Satguru I have attained Jnan, Yoga, and Bhakti. He is a perfect being and boundless in flow of inspiration. He is the living Lord of the world. It is difficult to describe the attributes of the Satguru. He is sweet of speech and is freedom loving. He has made me immortal by his touch and given me such divine knowledge as Vedas, Shastras and Puranas could not give."[49]

Thus Garib Das emphasises that no one can win the way to God without guidance from the Guru. Only when the light of the Guru shines in our heart can we move towards truth. The devout soul meets the heavenly Guide, the Satguru, and wins his grace by serving him. The very meeting with the Guru awakens his sleeping consciousness and his mind opens up to the supreme realisation of true knowledge and love of God. All

48. ऐसा सतगुरु हम मिल्या, सुन्न विदेसी आप ।
रोम रोम प्रकाश है, दीन्हा अजपा जाप ॥
ऐसा सतगुरु हम मिल्या, मगन किये मसताक ।
प्याला प्याया प्रेम का, गगन मण्डल गरगाप ॥
ऐसा सतगुरु हम मिल्या, सुरत्ति सिन्धु की सैल ।
बजर पौल पट खोल कर, ले गया झीनी गैल ॥
G.G.S., p. 2.

49. ऐसा सतगुरु हम मिल्या, सुरति सिन्धु की नाल ।
ज्ञान योग और भक्ति सब, दीन्हीं नजर निहाल ॥
ऐसा सतगुरु हम मिल्या, बे परवाह अबन्ध ।
परमहंस पूरण पुरुष, रोम रोम रवि चन्द ॥
Ibid.

obstacles disappear from the path of the aspirant. There is no other easy way or short cut to God except through the grace of the Guru.

"The Satguru" says Garib Das, "is an embodiment of the perfect Brahma. God reveals Himself through him. There is no difference between God and Guru. Spiritually they are one and the same. The Satguru is like the philosopher's stone. The human beings are like iron. His very touch makes us gold. He changes our whole being. He removes the hardness of our soul and like a blacksmith gives us a new from."[50] Death dare not come to the man who has met the Satguru. He is never afraid of death. The god of death becomes his servant. By meeting the Satguru man swims across the dread ocean of worldly life.[51]

We must distinguish betweet the real Guru and the false Guru. The real Guru has not only attained God but remains in perfect union with Him all the time. He is the perfect Man who sees the Light of God in every one and can easily discriminate between the true and the false. He is conscious of God's loving watch over him. Unshaken by joy and sorrow, wholly free from anger, virtuous and kind, delighting in the worship of God, without the least taint of worldiness or egoism, eager for humble service of the lowliest of men, such a Guru can guide us to the Lord he loves.

"In the Kali age," says Garib Das, "the Satguru is the only

50. सतगुरु पूरण ब्रह्म है, सतगुरु आप अलेख ।
सतगुरु रमता राम है, यामें मीन न मेख ।।
सतगुरु पारस रूप है, हमरी लोहा जात ।
पलक बीच कंचन करें, पलटें पिण्ड अरु गात ।।
हम तो लोहा कठिन हैं, सतगुरु बने लुहार ।
युगन युगन के मोरचे, तोडि घडे घन सार ।।
G.G.S., p. 4.

51. जम जौरा जासें डरें, धर्मराय धर धीर ।
ऐसा सतगुरु एक है, अदली अदल कबीर ।।
जम जौरा जासें डरें, मिटे कर्म के लेख ।
अदली अदल कबीर है, कुल के सतगुरु एक ।।
G.G.S., p. 5.

true Saviour. He is the Merciful Giver of life and wisdom. Without the aid of the Satguru, the path cannot be known. On meeting the Satguru, the unseen can be seen. Through his kindness, the Satguru changes the heart of men and all mental and spiritual darkness disappears. Without the help of the Satguru even Brahma and Siva could not attain salvation. The True Guru is the bestower of Bhakti (love) and Mukti (Liberation). He takes the soul of men to the Infinite. Without the knowledge of the True Guru all live in blindness. He alone destroys the fear of death and takes men to the abode of bliss. All doubts, delusions and sins depart on meeting the True Guru. I have taken refuge in the perfect one. I am his servant."[52]

There is no dearth of false Gurus in the wold. Inside them there is no spirituality and no light. "They put on the garbs of holy men, make pretentions of becoming Gurus and give *mantram* in the ears of the ignorant disciples. Such false Gurus live in darkness and lead others to darkness.[53] Blind are

52. सतगुरु दाता है कलि मांही । प्राण उधारन उतरे सांई ॥
सतगुरु दाता दीन दयालं । जम किंकर के तौरे जालं ॥
सतगुरु बिना पंथ नहिं पावै । सतगुरु मिलै तो अलख लखावै ॥
सतगुरु साहिब एक शरीरा । सतगुरु बिना न लागै तीरा ॥
सतगुरु दया करै दिल फेरै । कोटि तिमिर मिटि जांहिं अंधेरै ॥
सतगुरु बंकनाल हो आये । शिव ब्रह्मादिक पार न पाये ॥
सतगुरु भक्ति मुक्ति के दानी । सतगुरु बिना न छूटै खानी ॥
सतगुरु शाला कर्म बतावै । सतगुरु अगम द्वीप लै जावै ॥
सतगुरु बिना सकल सब अन्धा । सतगुरु काटैं जग के फन्दा ॥
सतगुरु जामन मरण मिटावैं । सतगुरु सुखसागर लै जावैं ॥
सतगुरु मिलै संदेह सब, छूटैं भरम बिकार ।
समरथ का सरणा लिया, हम चाकर दरबार ॥
G.G.S., p. 3.

53. कण्ठी माला सुमरणी, सबै सिलसिला मेट ।
कनफूका गुरुवा मिले, ज्यूं जम मारी फेट ॥
कण्ठी माला सुमरनी, पहरे सं क्या होय ।
ऊपर ढुंढा साध का, अन्तर राख्या खोय ॥
कनफूका गुरुवा मिले, जानैं भाव न भेद ।
जम के हिलकारे फिरैं, हाथौं में लिये बेद ॥
G.G.S., p. 141.

these Gurus and blind are their disciples. They are ignorant of divine knowledge and they have never heard the celestial music (*anahad sabda*).[54] These pretenders give *mantrams* which have no effect on the disciples. That is why he calls them *kanphuka Gurus*. "There is no end to these *kanphuka* Gurus. They bring moral and spiritual disaster to their disciples. Because they are hypocrites, their disciples also become victims of hypocrisy. A false Guru is the carrier of moral death. Like the *simbal* tree he bears no fruit and his disciples go empty handed. Many Kazis and Pandits who pose to be true Gurus and Pirs are like the ox yoked to an oil press. They ask their disciples to repeat something mechanically but it is of no avail.[55]

Garib Das gives the highest place to Kabir as the Ideal Guru. "He is sweet of tongue and manners and he is the Pir and the Guru of both Hindus and Muslims. Garib Das is happy that he has found Kabir, the Perfect Guru, who is profound and inscrutable."[56]

A devotee should sacrifice his body, mind and wealth to the True Guru. One should sacrifice his very life for him. One's head should be placed at the disposal of the True Guru. For such dedication, a man gets His grace and love. The narrow

54. अन्ध गुरु अन्ध शिष्य है, अन्ध जगत दहूँ दीन ।
षट् दरशन सब गुंग हैं, सुनी न अनहद बीन ।।
G.G.S., p. 140.

55. कनफूका गुरु बहुत हैं, अनगिन कोटि अनन्त ।
साधू होकर ना मिलें, सो सतवादी सन्त ।।
कनफूका गुरु काल है, फांसी देहि अड़ाय ।
मारत हैं मैदान मैं, छल बल बहुत बनाय ।।
कनफूका गुरु काल है, आये भेष बनाय ।
तन पर द्वादश तिलक हैं, सब जग गया पिताय ।।
G.G.S., p. 142.

56. मघर मुवा सो सतगुरु मेरा, हिन्दू तुरक का पीर ।
दोन्यौं दीन हरष भये सन्तौ, पाया नहीं शरीर ।
दास गरीब अगम अनुरागी, सतगुरु मिले कबीर ।।
G.G.S., p. 655.

and difficult path leading to God becomes easy and wide.[57]

The name of God or the *Sabda* (Word)

God has no form or colour. So the Nirguna saints and even the saints of the Semitic faith remember Him through His Name. The Name of God is His manifest form. It is generally a Divine word the meditation of which opens the mind to higher realisation. The only contact we can have with God is through His Name. There are many attributive Names of God but the Name which is given as a *mantram* by the Guru is always a special Divine word. "The soul without the Name is lost in the raging fires of egoism," says Aldous Huxley, "The simplest and the most widely practised form of spiritual exercise is repetition of the Divine Name, or of some phrase affirming God's existence and the soul's dependence on Him."[58]

Garib Das says: "The Name of God is His essence. They who concentrate their mind on the One realize it. He pervades within man and He is found everywhere outside him, unseen. One should not delay in repeating the Name of God. One should remember God ever and ever by uttering the Name. By repeating the Divine Name a man drinks the Nectar which makes us immortal. Repeating the Name is much more fruitful spiritually than giving millions of cows in charity or performing countless sacrifices or going to places of pilgrimage.[59] He who repeats

57. सतगुरु कुं क्या दीजिये, तन मन धन और सीख ।
पिण्ड प्रान कुरबान करि, जिन भक्ति दई बकसीस ।।
ऐसा सतगुरु हम मिल्या, महिमा कही न जाय ।
भवन चतुर्दश लोक सब, तिल में दिये दिखाय ।।
G.G.S., p. 28.

58. Aldous Huxley : *The Perennial Philosophy*, p. 317

59 राम नाम निज सार है, मूल मन्त्र मन माहिं ।
पिण्ड ब्रह्मण्ड से रहित है, जननी जाया नाहिं ।।
राम रटत नहिं ढील कर, हरदम नाम उचार ।
अमी महारस पीजिये, योहिं तत बारंबार ।।

Continued on next page

the Name of God realizes God within himself. Without the Name all meditations, all penances are useless. Garib Das calls himself a trader of the spiritual gifts of Divine Name, which gives him endless profit.[60]

The Divine Name is the most precious gem of life. Its value cannot be assessed. Its value goes on increasing two-fold and three-fold. The Name is Nirguna and pure. It is the eternal Spirit himself. Those who are absorbed in the Divine Name are really wealthy. All else is hypocricy.[61]

Some people wear a rosary to show that they repeat the Name regularly. Garib Das says that the rosary will not liberate any one. It is the Divine Name which alone can liberate the soul. He has laid stress on the repetition of such holy Names as Om, Soham, Hari and Ram. He gives great importance to the repetition of all these Names.[62] If properly pronounced, Om will represent the whole phenomenon of sound and no other word can do this; this, therefore, is the fittest symbol of Sphota, which is the real meaning of the word Om, And as the symbol can never be separated from the thing signified, Om and Sphota are

कोटि गऊ जे दान दे, कोटिक जगि जोनार ।
कोटि कूप तीरथ खने, मिटे नहिं जम मार ।।
कोटिक तीरथ बरत करि, कोटिक गज करि दान ।
कोटि अश्व बिपरों दिये, मिटै न खैंचातान ।।

G.G.S., p. 6

60. नाम बिना क्या होत है, जप तप संयम ध्यान ।
बाहरि भरमे मानवी, अब अन्तर में जान ।।

G.G.S., p. 7

61. रत्न खजाना नाम है, माल अजोख अपार ।
यह सौदा सत कीजिए, दुगनें तिगनें चार ।।

G.G.S., p. 72

62. माला मुक्ति न होत है, मुक्ति होत है नाम ।
एकै अक्षर बाहरा, ऊजड़ भला न गाम ।।

G.G.S., p. 328

ओम का नाम जपै निशि बासर, ज्ञान बुद्धि का खेलं ।
हरियं जाप हिरम्बर हीरा, लछमी सहित समीपं ।।
सोहं जाप सहंसर मेला, कोइ जन जाने भेदं ।

G.G.S., p. 328

One. And as Sphota, being the finer side of the manifested universe, is nearer to God and is indeed the first manifestation of Divine Wisdom, Om is truly symbolic of God. More than this. The Yogis claim that through meditation one may hear this word Om vibrating through the Universe.[63] Garib Das also says that Om is the key to Mukti. It is the spirit that pervades all. Its sound vibrates within and without man.[64]

The Saints

The saints are divine souls who have, through spiritual effort, attained and realised God. A saint is not to be judged by his holy garb and sectarian marks but by his inward enlightenment. "It is difficult", says Garib Das, "to describe the true greatness of the saints. The merit gained by bathing at the 68 places of pilgrimage is attained at their feet. Their glory is beyond description. On meeting a true saint a man meets God. Such great sages as Nārada and Prahlāda have been saved by association with the saints."[65]

It is the Will of God that no one should hurt his saints. He who causes any injury to a saint hurts God. When a saint suffers, God Himself suffers.[65] Blessed is the mother, blessed is the land, blessed is the city, blessed is the family in which a saint is born. Blessed is the womb in which a saint descends.[67]

63. Christopher Isherwood, *Vedanta For the Western World*, Pp. 152-53

64. ओम मूल भक्ति का रासा, तहं वहं लीन पवन करि साँसा ।
नाभि चक्र नरहरी विशेखा, हरियं हेत कला अनेका ।।
G.G.S., p. 320

65. संतों की महिमा कही न जाय । अठसठि तीरथ चरणों पाय ।।
संतों की महिमा अपरम्पार । पूरन ब्रह्म मिले करतार ।।
संतों की महिमा अगम अगाध । नारद से उधरे प्रह्लाद ।।
G.G.S., p. 673

66. राम कहै मेरे साध कूं, दुःख मत दीजो कोय ।
साध दुखाये मैं दुखी, मेरा आपा भी दुख होय ।।
G.G.S., p. 602

67 धन जननी धन भूमि, धन नगरी धन देश ।
धन करणी धन कुल धन, जहां साधू प्रवेश ।।
G.G.S., p. 118

The saint is the embodiment of God. There is no difference between the two. The saint belongs to God. His caste and creed is the caste and creed of God. He is ever absorbed in God.[68]

Holy Company *(Satsanga)*

The saints are always in God's presence, and where God is there is Heaven. The association with holy men is very inspiring to all seekers of God. That association is won by moral and spiritual effort only. In the company of holy men, one forgets evil deeds and remembers God. In the company of the saints, a man learns discrimination, acquires divine knowledge, and walks on the path of enlightenment.

So Garib Das calls on people to seek association with the saints. Worldly associations throw a man into confusion. But the association with holy men should be based on discrimination (*viveka*), otherwise it may prove useless." One must avoid evil company at all costs. Evil company breeds desire for committing sin. Blessed is the man who keeps company with lovers of truth and the real saints. He loses all his doubts and delusion and helps others on the path to God.[69]

Pilgrimages, Sectarian Symbols, Rituals and Renunciation

Garib Das was dead against idolatory. For him all types of idolatory and image worship was the worship of dead matter.

68. सांई सरीखे संत हैं, यामैं मीन न मेष ।
पडदा अंग अनादि है, बाहर भीतर एक ।।
सांई सरीखे देख ले, पिरतावै जै कोय ।
सप्त कोस जल चढ़ि गया, जहाँ साधू मुख धोय ।।

69. संगत कीजै साध की, संसारी भटकन्त ।
पिंजर सूवा पढत है, किस कूँ बूझै पंथ ।।
सतगुरु की संगति भली, हंसा थीर मुकाम ।
जुगन जुगन के बीछड़े, परसे लोक निधान ।।
साधौं की संगति करैं, बड़भागी बड़ देव ।
आपन तो संशय नहीं, और उतारैं खेव ।।
संगत हुई तौ क्या हुआ, हिरदै नहीं बिवेक ।
छलनी कन्दा छानिहीं, कूकस राख्या देखि ।।

G.G.S., p. 110

He was also strongly against caste prejudices, empty rituals and symbols. As he led a householder's life, he was against renunciation of homes and normal life. "What is the use, offering flowers and prayers," says Garib Das "to dead stone gods. By the worship of the stone, God will not be pleased. The idol is made by the chisel and hammer of the artisan. While making it he held it under his feet and struck hard on its forehead. Even a god of silver and gold is of no avail.[70]

Caste system has been the curse of our country for many centuries. Garib Das had very strong feelings against the caste system. He treated all people equally. Spiritual life was open to everyone. "What matters if a man is a brahmin or a sweeper. The same God speaks through them"[71] Many persons of low caste rose to be great Saints and they were revered by all castes. Kabir, Ravi Das, Sain and Sadhna were all born in low castes.

Wandering to the places of pilgrimage without any inner search for light is of no avail. All the sixty-eight places of pilgrimage are within man. All external meditation and penances are useless. Garib Das laid emphasis on the inner life of man. God was to be searched within the soul and not in holy places.[72]

Garib Das was strongly against the so-called renunciation of Yogis and Sanyasis. Some of them pretend to be living on milk only. But within their heart there is nothing but darkness.

70. कहां पाहन फूल चढ़ावै । जड जूनी घण्ट बजावै ॥
याह जड पूजा नहिं कीजै । जासैं पारब्रह्म नहिं रीझै ॥
एक घड़ी ठठेरा बीनां । तन टांकी चीतन कीना ॥
जै सौनें का शालिगरामा । सो क्या आवै तुम्हरै कामा ॥
जै चांदी का बी होई । तेरी भूख बिडारें सोई ॥
कहा पांहन पूजै पाढा । जैसें छेली गलि थन काढा ।
G.G.S., p. 534

71. को पंडत, किस कहो चुहड़ा, एकै बोलनहारा ।
ज्यों मटकी मैं झिलकै चन्दा, है माँही पर न्यारा ॥
G.G.S., p. 653

72. अठसठि तीरथ हैं मनमाहीं, गंग सहंस मुखधार ।
ब्रह्मा विष्णु महेशर शेषा, जाप जपै ररंकार ॥
G.G.S., p. 656

To wander about in the forests is not Yoga but a disease. It matters little if a man has put on a holy garb. The chains of *karma* will not break unless a spiritual effort is made. Of what use is self-mortification? This body is very precious and it should not be treated with cynical contempt. What use is it to leave cities and towns and go to mountain caves and forests? Those who have the light of God in their hearts, for them the cities and forests are alike.[73] Love of the Infinite and Immortal God alone can save men.

Grace of God

In Garib Das, as in most of the Bhaktas, much stress is laid on the grace of God. Man can never acquire communion with God by his own effort. He can have a vision of God only when God chooses to reveal Himself. God can be attained only by His grace. He cannot be bought for any price or gift. No human attainments, physical, intellectual, moral or spiritual, are adequate for the attainment of God.[74]

73. दूधाधारी सिद्ध हैं, पान फूल फल खांहि ।
घट में नाम न संचरै, बंधे जमपुर जाहिं ।।
चुंडित मुंडित भदरा, मौनी महल न पाय ।
धूंमर पान ठढेसरी, दोजख धक्के खाहिं ।।
जोग नहीं यौह रोग है, जब लग नाम न चीन्ह ।
घर घर द्वारे भटकते, भेष बिना आकीन ।।
भेष लिया तौ क्या हुआ, जब लग नहीं विवेक ।
तीन काल निपजै नहीं, मिटै कर्म नहिं रेख ।।
उरध कपाली तपत हैं, तल शिर ऊपर पैर ।
दम का खोज न जानहीं, कहा देह सूं बैर ।।
याह देही सौंहगी नहीं, महंगी रत्नौं मोल ।
जो जानै तौ राम जप, कुलफ कपाट न खोल ।।
पर्वत डूंगर क्यूं चढौ, बस्ती तजो न गाम ।
बन बसती मैं एकसा, जाकै हिरदै राम ।।
अविनाशी सें प्रेम होय, प्रेम सहत ह्वै नीर ।
सकल सुंन सब गहबरै, पांचौं तत्त्व खमीर ।।

G.G.S., p. 138

74. *The Cultural Heritage of India*, Vol 4, p. 147

Defined in psychological terms, grace is someting other than our self-conscious personal self, by which we are helped. We have experience of three kinds of such help: animal grace, human grace and spiritual grace.[75] Garib Das emphasises on the spiritual grace of the Guru and God. The grace of God comes to all men equally. It is through God's grace that the Guru is met. It is through His grace that the divine Name is achieved. It is through His grace that a vision of the Lord is attained. It is through His grace and not through our mental and other efforts that our sins are destroyed.

Salvation and Death

Death is inevitable; life is transient. Everything mortal will pass away. We should not stick our minds to worldly things. The *atma*, the soul, is immortal. Conquest of death is the purpose of our life. Everyone is the victim of death. Garib Das devotes a whole chapter to Death as he sees it. The end of salvation is to escape the cycle of birth and death. Men may rise higher or may fall lower in the cycle of birth and death spread over 84 lakh forms of life. To escape this cycle is to escape hell. Salvation is union with God.

Mysticism in Garib Das

In Garib Das there is more mysticism than philosophy. As a matter of fact, his faith can be called a deeply mystic faith. He falls under the same category of mystics as Kabir. The opinion of Dr. S.N. Das Gupta aptly applies to Garib Das in all its details. Prof. Dasgupta says: "There was, therefore, nothing particularly novel in Kabir's insistence that the time honoured distinctions of caste, creed and social status are absolutely valueless or in his emphasis upon the need of Bhakti for all, as that which alone exalts a man. But in Kabir we find a reformatory zeal. He never tires of reiterating the worthlessness of all these superstitions of caste, creed, social status, external purity and impurity, penances, asceticism and all sorts of formalities which passed by the name of religion though in fact having nothing to do with it. Thus on the one hand Kabir waged war against the

75. Aldous Huxley, *The Perennial Philosophy*, p. 191

prevailing superstitions, rituals and litanies of all religions and religious sects, and on the other hand he dived deep in the depth of God's love and he beheld nothing but God on all sides becoming as it were one with Him in spiritual union. The motto of his life was, as he often said : 'Remember God, Remember God, my brethren,' and in his own life he felt he was absorbed in the Infinite."[76]

Mysticism has been described in various ways. It is a term applied to occult sciences and even black magic. The best definition we have is given by Evelyn Underhill when she says : "Mysticism is not an opinion. It is not a philosophy. It has nothing in common with the pursuit of occult knowledge. On the one hand it is not merely the power of contemplating Eternity ; on the other hand it is not to be identified with any kind of religious queerness. It is the name of the organic process which involves the perfect consummation of the Love of God : the achievement here and now of the immortal heritage of man. Or if you like it better—for this means exactly the same thing—it is the art of establishing his conscious relation with the absolute."[77] This is the definition which exactly defines Garib Das' mysticism. To this we may add the observation of Rudolf Otto, who, while discussing Christian and Indian Mysticism, describes Indian mysticism as the mysticism of experience or the mysticism of *atma*.[78]

Evelyn Underhill applies four cardinal tests to all true mysticism. The first one is that it is "active and practical and it goes beyond the intellect". Garib Das time and again says that the intellect is of no avail. Only intuition awakened by the Guru's inspiration can help man to the highest realisation.

The second important test of higher mysticism is that its aim is wholly transcendental and spiritual. It is in no way concerned with adding to and exploring the universe. The whole philosophy of Garib Das described in the previous chapters bears witness to this important fact.

The third important test is that "The One is for a mystic not merely the Reality of all that is, but also a living and personal

76. S.N. Das Gupta : *Hindu Mysticism*, Pp. 159, 161-162
77. Evelyn Underhill, *Mysticism*, p. 81
78. Rudolf Otto, *Mysticism East and West*, p. 223

object of love, never an object of exploration. It draws its whole being homeward but always under the guidance of the heart.'' Fourthly, "Living union with the One which is the term of his adventure, is a definite state or form of enhanced life. It is arrived at by an arduous psychological and spiritual process, the so called Mystic Way, entailing complete remaking of character and liberation of a new or rather latent form of consciousness, which imposes on the self the condition which is sometime inaccuratly called ecstasy."[80]

Garib Das has written whole chapters on the spiritual union with the Infinite as the ultimate aim of his mystic faith. "The essence of Bhakti is that it is pursued for its own sake and not for any ulterior motive. The boundless grace of God wins from man a response in adoring and self-giving love. But such devotion has its necessary fruit in the purification of the soul, in its deliverance from the necessity of rebirth. It is universally assumed in India that ignorance and selfish desire alone are responsible for the soul's implication in this necessity."[81] This analysis of Sydney Spencer applies to all Bhakti schools. The mystic moves towards God by the same stages which have been marked out by various saints. Garib Das also reflects the same approach. The early stage is that of intense yearing, which Garib Das calls *biraha.* The Western mystics call it the separation from the Beloved and pining for Him.

Garib Das has written a whole chapter on *biraha.* "I am a mad devotee," says Garib Das, "the cup of devotion and prayer is in my hand. It is full of nectar. I am imbued with the love and longing for God.[82] The longing for God has taken possession of me. I am madly in love with Him. There is a deep pain in my heart and no one can remove it. I cherish this burning passion for the Beloved. It is the storm of love that is raging within me. There is sadness and sorrow in the heart but it is the sadness of separation from Him." It is passionate longing for Him in which all distractions are forgotten. The Bhakta cannot live

80. Evelyn Underhill, *Mysticism*, p. 81
81. Sidney Spencer, *Mysticism in Word Religions* p. 62
82. सजन सुराही हाथ है, अमृत का प्याला ।
हम बिरहन बिरहे रंगी, कोइ पूछै हाला ॥
G.G.S., p. 595

even for a moment without Him. His love alone is all satisfying. The Bhakta lives in prayer and rememberance of the Beloved. The love of God overpowers all his thoughts and feelings and he longs for total absorption in the Divine.[83]

The highest spiritual state is described as *turiya*. It is achieved by the service of the true Guru and by repeating the Name of God. Beyond this *turīyā* state is the heaven of God, the place where He alone exists. That place or heaven where God alone resides is called *Parbrahma kā sthana* or *Parbrahma ka desa, gagan mandala, sunya sikhara.* Garib Das says :

Serve such a *Satguru*,
Who helps in meeting the Supreme through *Soham*.
The mind then rests in the *turiya* state,
The three torments are removed.
Higher than *turiya* is the city and palace of God,
It is the land where He alone is.
Serve such a *Satguru* who gives you the *Sabad*,
Through which the highest state is reached.[84]

... ...

In the highest seat of consciousness,
Is the throne and abode of God;

83. बिरहा हम घर आइयां, कही बिरह की बात ।
बिरहिनि सैं बांनी कही, सूके पिण्ड अरु गात ।।
सुनत उदासी हो गई, लगी बिरह की दाह ।
बिरहा वेदनि मेटि हैं, हम बिरह की चाह ।।
बिरहा बादल प्रेम का, श्याम घटा घनघोर ।
दामिनिही में गरज है, बिरहनि कठिन कठोर ।।
दाह लगी कैसे मिटै, खिमि खिमि होय उजास ।
उनमनी सैं होइ ऊंझना, बिरहनि अधिक उदास ।।
G.G.S., p. 11

84. गरीब ऐसा सतगुरु सेइये, सोहं सिंध मिलाप ।
तुरिया मध आसन करै, मेटै तीनूं ताप ।।
गरीब तुरिया पर पुरिया महल, पारब्रह्म का देस ।
ऐसा सतगुरु सेइये, शब्द विग्याना नेस ।।
R.S., p. 58-59

It is the *tuviya* state, where pure saints reside.[85]

The Hatha Yogis try to achieve the highest state by a series of physical feats called *āsana* and breathing practices called *prānāyāma*. Through control of breath, an attempt is made to cleanse the nerve centres *(nadis)*. In *prānyāma* (breath control), filling is called *purak*, expelling is called *rechaka*, and retaining is called *kumbhaka*. The three main nādīs are *Idā* also called Ganga, *pinglā* also called Yamuna and *susumanā* also called Saraswati. By closing the first two, the flow of breath is directed to *susumanā* All these Hatha Yoga practices are aimed at awakening the serpent power *(kundalini)*. When the *kundalini* rises up through various *chakrās*, the highest realization is attained.

He practices *kumbhak* and *rechak* through Hatha Yoga,
Says Garib, very few succeed in controlling the Serpent Power.
The breath is controlled after *kumbakh* and *rechak*,
Then after passing the breath through *ida* and *pingla*
Sushmana is opened, which leads to union.[86]

After the awakening of *kundalini*, which rests below the navel in a serpent coil, the *prānashaktī* passes through *chakrās*.

The Kundalini rests near the navel in three coils
From its mouth comes out fire which rises to skies.[87]

This leads us to six centres which are : (1) *mūlādhāra*, which is situated above the organ of generation and is the region of earth ; (2) *svādhisthāna*, which is just above the previous one

85. गरीब गगन मंडल गादी जहां, पारब्रह्म अस्थान ।
सुन्न सिखर के महल मैं, हंस करैं बिसराम ॥
Ibid

86. कुंभक रेचक सब करैं, अनि करत उदगार ।
गरीबदास उस नागनी कूं, जीतै सोई खिलार ॥
कुंभ भरै रेचक करै, फिर टूटत है पौन ।
आगे घाटी बन्द है, इंगला पिंगला दोय ।
गरीबदास सुषमन खुलै, तास मिलावा होय ॥
G.G.S., p. 202

87. तीनि पेच है कुंडलिनी, नाभी कै पासा ।
जाकै मुखसें नीकसै, जल अग्नि अकाशा ॥
G.G.S., p. 240

and is the region of water ; (3) *Manipura,* which is in the spinal cord opposite the navel and is the abode of fire; (4) *anāhata,* which is opposite the heart and is the abode of air; (5) *viśuddha,* which is opposite the base of the throat and is the region of ether; and (6) *ājnā,* which is opposite the junction of the eyebrows and is the centre of psychic vision. The piercing *(bheda)* of the six *chakras* is a process whereby the elements of which the body is composed are purified.[88] Garib Das describes these chakras as follows:

Above the genital organ is the *mūlsthana,*
Above the *mulsthana* is *svād chakra,*
Above the *svād chakra* is *nabhi kaval;*
Take care of this *nabhi kuval.*
At the *chakra* near the heart you can see the mind,
The consciousness is unveiled through *soham.*
Near the *kañtha sthān,* the word is meditated upon,
Without using the tongue the *mantra* is repeated.
The consciousness is realized at *trikuti* ;
Above it is the *kailasha* palace, the wonderful heaven,
Where a thousand lotus petals can be seen;
Garib Das says, that is the seat of God.[89]

Garib Das' mysticism has not only been expressed in emotional terminology of the Bhaktas but also in the psychological terminology of the Yogis. The saint in his highest state of consciousness hears the *anhada sabda* (unstruck music). This state is achieved after the *kundalini* is awakened, the *prānās* move along the *chakras* and reach the tenth door *(dasam dvar).* Within every heart there is the sound of the Infinite God. The higher the spirit soars, the purer and diviner the music it hears.[90]

88. *The Cultural Haritage of India,* Vol IV, p. 249

89. गुदा असथांन पृर मूल असथांन है, मूल असथांन परि स्वाद चकरं ।
स्वाद के चकर परि नाभ का कवल है, नाभ के कवल का करौ फिकरं ।।
हिरदै अस्थांन मैं मनमूरति लखौ, सुरति सारंग सोहं सराफा ।
कंठ असथांन मैं ररं रस रीति है, बिना मुख रसन जपि अजपा जापा ।।
त्रिकुटि कमल परि किला कैलास है, अजब बैकुंठ बैलोक नगरी ।
सहंस दल कमल परि अगम, आसन पुरुष दास गरीब नहीं पंथ डगरी ।।
G.G.S., p. 579

90. घट घट में नाद उचार वाणी, मीही महल में मारफत गावता है ।

The highest seat of consciousness is called the *dasam dvār*. or the tenth door. Here one hears the *anahad śabad* and also sees the light of God in its supreme form. This is the *turiya* state and the actual realisation of God in the highest mystic experience. Garib Das also calls it *brahma dvar*.

If you wish to see the light within,
Sing the *anahad sabad* in pure mind.
He who conquers the lower self is *Brahmajnani*,
He enjoys bliss through self-control.[91]
He who reaches the highest consciousness,
After controlling all the doors of self,
Reaches the *brahma dvār*; he sees the light of God.[92]

Garib Das is never tired of describing this experience where all darkness and delusion disappears and all is light and music of heaven. The achievement of this highest Yoga, the *Sabda Yoga*, is possible not by Hatha Yoga or such practices as make the life abnormal. It is attainable by pure Bhakti. As Sydney Spencer puts it: "The goal is absorption in God. When the body dies, to what abode shall the pious man go? It shall unite with Him who is beyond expression and indestructible. When the idea of birth and death departs from man's mind, he shall for ever be absorbed in God."[93] For Garib Das this was the goal. He believed in total absorption in God like a stream merging in the ocean. This state is called *sahaja*. Through *sahaja* one meditates. Through *Sahaj* one attains the fruit of salvation. A whole Chapter, *Sahaj ka Anga* (G.G.S. Pp. 106-107), is devoted to it.[94]

ताल मृदंग जहा संख सुर पूरिए, बिन मुख नाद बजावता है ॥
R.S,, p. 221

91. जो तुझ दीपक जोया चहिये । तो शब्द अनाहद हसां गहिये ॥
कंदर्प जीते सो ब्रह्मज्ञानी । बंक नाल बंधे रस पानी ॥
G.G.S., p. 481

92. औघट घाटी नाद सुर, कुम्भ भरे भरपूर ।
ब्रह्म दुआरा जद खुला, देखे नूर जहूर ॥

93. Sydney Spencer, *Mysticism in World Religions*, p. 65

94. सहजै बरषा होत है, सहजै ऊगै बीज ।
सहजं ही परवान फल, सहजै सतगुरु रीझ ॥
सहजै सिद्धि प्रकासिया, सहजै चलैं विमान ।
सहजै ज्ञान विवेक बुधि, सहजै दीजै दान ॥
G.G.S., p. 106

CHAPTER V

Influence of Kabir on Garib Das

Out of all the medieval saints the impact of Kabir and Guru Nanak on contemporary religious and social thought was the greatest. We will discuss the influence of Kabir on Garib Das in this chapter and that of Guru Nanak and *Adi Granth* in the next chapter.

The influence of Kabir's thoughts, language and philosophy on Garib Das is tremendous. This has been acknowledged not only by the biographers and followers of Garib Das but also by the Saint himself. Although he never met Kabir in his life time, he adopted Kabir as his inspirer, as his Guru and as his ideal *avatara.* Garib Das says :

> Kabir is the Chief among all Saints.
> He is the True Guru and embodiment of Justice.
> Kabir is the Primal and beginningless Spirit,
> His vast light is spread in the fourteen regions;
> There are innumerable gems and precious stones,
> Kabir is the most precious amongst them all.[1]

Kabir is not only a historical figure for Garib Das, but also an eternal Spirit, whom he can meet in spiritual vision and from whom he can take guidance and inspiration. For him, Kabir is the living Spirit of God in the form of an ever living Divine Teacher.

> Love is the lotus leaf,
> Through it the state of *Sunya* is attained,
> Humble Garib has been liberated,
> He has met the True Guru Kabir.[2]

1. सब सन्तन सिरताज है, सतगुरु अदल कबीर।
गरीब आदि अनादि कबीर है, चौदा भवन विशाल।
हीरे मोती बहुत हैं, कबीर लालन सिर लाल।।
R.S., p. 95

2. अलल पंख अनुराग है, शून्य मण्डल रहै थीर।
दास कबीर उधारिया, सतगुरु मिले कबीर।।
G.G.S., p. 6

It is not a matter of coincidence but a revealing fact that Garib Das wrote on the same topics in the same strain and in the same poetic forms as Kabir Das did.

Kabir Granthavali	*Garib Das' Granth*
गुरुदेव को अग	गुरुदेव का अंग
सुमिरण को अंग	सुमिरण का अंग
बिरहा को अंग	बिरहा का अंग
ग्यान बिरह को अंग	ग्यान बिरह का अंग
परचा को अंग	परचा का अंग
रस को अंग	रस का अंग
लम्ब को अंग	लाम्बी का अंग
जरना को अंग	जरना का अंग
हैरान को अंग	हैरान का अंग
लय को अंग	लय का अंग
निहकर्मी पतिव्रता को अंग	निष्कर्मी पतिव्रता का अंग
चितावनी को अंग	चितावनी का अंग
मन को अंग	मन का अंग
सूछम मारग को अंग	सूछम मारग का अंग
सूछम जनम को अंग	सूछम जनम का अंग
माया को अंग	माया का अंग
चणक को अंग	चणक का अंग
करनी बिना कथनी को अंग	करनी बिना कथनी का अंग
कथनी बिना करनी को अंग	कथनी बिना करनी का अंग
कामी नर को अंग	कामी नर का अंग
सहज को अंग	सहज का अंग
साँच को अंग	साँच का अंग
कुसंगत को अंग	कुसंगत का अंग
संगत को अंग	संगत का अंग
असाध को अंग	असाध का अंग
साध को अंग	साध का अंग
सारग्राही को अंग	साहग्राही का अंग
उपदेस को अंग	उपदेस का अंग
विश्वास को अंग	विश्वास का अंग
कुशब्द को अंग	कुशब्द का अंग
जम को अंग	काल का अंग

Garib Das has written almost on all the topics on which Kabir has written in the same way as Kabir did. The couplets *(slokas)* express and cover the same themes, though in a slightly different language. Garib Das' writings are as voluminous as those of Kabir, and the Saint of Haryana made his whole life and writings an imitation of Kabir's genius and creative faculties. Garib Das wrote almost in the same Ragas, Ramainis and Padavalis, as Kabir did. Poetry set to the following Ragas is found both in Kabir and Garib Das : Raga Gaudi, Raga Ramkali, Raga Asavari, Raga Sorath, Raga Kedara, Raga Maru, Raga Todi, Raga Bhairava, Raga Bilawal, Raga Basant, Raga Kalayan, Raga Malhar and Raga Dhanasari. Thus even in music we note that the aspirations and inspiration of Garib Das were guided mainly by Kabir.

If we take up the views of Kabir and Garib Das on various religious topics we will notice that Garib Das drew his major inspiration mainly from his Master, Kabir. It would be convenient to study the influence of Kabir on some salient subjects.

Concept of the Guru

According to Kabir,the Guru is indispensable and invaluable. The Guru gives the key to spiritual treasures. What the mind cannot attain can be attained through the powers of the Guru. He sings the greatness of the Guru and identifies his spirit with that of God. Explaining Kabir's conception of Guru, Dr. Ram Kumar Verma says : "Acccording to Kabir, the Guru is greater than God even. Without the elevating help of the Guru, an unclean soul can never attain God. Only by the grace of the Guru can the soul be led to walk on the path of realisation of God. The Guru becomes more important than God because without him God cannot be attained. That is why Kabir says that when both Guru and Gobind (God) stand before me I do not know whose feet I should touch first."[3] According to Kabir the Guru is the medium between God and soul. He brings about the union between the two. Spiritually the Guru and God are one.

The Guru and God are one; they are one spirit in two

3. Dr. Ram Kumar Verma, *Kabir Ka Rahasyavada*, p. 52.

forms; He who effaces himself and dies while living, he attains God."[4]

Garib Das also says in the same strain that Satguru and Brahma are one. There is not the slightest difference between them. According to him :

> Satguru is the Perfect Brahma; Satguru is Infinite God Himself, Satguru is the all-pervading spirit: There is absolutely no difference between the two.[5]

Guru is the bestower of divine knowledge. He inspires the seeker after truth with love and light. Kabir says :

> Maya is the flame of the lamp, man is the moth.
> He is misled again and again into the flame;
> Kabir says, the guidance of the Guru saves a few.[6]

Garib Das also says the same thing :

> After being absorbed in *maya*, I was deluded and lost;
> I met the Satguru who revealed the Yoga of knowledge.[7]

The Guru strikes the disciple with the arrow of love, like god Cupid. This arrow of love destroys all that is unworthy of a devotee and gives him a new life of love and devotion. On this point the views of Kabir and Garib Das are identical.

> The Satguru has shot the arrow, aiming it straight with his hand. It has pierced the body, the flame of passions

4. गुरु गोविन्द तो एक है, दूजा ये आकार ।
आप मिटै जीवत मरै, तो पावै करतार ।।
K.G., p. 3

5. सतगुरु पूरण ब्रह्म है, सतगुरु आप अलेख ।
सतगुरु रमता राम है, यामें मीन न मेख ।।
G.G.S., p. 4

6. माया दीपक नर पतंग, भरम भरम पड़न्त ।
कहै कबीर गुरु ज्ञान से, एक आधा उबरन्त ।।
K.G., p. 3

7. माया का रस पीयकर, हो गये डामाडोल ।
ऐसा सतगुरु हम मिल्या, ज्ञान योग दिया खोल ।।
G.G.S., p. 3

has been extinguished.[8]

Satguru has shot the arrow drawing it with all his strength. As it struck, all the *karmas* and delusions have been burnt.[9]

And yet the Guru is he who is fully enlightened. The Guru is perfect and has all the spiritual powers of making others perfect. There are many false Gurus and we should beware of them. Both Kabir and Garib Das warn us against blind Gurus *(andha gurus)* in the same terms:

The disciple whose Guru is blind, is bound to remain utterly blind,
When the blind leads the blind, both are annihilated.
Blind is the Guru and blind the disciple,
And blind is the faith of both.
They remain deaf to truth
and never hear the Divine Music.[11]

Sumiran (Rememberance of God)

Nama (the Name of God) is the essence of the creed of Kabir and Garib Das. Both call it the *sumum bonum* of religious life:

Says Kabir, I have said, and Brahma and Siva have said,
The Name of God is the sum and substance.[12]

8. सतगुरु मार्या बाण भर, धर कर सूधी मूठ।
अँग उघाड़े लागिया, गई दवा स्यों फूट॥
K.G., p. 2

9. सतगुरु मार्या बान कसी, खेबर ग्यासी खेंच।
भर्म कर्म सब जरि गये, लई कुबुद्धि सब ऐंच॥
G.G.S., p. 3

10. जाका गुरु भी आँधला, चेला खरा निरन्ध।
अन्धे अन्धा ठेलिया, दोनू कूप पड़न्त॥
K.G., p. 2

11. अंध गुरु अंध शिष्य हैं, अंध जगत दुंहु दीन।
षट दरशन सब गुंग हैं, सुनी न अनहद बीन॥
G.G.S., p. 14.

12. कबीर कहे मैं कथ गया, कथ गए ब्रह्म महेश।
राम नाम मत सार है, सब काहूँ उपदेश॥
K.G., p. 5.

Garib Das also says :

The Name of God is of the essence and supreme,
On which the mind should be fixed with *soham* ;
Sit on the carpet of knowledge and bathe in the lake of Bliss.[13]

Like Kabir, he calls the Name of God *nirmala* (pure), *nishchal* (eternal), *agadha* (unfathomable), *parasa* (philosopher's stone). Kabir has again and again described the Godhead as *Niranjana* (ineffable). Garib Das also uses the word *Niranjan* in the same sense as Kabir does, both for God and *Nama* which represents God :

O Saints, Name of the Absolute and
Perfect God is good,
Fasting and going to pilgrimages are hollow ;
Fruitless are prayers, penances and self-mortification.[14]

The Bhakti of both Kabir and Garib centres around the name of God. Kabir says :

The Real Bhakti is rememberance of the Name of God,
Anything else leads to pain and great sorrow ;
The Name of God should be remembered in mind, speech and actions.[15]

Garib Das follows :

Bhakti, worship, yoga, knowledge, meditation and faith,
They all reside together in the Name of the Lord.[16]

13. नाम शिरोमणि सार है, सोहं सुरत लगाय ।
ज्ञान गलीचे बैठ कर, सुन्न सरोवर न्हाय ।।
G.G.S., p. 8.

14. नाम निरंजन नीका, संतो राम निरंजन नीका ।
तीरथ बरत थोथरे लागें, जप तप संजम फीका ।।
G.G.S., p. 517.

15. भक्ति भजन हरि नाम है, दूजा दुःख अपार ।
मनसा वाचा कर्मणा, कबिरा सुमिरण सार ।।
K.G., p. 5.

16. भक्ति बंदगी योग सब, ज्ञान ध्यान परतीत ।
सुन्न सिखरगढ में रहें, सतगुरु शब्द अतीत ।।
G.G.S., p. 8.

Pangs of Separation *(Biraha)*

Longing for the Beloved is common to all Bhaktas. The Sagun Bhaktas express this longing for a historical personality or *avatara*. But Garib Das follows Kabir in his poignant longing for the Supreme Beloved. They both use the same symbolism of the moth and the fire, the *chakvi* and *chakva*, the frog and the cloud to describe the pangs of separation.

1. As the *Chakva* and *Chakvi* wait for the moon,
   And the frog croaks on hearing the thunder of cloud,
   So also a passionate Bhakta longs for his Beloved.[17]
2. The *Chakvi* anxiously waits in separation for the night,
   And meets the Beloved in the morning.
   But those who are separated from the Beloved
   Thirst for Him day and night.[18]
3. The cranes are crying in the sky, the clouds are athunder,
   And rain has fallen and filled the ponds,
   What can be the condition of those
   Who are separated from God.[14]
4. The cranes fly far but all the time,
   They cry aloud for their young;
   Those who are madly in love with the Beloved
   Should long for Him like this.[20]

17. जैसे चन्द चकोर है, ज्यूं चकवी चित होई ।
    बोलें दादुर गरज सुनि, बिरह लगी दिल सोई ।।
    G.G.S., p. 12.

18. चकवी बिछड़ी रैन की, आय मिली परभात ।
    जै जन बिछड़े राम स्यूँ,ते दिन मिले न रात ।।
    K.G., p. 7.

19. अम्बर कुन्जा कुरलियाँ, गरज भरे सब ताल ।
    जिन सें गोबिन्द बीछड़े, तिनके कौन हवाल ।।
    K.G., p. 7.

20. ज्यों कुंजी कुरलात है, अण्डे पारें पोष ।
    ऐसे बिरहनि ध्यान धर, उस बिरहा के लोक ।।
    G.G.S., p. 12.

5. When the lamp, the flame and the oil
are brought together,
The moth flies and burns itself in it.[21]

6. The moth, full of pain in his heart,
Is attracted by the love of the flame;
He cares not for anything else and offers his all.[22]

The views of Kabir and Garib are so identical in theme and expression both in *birhe ka anga* and *gyan birhe ka anga* that it is easy to conclude that Garib Das has derived his main inspiration from Kabir for writing his work. The terminology, the symbology and poetic expressions of *birah* are used by Garib Das in the same tone as Kabir Das does.

Nature of Experience

We find that Garib Das gives expression to his spiritual experiences, almost exactly in the same way and in the same terminology as Kabir does.

1. I have seen the Beloved with concentrated mind;
He is full of Light and like the philosoper's stone;
He is absorbed in my eyes.[23]

2. The moonlight is the Light of God.
The blazing light of God is spread everywhere;
His Light is the light of the world,

21. दीपक पावक आनिया, तेल भी आन्या संग ।
तीनों मिलकर जोहिया, उड़ उड़ पड़े पतंग ॥
K.G., p. 11.

22. पडै पतंग व्यथा भरा, दिल दीपक दरियाव ।
तन मन अरपै प्राण कूं, भावें सरबस जाय ॥
G.G.S., p. 12.

23. कबिरा देख्या एक अँग, महिमा कही न जाय ।
तेजपुञ्ज पारस धणी, नैना रहे समाय ॥
K.G., p. 15.

There is no end to His Light.[24]

3. God is unfathomable, unknowable and unseen,
Only His Light shines ;
Those who serve him are saved
From vice and virtue and injury.[25]

4. His light shines in all its splendour,
His eyes are shining with joy;
Kabir stands near His throne,
And waves the *chauri* over His head.[26]

Garib identifies the light of Kabir with the light of God and thereby acknowledges his highest respect for Kabir. He points out that Kabir is the source of his inspiration. All light comes to him from Kabir.

1. Leaving the finite, the soul went to the Infinite,
And there took a lasting abode;
The lotus has bloomed without flowers,
Only a devotee of God can see it.[27]

2. By repeating the Name,
The mind is concentrated on *Soham* ;
The finite soul is absorbed in the Infinite

24. तेजपुंज की चाँदनी, तेजपुंज झलकन्त ।
तेजपुंज निज नूर है, तेजपुंज नहीं अंत ।।
G.G.S., p. 24.

25. अगम अगोचर गम नहीं, तहाँ जगमगै जोत ।
जहाँ कबीरा बन्दगी, पाप पुण्य नहीं चोट ।।
K.G., p. 12.

26. झिलमिल ज्योती जगमगै, नैना बैन बिलास ।
सत्य पुरुष सिर चंवर है, तखत कबीर खवास ।।
G.G.S., p. 25.

27. हद्द छाँड़ बेहद गया, हुआ निरन्तर बास ।
कवल ज्यूं फूल्या फूल बिन, को निरखै निज दास ।।
K.G., p. 12.

Man is then free from birth and death.[28]

Another common feature between Garib Das and Kabir is the concept of *suratī* and *niratī* which have been variously interpreted. Kabir says :

The *surati* has been absorbed in the *nirati*,
Nirati is stable and stationary ;
When I came to know
The secret of *surati* and *nirati*,
Then the door to realization opened.[29]

Garib Das follows :

The mind is absorbed in *surati* and *nirati* experience,
After remembering the name of God,
My soul has become immortal.[30]

The joy of spiritual experience is considered a *rasa* and the alchemy of this *rasa* is called *Ram Rasayan.* It is compared to wine. Kabir says :

The alchemy of Divine Name is the bliss of love,
Those who know the joy, drink the wine,
It is a precious drink,
But the wine seller wants your head as the price.[31]

Garib Das follows :

The alchemy of Divine Name is the bliss of love,
It is not easy to get it, listen to one thing of all,

28. ररंकारतों धुन लगै, सोहं सुरत समाय ।
हद बेहद पर बास है, बहुर न आवै जाय ॥
G.G.S., p. 8.

29. सुरति समानी निरति में, निरति रही निर्धार ।
सुरति निरति परचा भया, तब खुले स्वयं द्वार ॥
K.G., p. 14.

30. सुरति निरति मन पवन पर, सोहं सोहं होय ।
शिव मन्तर गौरज कह्या, अमर भई है सोय ॥
G.G.S., p. 6.

31. राम रसायन प्रेम रस, पीवत अधिक रसाल ।
कबिरा पीवण दुलभ है, माँगे सीस कलाल ॥
K.G., p. 16.

You have to give your head as the price.[32]

Like Kabir, Garib Das compares the *rasa* of spiritual experience with the *rasa* of wine. A dedicated spirit like that of the Sufi saint Mansur alone is fit for it. Says Kabir :

Around the fire-place of the brewer
Many people come and sit ;
He alone gets a drink of wine who offers his head,
Otherwise one cannot drink it.[33]

Garib Das follows :

Mansur received a drop of wine,
From the Jug of the wine-seller.
The Light emanated from his words,
And spread to every flower.[34]

Not to reveal the inner secret of spiritual life and to endure with humility the gift of divine powers is a common feature of all saints of this period. In the chapter on *Jarna ka Anga*, Kabir had written five couplets but Garib Das elaborated it into eighty couplets. The spiritual powers of God should be received with humility and humanity. Kabir says :

So wonderful is His experience that its wonderment
Cannot be described ; It should be kept concealed ;
The Vedas and Koran have not known His end,
No one will accept the truth.

Garib Das follows :

Such should be a man's endurance as of the earth,

32. राम रसायन प्रेम रस, सौंहगा सौदा जान ।
सो बातन की एक है, सीस दीजिए दान ।।
G.G.S., p. 31.

33. कबिरा भटी कलाल की, बहुतक बैठे आय ।
सिर सौंपे सोई पिबै, नहीं तो पिया न जाय ।।
K.G., p. 16.

34. कल्लाली के कलस की, लगी छींट मन्सूर ।
फूल फूल परबेस है, शबद समाया नूर ।।
G.G.S., p. 31.

35. ऐसा अद्‌भुत जिन कथै, अद्‌भुत राख लुकाय ।
बेद कुरानैं गम नहीं, कह्या न को पतियाय ।।
K.G., p. 18.

Even when someone digs it, it is silent in pain,
Such are the endurance powers of its body.[36]

Both Kabir and Garib Das practised this in their life. Their tolerance and powers of endurance were infinite. Both of them preached tolerance as the keystone to spiritual life. In the *Chitavani ka Anga* Garib Das reminds men of the impermanance of this life and body and urges them like Kabir to think of God. Man comes naked to the earth and goes naked leaving his millions behind him. Says Kabir :

This body is about to perish,
Save it if you can ;
People who owned millions,
Have left the world empty-handed.[37]

Garib Das follows :

Naked you came to the world ;
And naked you will depart ;
Life in between is a dream,
The mind has been misled by *maya*.[38]

The body is transient. Man is ignorantly absorbed in the pleasures of the body. He will repent when the soul has left the body. Kabir says :

Why are you proud of your body
Which you think of as beautiful ;
Once you leave the body you will never meet it again,
Just as a snake never regains it skin.[39]

36. ऐसी जरना चाहिए, ज्यों पृथ्वी तत थीर ।
खोदे से खसकै नहीं, ऐसा बजर सरीर ।।
G.G.S., p. 35.

37. कबिरा ये तन जात है, सकै तो लेय बहोड़ ।
नंगे हाथों ते गए, जिनके लाख करोड़ ।।
K.G., p. 24.

38. नंगा आया जगत में, नंगा ही तू जाय ।
बिच में ख्वाबी ख्याल है, मन माया भरमाय ।।
G.G.S., p. 32.

39. कबिरा काहे गरबियो, देही देख सुरंग ।
बीछड़ियाँ मिलबे नहीं, ज्यों काँचली भुजंग ।।
K.G., p. 21.

Garib Das follows :

Why are you so absorbed in this body,
O fool, it is nothing but a dwelling of mud ;
Worship thy Lord and search the supreme Being.[40]

Following Kabir in his philosophy of the Self, Garib Das says that the original home of the Self was heaven. From there it fell to the lowest level of *maya* and is suffering ever since. Says Kabir :

Mind is the bird which rose very high in the sky,
But the pull of *maya* brought it down soon.[41]
Garib Das follows :
The mind has fallen from the skies,
And has got mixed up with dust.
He has forgotten God and is lost in the cycle of births.[42]

The path of the seeker is very difficult. Both Kabir and Garib Das call it *sookham* (subtle). It is not easy to travel over it. It requires a great moral discipline and deep faith. Kabir says :

The path is very difficult,
Only a few can traverse it.
Those who reach it return not,
Who shall report back their well-being ?[43]

Garib Das follows :

The words they speak are subtle,

40. या माटी के महल में, मगन भया क्यूँ मूढ ।
कर साहिब की बन्दगी, उस साँई को ढूँढ ।।
G.G.S., p. 70.

41. कबिरा मन पाँखी भया, बहुतक चढ्या अकास ।
ऊहाँ ही ते गिर पड्या, मन माया के पास ।
K.G., p 30.

42. यो मन गिर्या अकास ते, हो गया धामा धूल ।
लाख चौरासी मन बसी, पारब्रह्म गया भूल ।।
G.G.S., p. 72.

43. कबिरा मारग कठिन है, कोई न सकिया जाय ।
गए तो बहुड़े नही, कुसल कहे को आय ।।
K.G., p. 31.

Subtle is the message they give.
The subtle can get at the subtle,
There is no need for outer trappings.[44]

The concept of *māyā* pervades the whole religious philosophy of India. Like Kabir, Garib Das describes *māyā* as *mohinī*, *dutani* and *parpancanī*. Kabir says :

Maya is the magician which has bewitched every one
And overpowered the whole world ;
Only a few souls are saved ;
They broke away from the beaten path.[45]

He says again :

Maya is a witch who has swallowed everyone,
If she comes near the Saints her teeth will be taken out.[46]

Garib Das follows :

Maya is the magician which has bewitched the whole world.
It has spread the net of its poison over earth, heaven and hell.[47]

Maya is the devil which has destroyed the world,
Maya is blood-thirsty which is not controlled by anyone.[48]

44. सूखम बाणी बोलते, सूखम सबद सँदेस ।
सूखम सै सूखम मिल्या, काह दिखावें भेष ॥
G.G.S., p. 81.

45. कबिरा माया मोहनी, सब जग घाल्या घान ।
कोइ एक जन ऊबरे, तोड़ी कुल की आन ॥
K.G., p. 33.

46. कबिरा माया डाकनी, सब किस ही को खाय ।
दाँत उपाड़े पापनी, जै सन्तों नेडे जाय ॥
K.G., p. 34.

47. ऐसी माया मोहनी, मोह्या सब संसार ।
स्वर्ग मिरत पाताल लग, डारे बिस के जाल ॥
G.G.S., p. 85.

48. ऐसी दूती जोगनी, जगत कीन बैरून ।
आन अटक मानै नहीं, माया चढ रही खून ॥
G.G.S., p. 87

Garib Das' monotheism and his hatered for all types of idolatory is solely inspired by the strong feelings of Kabir about it. For them this *pāhan-pūjā*, stone-worship, is the most misleading faith.

Says Kabir :

Man makes an image of stone and worships it as the Creator,
If he continues to worship with this faith, he will sink in the river of death.[49]

Again :

I too might have been an idol worshipper,
And might have been carrying idols on my head,
Just as an ass carries loads in a battlefield ;
But by the grace of the Guru I have thrown away the weight.[50]

Garib Das condemns idolatory in similar strong words :

He who loves the stone-god ignores the Living Spirit,
He will fall into hell and never be liberated.[51]

Again :

People call a stone by the name of God,
I am full of misgivings for them ;
How can iron be converted into gold.
Unless it touches the philosopher's stone.[52]

49. पाहन केरा पूतला, कर पूजे करतार ।
इहि भरोसे जो रहे, ते डूबे कलि धार ॥
K.G., p. 43.

50. हम भी पाहन पूजते, खोते रण के रोज ।
सतगुरु की किरपा भई, डार्‌या सिर का बोझ ॥
K.G., p. 44.

51. पाहन सेती प्रीतड़ी, चेतन सेती दोष ।
दोजख धारे जायँगे, कभी न पावैं मोख ॥
G.G.S., p. 88.

52. पाथर परमेसर कहैं, बड़ा अँदेसा मोह ।
पारस से भेट्‌या नहीं, कैसे पलटे लोह ॥
G.G.S., p. 88.

When man preaches one thing and does the opposite it is called *Karnī binā Kathnī* by both Kabir and Garib Das. On this theme also, Garib Das closely follows Kabir's thoughts and gives it an identical expression. Kabir Says :

What is the use of talking if you do not do what you say,
Your life will be like a temporary structure which will fall in no time.[53]

Garib Das follows :

There are many who preach and preach,
They talk and bray like an ass,
The man who practises is silent and never sells his faith.[54]

Lust is one of the main hinderances in spiritual life. While legitimate indulgence within the family life is permissible, adultery is considered a great sin by all religions. Lust for another man's wife is considered the greatest sin. Kabir says :

Few escape lust for other men's wives and paramours,
They taste sweet to start with,
But become poison in the end.[55]

Garib Das follows :

Do not covet the wife of another,
You will suffer for this sin.
Do not waste your precious wealth,
Do not exchange diamonds for dust.[56]

53. कथनी कथी तो क्या भया, करनी ना ठहराय ।
कालबूत के कोट ज्यों, देखत ही ढह जाय ।।
K.G., p. 38.

54. बक्ता बादी बहुत है, गदहे ज्यों अरड़ाय ।
करनी करै सो मौन है, साख बेच नहीं खाय ।।
G.G.S., p. 97

55. परनारी परसुन्दरी, बिरले बन्चे कोय ।
खाते मीठी खाण्ड सी, अन्त काल विष होय ।।
K.G., p. 39.

56. परनारी नहीं परसिए, होगा हाल बेहाल ।
पारस पूंजी जात है, कांकर सांटे लाल ।।
G.G.S., p. 104.

The idea of *Sahaja* has been present in Indian thought since many centuries. The Vaishnavas, the Buddhists and even the Shakta cults and Nathpanthis gave it many forms and expressions. Saint-Poets like Chandidas gave it a romantic but morally refined form. Garib Das, following Kabir, makes it an ethically pure and balanced way of life. Both have written much on *Sahaja*. Although *Sahaja* is said to be an easy way of spiritual life yet they point out firmly that it is not so easy. It requires great moral effort. Chandidas says :

> *Sahaja*, *Sahaja*, everyone speaks of *Sahaja*,
> But who knows what is *Sahaja* ?

Dr. Ananda Coomaraswamy calls *Sahaja* "the last achievement of all thought" and says that it is "a recognition of the identity of spirit and matter, subject and object ; and this reunion is the marriage of Heaven and Hell, the reaching out of a contracted universe towards its freedom, in response to the love of Eternity for the production of time. There is no sacred or profane, spiritual or sensual, but everything that lives is pure and void".

While the Vaishnavas like Chandidas practised *Sahaja* through the love of women they never married, Kabir and Garib Das practised *Sahaja* through married life. Kabir says :

> *Sahaja Sahaja*, everyone speaks of *Sahaja*
> They do not know what *Sahaja* is ;
> He who has abandoned all poison of evil easily,
> He deserves to know *Sahaja*.[57]

Again :

> *Sahaja*, *Sahaja*, everyone speaks of *Sahaja*
> People know not what *Sahaja* is.
> He who meets God easily knows what is *sahaja*.

Garib Das accepts *Sahaja* and praises it as the noblest creed, but it is the *Sahaja* of Kabir and not of Chandidas :

> Through *Sahaja* meet the true Guru,

57. सहज-सहज सब को कहैं, सहज न चीन्है कोय ।
जिन सहजै बिख्या तजी, सहज कहीजै सोय ॥
K.G., p. 41.

58. सहज सहज सब को कहैं, सहज न चीन्है कोय।
जिन सहजै हरिजी मिलै, सहज कहीजै सोय ॥
K.G., p. 42.

Through *Sahaja* knowledge in acquired.
Through *Sahaja* ecstacy is reached,
Through *Sahaja* spiritual joy is attained.[59]

Speaking of the influence of Kabir on Garib Dasi Panth, Swami Yogindrananda of the Udasi sect writes : "To calm down the fiery conflict between Hinduism and Islam, a number of saints like Kabir and Garib Das were born whose aim was to remove the bitterness between the followers of Allah and Ram by showing that religion of love was one : *'doū dīn madhya ek hai, allah alakh pachān'*. The God whom both the creeds worshipped was one. Allah of the Muslims and Alakh of of the Hindus was one. Garib Das had unbounded faith in the humility and the *Bani* (writings) of Kabir. He looks at Kabir in two forms. He identifies Kabir with God and yet with unbounded faith in Kabir he gives many detailed anecdotes from the life of the historical Kabir. He describes his birth, his stay in Kashi, his meeting with Ramananda, his clash with Emperor Sikander and many other stories. Out of all saints he has described in detail, only the various anecdotes of Kabir's life are given by him though he respects other saints equally."[60]

Dr. Hazari Prasad Dwivedi points out that a distinguishing feature of Kabirpanthis is that "*maya* is a *shakti* of *Niranjana*. What is in the *Brahmanda* (universe) is also in the *Pinda* (body). *Kundalinī* is the *maya* and *adi-shakti*, the serpent power. From *Omkar* all have been created."[61]

In the words of Evelyn Underhill we can include Garib Das among those saints "who have resolved the perpetual conflict between the personal and the impersonal, the transcendent and the immanent, the static and the dynamic aspects of the Divine Nature, between the Absolute of philosophy and the sure true Friend of devotional religion. They have done this, not by taking these apparently incompatible concepts one after the other ; but by ascending to a height of spiritual intuition at

59. सहजै सतगुरु मिलेंगे, सहजै उपजै ज्ञान ।
सहज खुमारी लग गई, सहजै ही रसपान ॥

G.G.S., p. 106.

60. *Grantha Sahib Garib Das*, Second Edition, Introduction, Pp. 17-19.

61. Hazari Prasad Dwivedi, *Kabir*, Pp. 108-109.

which they are as Ruysbroeck said, 'melted and merged in the Unity', and perceived as the competing opposites of a perfect whole."[62]

Kabir and Garib Das divide religious people not into Hindus and Muslims but into those who love truth and those who follow falsehood. Those who are on the side of truth are never misled by false and fanatic representations of truth. Kabir says:

> When a man of falsehood meets a false man,
> They become fast friends ;
> When a truth-loving man meets a man of falsehood
> There is no bond between them,
> They part company.[63]
> Meet and face the truth-loving man,
> What use is it to meet those who are false ?
> They will suffer for countless ages.[64]

Both Kabir and Garib Das condemn the path of fanaticism shown by Qazis, Mullas and Brahmins as the path of falsehood. Truth never divides humanity. Truth is the meeting ground of the lovers of God. Wherever the word *Sanch* occurs in the writings of Kabir and Garib Das it is synonymous with God. God alone is the Supreme Truth. Anything that takes us away from Him is falsehood and anything that leads to the love of God is Truth.

The saints and the association of the saints, *sadhu ki sangat*, is another important and common feature of the religious thoughts of Kabir and Garib Das. The glory of the saints is sung by Garib Das in the same glowing terms. Kabir says :

62. Rabindra Nath Tagore, *Kabir*, Introduction, Pp. xxiii-xxiv.

63. झूठे को झूठा मिलै, दूना बढ़ै सनेह ।
भूठे को साँचा मिलै, सभ ही टूटे नेह ॥

K.G., p. 43.

64. साँचे से सन्मुख रहै, झूठे से क्या नेह ।
सख जुगन जुग पड़ैगी झूठे के मुख खेह ॥

G.G.S., p. 107.

The family which produces a servant of God is blessed,
The family which does not produce a saint is like a fruitless tree.[65]

Again :

Blessed is the mother who gives birth to a Vaisnava son;
A Vaisnava is one who remembers God,
The world without Him is barren.[66]

Garib Das also expresses the same view :

Blessed is the mother, blessed is the land, blessed is the city and blessed is the nation ;
Blessed is the family and blessed are its deeds where a Saint is born.[67]

Again :

The Saints are like God, there is no difference between them.
There is a thin veil outside, within they are one and the same.[68]

One of the greatest fights which both Kabir and Garib Das fought on the social and religious level, was against hypocrisy and outward show of religion. Unlike innumerable mendicants in India (and there still are thousands of so-called Saints who put on the holy garb, carry a rosary and religious symbols and lead a very irreligious life), both Kabir and Garib Das wore ordinary dress. They did not distinguish themselves by any religious garb, symbols or any outward signs. And they disapproved of all religious garbs and pretentions. Kabir says :

65. कबिरा कुल तो से भला, जे कुल उपजे दास।
जेहि कुल दास न ऊपजे, से कुल आख पलास ॥
K.G., p. 53.

66. कबिरा धन ते सुन्दरी, जिन जाय वैष्णो पूत।
राम सिमिर वैष्णो हुआ, सब जग गया ऊत ॥
Ibid.

67. धन जननी, धन भूमि, धन नगरी, धन देस।
धन नगरी धन कुल, धन जहाँ साध परवेस ॥
G.G.S., p. 118.

68. साँइ सरीखे सन्त हैं, यामे मीन न मेख।
पड़दा अंग अनादि है, बाहर भीतर एक ॥
G.G.S., p. 119.

It is no use wearing a rosary,
Open your heart to the love of God;
Concentrate on the feet of God
Then only you can attain immortality.[69]

Again :

What matters if you have become a Vaishnava,
When you have not realised Him through discrimination
By imprinting frontal marks on your forehead
You are only misleading the people.[70]

Garib Das also says in the same strain :

You cannot be liberated through the rosary,
You can be liberated only through Name of God.
Without the Name of God neither the forest nor the
cities are worth living.[71]

Again :

Outwardly you have the garb of a Vairagi,
But you drink wine and indulge in sin ;
Those who have not attained Bhakti
They suffer from low passions inside them.[72]

Faith in the Supreme Being is the main source of inspiration for both Kabir and Garib Das. This faith is based on sincere love and dedication and they both preach this kind of faith. Kabir says :

69. माला फेर्या कुछ नहीं, गाँठ हृदय की खोय ।
हरि चरणां चित राखिए, तो अमरापुर होय ।।
K.G., p. 46.

70. वैष्णव भये तो क्या भए, बूझा नहीं बिबेक ।
छापा तिलक बनाय कर, ठगिया लोक अनेक ।।
K.G., p. 46.

71. माला मुकत न होत है, मुकत होत है नाम ।
एकै भीतर बाहरै, ऊजड़ भला न गाम ।।
G.G.S., p. 139.

72. ऐसे भेख बैराग है, मधहारी चण्डूल ।
जिन्हो भक्ति भावै नहीं, अन्दर सूल बबूल ।
G.G.S., p. 141

Why are you worried, on your head is the Hand of God,
If thousands of dogs bark,
They cannot sway an elephant.[73]

Garib Das follows :

Have faith and be firm in your belief
What God Wills will happen ;
By restraining your mind fix your mind on higher consciousness,
And you will attain the supreme state.[74]

So it is faith which protects man from all harm and it is unstinted faith coupled with meditation on Him that leads to the Supreme State. Death is a reminder of the transience of this life. Man is so absorbed in his surroundings that he forgets death which may come unawares and suddenly cut him from his attachments to this world. Death is inevitable and both Kabir and Garib Das make us deeply conscious of the call of death. Kabir says :

Death stands on your head, wake up my dear man,
Without the love of God, why do you sleep in ignorance.[75]

Garib Das follows :

Death laughs at you like a merciless butcher
It will in time swallow everyone ;
Satguru alone has controlled death,

73. कबिरा तू काहे डरै, सिर पर हरि का हाथ ।
हस्ती चढ़ न डोलिए, कुकर भोंसैं जो लाख ।।
K.G., p. 58

74. कर विश्वास यकीन रख, धनी करे सो होय ।
त्रिकुटी संयम ध्यान धर, देख परम पद लोय ।।
G.G.S., p. 155

75. काल सिरहाने यो खचा, जाग पियारे मींत ।
राम सनेही बाहिड़ा, तू क्यूँ सुवै नचींत ।
K.G., p. 72

With the hatchet of God's name.[76]

Besically, the mysticism of Kabir as interpreted by scholars like Dr. Hazari Prasad Dwivedi, Evelyn Underhill, Dr. Ram Kumar Verma and Parasuram Chaturvedi is found in Garib Das in all its aspects. The terms like *ajapā jāpa*, *anhada śabda*, *unmana avasthā*, *gagan* or *sunya* express the common views of the two great saints. The concepts of *surati* and *nirati* and other mystic concepts are absolutely identical. Both of them made their creed distinct from the orthodox Hindu and Muslim creeds. Both of them gave up all superstitions and formalism. Both of them believed in unblemished Bakhti of one God who is worshipped by all. And both of them were fearless in condemning injustice and kept away from the rich and the power-thirsty men of the court.

76. काल कसाई हँसत है, सरब लोक कूं खाय ।
अँकुस निरगुन नाम का, सतगुरु प्रकड़्या जाय ॥
G.G.S., p. 168

CHAPTER VI

Influence of Adi Grantha on Garib Das

The *Adi Grantha*, the scripture of the Sikhs, was compiled by Guru Arjan, the fifth Guru, in 1604 A.D. It was the first Holy Book that brought together the best writings of the Nirgun and Sufi saints along with the writing of the Sikh Gurus. "The *Adi Grantha*, presents before us a universal and practical religion, preached by the Sikh Gurus as well as other Indian saints belonging to the Bhakti movement. There is a parliament of saints in which Brahmins, Kshatriyas and Vaishyas sit with the Shudras, the Hindus sit with the Muslims, the kings sit with the lowly. There is no distinction of caste or birth. They are poets of the people who are absorbed in the Name of the Lord. They are without any hypocrisy and formalism. They are frank and sincere. The *Adi Grantha* is not a philosophical treatise, but philosophy is propounded through the songs of love and devotion. The message of love, truth, contentment, humility, fatherhood of God, brotherhood of man, restraint on passions, kindness to living beings, purity of mind and body, search for the Self, equality of man and woman, service of others, liberalism in food and clothing, make the religion of the *Adi Grantha* a universal religion."[1]

There is considerable external and internal evidence that the *Adi Grantha* had a great influence on Garib Das' vision and poetry. Garib Das' *Grantha* was compile on the very pattern of the *Adi Grantha* and Dadu's *Grantha*. Even the present day Garib Dasi *mahants* (Priors) acknowledge the fact that the compilation, ceremonial readings and rituals attached to Garib Das' *Grantha* are all inspired by the *Adi Grantha*.

Coming to internal evidence, the two most outstanding features are :

(1) Garib Das pays homage to the same Bhaktas of the Nirgun tradition as are included in the *Adi Grantha*,

1. Dr. S.S. Kohli, *A Critical Study of Adi Grantha*, p. 370.

viz., Jaideva, Ramananda, Kabir, Namdeva, Pipa, Sain, Sheikh Farid, Bhikan, Ravidas etc. The other saints to whom he pays homage and whose writings are not included in the *Adi Grantha*, are those who either lived after the *Adi Grantha* had been complied or whose names could not be included in the Nirgum School, such as Mira Bai, Tulsi Das etc. (2) Garib Das never went to purely Punjabi speaking areas and, although Punjabi has some influence on Western Hindi as a whole and quite a good influence on Haryanavi, yet when we note that Garib Das has written poems in pure Punjabi language, we cannot but conclude that this linguistic influence was mainly due to the influence of the *Adi Grantha* and Sufi poetry. Many Punjabi poems of Garib Das are very much akin to the Punjabi poems of the *Adi Grantha*. Many Hindi poems are also very much akin to those in the *Adi Grantha*. This will be discussed in the Chapter on language.

We may add two more reasons for the easily deducible influence of the *Adi Grantha* on Garib Das. Firstly, the poetry of Sheikh Farid and Bhikhan was available mainly in the *Adi Grantha*. It has been recognised that many other verses attributed to Sheikh Farid are imitation poems of other poets. But the verses of Farid and the language which has mainly influenced Garib Das' *Birahā* and *Vairāgya* are those found only in the *Adi Grantha*. Secondly, there are many hymns of Kabir in the *Adi Grantha* which are not found in any other collection of Kabir's works, however old. We find that Garib Das had not only read them but also copied them. Thus for Kabir's influence also, Garib Das was considerably indebted to the *Adi Grantha*. There are a number of autobiographical stories of Kabir which are found only in the *Adi Grantha*, and which have been repeated by Garib Das. Thus the influence of the *Adi Grantha* on Garib Das has been tremendous.

Another salient influence of the *Adi Grantha* is the choice of *Ragas* in which Garib Das writes his poetry. Such *Ragas* as Kafi,* are found only in the *Adi Grantha* and not in Kabir's works outside the *Adi Grantha*. Kafi *Raga* was used mainly by

* For discussion on Kafi, see Chapter VIII.

Guru Nanak and some Sufi saints.

Yet, it would be wrong to conclude that the vision of Garib Das is absolutely identical with that of the *Adi Grantha*. If Guru Arjan were to apply the test he applied while selecting the writings of medeival saints for inclusion in the *Adi Grantha*, he might reject half of Garib Das's work, which shows a great respect for Hindu traditions, mythology, and the Bhagvata cult, all of which the Sikh Gurus rajected. The influence of the *Adi Grantha* on Garib Das is confined to the tenets of Nirgun ideology.

Monotheism

Duncan Greenless gives the following Names of God used to describe the Nirgun Absolute God :

> "Bhagvān, Bishan, Brahmā, Gobiñd, Gopāl, Harī, Īshar, Mādho, Murārī, Prabhū, Pārbrahma, Rām, Harī, Allāh, Khudā, Karīm, Rabb, Rahīm, Rāzik, Sāhib, Prītam, Oṁkār, Anek, Kartār, Khāliq, Karan Kāran, Jagjīvan Tek, Prānpatī, Nirgun, Sargun Mālik, Atmā, Sarbjot, Sarbnivāsī, Sohāg, Tāt, Nirlep, Niranjan, Agama, Agādh, Sat, Sañch, Nirañkār, Anil, Abīnāshī, Achala, Abhed, Bharpūr, Ached, Nirākār, Amolak, Sāgar, Adī, Anādī, Beañt, Akāl, Adesha, Sarab-byāpi, Hadurī (Hazurī), Dānā, Añtarjāmī, Sukhasāgar, Gunanidhān, Dīnadayāl, Dātār, Anātha-Nātha, Dukhabhañjan, Patita-pāvana, Bābā, Pitā, Mātā, Nirbhaya, Nirvaira, Abhūl, Adol, Pavitra, Suñdara, Manmohan, Thākur, Alekh."[2]

All these names have been used by Garib Das to express the attributes of the Supreme Being.[3]

2. Duncan Greenless: *Gospel of Guru Granth*, p. CIXIV
3. अल्लाह अबिगत राम है, बेचगून निरबान ।
   मीरा मालिक है सही, महल मढी नहीं थान ।
   G.G.S., p. 6

   निर्गुण सरगुण दो पखा, मात पिता का साज ।
   हारी जीती है नहीं, उस पूरुष कूँ लाज ॥
   G.G.S., p. 154

Contd.

Creation

In the *Adi Grantha*, there is a strong belief that the world was created out of *Śabad* (Word)

> The creation and dissolution are through *Śabda*
> After the dissolution there is creation again through *Sabad*[4]

Garib Das also supports the same views:

> The subtle form and the many coloured creation,
> Is all created from One *Sabad*, such is its power.[5]

The True Guru (*Satguru*)

The concept of the True Guru as found in Garib Das is mainly derived from the *Adi Grantha*. No one can win the way to God by his own effort. Only with the help of the True Guru

Contd.

अबिगत, आदि, जुगादि जोगी सत्यपुरुष ल्योलीन है।
गगनमण्डल गलतान गैबी, जाति अजाति बेदीन है।।

G.G.S., p. 327

अगम नूर अघई, सुझलकत ज्योति।
निरंकार, निर्गुण, निरन्तर निराला।।

G.G.S., p. 340

अकाल अभूमि आदि है, जाकै नाहीं अन्त।
दिल ही अन्दर देव है, निर्मल, निर्गुण तन्त।

G.G.S., 18

सरबंग, अभंग, अनाहद है, जलथल पूरण है शून्य सिला।
दरवेश, दयाल निहाल करै, करणी भरणी डूबै न जला।।

R.S,, p. 215

4. उत्पत परलो सबद होवै, सबद फिर उत्पत होवै।

A.G., *Magh* III

5. सूखम मूरत सोहणा, बहुरंगी विस्तार।
एक शब्द से सब किया, ऐसा समरथ सार।।

G.G.S., pp. 27-28

can God be found. It is by serving Him that His grace is won and the road to Him is thrown open. The True Guru is eternal. "Without the True Guru, the path is not revealed. Without the Guru, no one has attained to God, no matter how tall he talks; it is He who knows the way and fixes true devotion in the pupil. When the Guru is met, the fear of God dwells in the heart. When the Guru makes the disciple perfect, he gains the Incomparable Reality."[6]

"The disciple feels himself in an ecstatic mood when he meets the True Guru He places all his belongings i.e. body, mind and material wealth at the feet of the Guru and, using them under His instructions, he achieves the end. The Guru loves such a disciple as a mother loves her child. The True Guru is an ocean of Truth and knowledge. The knowledge imparted by the True Guru is always faultle s. Since the Guru himself is the light of knowledge, his words are light of the world. The words of the True Guru are always about Brahman; the person who follows these words attains the state of bliss. The words of the Guru are like the divine nectar. The name of the Lord lies hidden in the words of the Guru. The knowledge of the Lord cannot be attained without the instructions of the True Guru."[7]

Garib Das describes the *Satguru* in similar terms :

Such a True Guru have I met in my consciousness,
As has blessed me with Gyan, Yoga and Bhakti.
My *Satguru* is a Living Yogi,
World Teacher, Lord and Spiritual Guide,
He has shot an arrow of love and awakened knowledge in me.
Such a *Satguru* have I met as is an embodiment of divine Light
I must offer my body, mind and everything, caring not for what might happen.[8]

6. Duncan Greenless : *Gospel of Guru Granth*, Pp. 86-87.
7. Dr. S.S. Kohli, *A Critical Study of Adi Granth*, Pp. 349-50
8. ऐसा सतगुरु हम मिल्या, सुरति सिन्धु के नाल ।
ज्ञान, योग और भक्ति सब, दीन्ही नजर निहाल ।।

Contd.

Through the teaching of the Guru,
The most difficult peaks have been climbed.
The perfect state has been revealed to me
I have entered Knowledge and Yoga.[9]

Garib Das also identifies the *Satguru* with his divine teachings and makes him the eternal Spirit able to guide all seekers of Truth. He is an embodiment of love and a liberator from the fearful ocean of life.

Divine Name

The Name of God is the saviour of man. This is a theme around which the whole religious philosophy of the *Adi Grantha,* is constructed. The soul without Name is lost in the raging fire of igoism and passionate desire, unable to win its way out of misery and to God's company where there is peace and joy. When God wants to save a suffering soul, He send His messenger with His Name, revealing Himself in a poor sinner's heart. So the *Adi Grantha* and Garib Das' *Grantha* use the same language to exhort people to repeat the Name of God. The *Adi Grantha* says :

Remeber God, Remember God, this is thy main work ;
Discard *māyā* and seek refuge in God
Consider as false the joys of this world.[10]

Contd.

जिन्दा जोगी जगतगुरु, मालिक मुरशिद पीर।
मार्या भलका भेद से, लगे ज्ञान के तीर ॥
ऐसा सतगुरु हम मिल्या, तेजपुंज की लोय।
तन मन अरपण शीशकूँ, होनी हो सो होय ॥

G.G.S., p. 2

9. औघट घाटी ऊतरे, सतगुरु के उपदेश।
पूरन पद परकासिया, ज्ञान योग परवेश ॥

G.G.S., p. 5

10. राम सिमिर राम सिमिर, एहि तेरो काज है।
माया को संग त्याग, प्रभु जी की सरन लाग,
जगत सुख मान मिथ्या, झूठो सब साज है ॥

A. G., Guru Tege Bahadur, 1352.

Garib Das follows :

Remember God, Remember God, Remember God, O mad man
With every breath repeat His name ceaselessly and worship Him ;
Within you the five senses are like the five devils,
Lust, anger, attachment are raging within you in full swing ;
Avarice has ensnared you. How shall you break it ?[11]

The name of God is spotless and one with the Spirit of God According to the *Adi Granth* :

Name, the spotless, is within man ; How to attain it ?
Name, the spotless, is all-prevading Spirit.
It can be attained with the help of the perfect Guru
Who reveals it in the heart.[12]

Garib Das also says :

The Name is pure and beautiful, the Name is spotless :
Going to pilgrimages, *japa* and *tapa* are all useless ;
Only rememberance of the Name liberates man,
And makes life worthwhile.[13]

11. राम सुमर, राम सुमर, राम सुमर बावरे ।
हरदम तो अजपा जाप, साहब को भजो रे ॥
इन्द्री घट पाँच भूत, दूत हैं दिवाने ।
काम सहर, क्रोध कहर, लोभ लहर ऊठें ।
मोह के तो पड़े फँद, कैसे करि टूटें ॥

G.G.S., p. 588

12. नाम निरंजन नाल है, किउ पाइए भाई ।
नामु निरंजन वरतदा, रविआ सभ ठाँई ॥
गुरु पूरे ते पाइए, हिरदय देय दिखाई ॥

A.G., p. 1242

13. नाम निरंजन नीका सन्तो, नाम निरंजन नीका ।
तीरथ बरत थोथरे लागैं, जप तप संजम फीका ॥
भजन बंदगी पार उतारै, सारथ जीवन जीका ॥

G.G.S., p. 517

As in the *Adi Grantha*, Garib Das calls the Name *Abigat* (without form) *nirmala* (pure), *agādh* (fathomless), *amar* (immortal) and *abināshī* (eternal).

The Body of Man

In the *Adi Grantha* the body of man is called the temple of God. Everything is to be found within the human body. Garib Das closely follows the *Adi Grantha* in its philosophy as regards the human body. According to the *Adi Grantha*:

> This body is a vast city in which are many shops,
> The *Gurmukhs* who strike a bargain buy the Name of Hari;
> They buy the Name and consider it more precious than jewels,
> Those who search for Truth anywhere except in the body,
> Are fools and wander in wilderness like the deer
> Who looks for fragrance in the forest,
> Though it comes from within him.[14]

Garib Das gives expression to similar ideas:

> Search the body, O man, in it resides the Supreme Being;
> Give up association with the misguided
> And do not be led away by them.
> In this body is the realm of God,
> There is the melody of Unstruck Music.
> The swans have come home and there is brightness everywhere.
> In this body are bathing ghats, all your dirt will be washed,

14. काया कोट अपार है, अन्दर हाट नाले ।
गुरुमुख सौदा जो करे, हरि बस्त सम्भाले ॥
राम निधान हरि बनजीए, हीरे परवाले ।
बिन काया जो हरि थाइ धन, खोजदे सो मूढ बेताले
सो ओजड़ भरम भवै, ज्यों जड़ मृग भाले ॥

A.G., p. 514

Give up your self and meet the Lord,
You will conquer the cycle of life and death.[15]

It is the Nirgun movement depicted in the *Adi Gantha* which first started fighting against social evils like the caste system and untouchability and for equality in social and religious spheres. Garib Das also fought against these evils equally vigorously. The subject has been discussed in an earlier chapter.

In north India, the *Adi Grantha* and the progressive movement behind it became the bridge between Islam and Hinduism. The Hindus lived in cultural isolation and a false sense of superiority calling the Muslims *malechhas.* The Muslims lived in pride and glory of their superiority as a ruling race looking down on the Hindus as *Kafirs.* The *Adi Grantha* became a cultural bridge between the two. It condemned false pride and the spirit of isolation in both and showed a common path and meeting ground in the love of God. It says :

The One Lord, Allah, is my God,
I have detached myself from both Hindus and Muslims.[16]

Again :

The Hindu is blind, the Muslim is one-eyed,
Among both of them the enlightened one is wise.
The Hindu worships in the *mandir,*
The Muslim worships in the mosque,
Namdeva serves and worships Him
Who is neither in the *mandir* nor in the mosque.[17]

15. काया खोज ले रे, काया में रहता पुरुष अलेख ।
बिभचारण का संग छाड़, क्या दिखलावे भेष ।।
इस काया में राम मण्डल है, बाजै अनहद तूर ।
सोहं हंसा सिन्धु मिले हैं, झिलमिल नूर जहूर ।।
इस काया में घाट पटन है, मल मूतर सब धोई ।
आपा मेट भेंट साहब कूँ, बहुर न आवन होई ।
G.G.S., p. 583

16. एक गुसाँई अल्लाह मेरा, हिन्दू तुरक दुहाँ नेबेरा ।
A.G., p. 1136

17. हिन्दू अन्धा, तुरक काणा, दुहाँ ते गिआनी स्याणा ।
हिन्दू पूजै देहरा, मुसलमान मसीत,
नामे सोई सेइया, जह देहरा न मसीत ।।
A.G., p. 857

And again :

Allah, the Invisible, is in every heart; reflect seriously;
Kabir loudly proclaims that God is the same in both Hindus and Muslims.[18]

Garib Das follows :

In both the religions, Hinduism and Islam,
Recognise One God to be the only Lord.
Remember His Name ever with love.[19]

Again :

Some go to the mosque, some to the *mandir*,
They think it is the house of God;
The Pandit and the Qazi have ruined the game,
They cannot distinguish Truth from falsehood.[20]

Although Garib Das expressed himself strongly against the sectarian attitude of Hindus and Muslims, for which he definitely received inspiration from the *Bhaktas* of the *Adi Grantha* including Kabir, he also showed a strong bias for Hinduism in preference to Islam. He believed in many Hindu practices like cow-worship, and felt admiration for the *Puranas*, Krishna and Shiva as is clear from his *Krishna Stotra*, and *ShivStotra*. He, however, identified Krishna and Shiva with God. And he condemned idolatory as vehemently as in the *Adi Grantha*. Like the *Bhaktas* of the *Adi Grantha*, he believed that worship of stone gods had been the curse of Hindu culture. The *Adi Grantha* declares :

The Hindus waste their time worshiping idols,
The Muslims waste it by to bowing their heads ;

18. अल्ला गैब सकल घट भीतर हिरदै लेई बिचारी ।
हिन्दू तुरक दोउं में एकै, कहै कबीर पुकारी ।।
A.G. p. 483

19. दोउ दीन मध एक है, अलह अलेख पिछान ।
नाम निरन्तर लीजिए, भक्ति हेत उर आन ।।
G.G.S., p. 6

20. देवल जाहीं महजद माहीं, साहिब का सिरज्या भानत है ।
पंडत काजी डोबी बाजी, नहि नीर छीर कूँ छानत है ।।
R.S., p. 216

The Hindus burn their dead, the Muslims bury them,
Niether knows the secret of God.[21]

Garib Das says :

He calls a stone his God; this worries me most;
Without coming into contact with *paras*,
How can iron turn into gold.[22]

Maya

Basing it on quotations from the *Adi Grantha*, Dr. S.S. Kohli interprets the concept of *maya* as follows : "According to the *Adi Grantha*, Prakirti or *maya* is not a separate ultimate reality. It has been created by God. The word *maya* is as old as the *Rig Veda*, but *Māyavāda* came into existence with Sankara in the 9th century A.D. Sankara's position is *brahma satyam jaganmithyā jīvo brahmaiva na parah* : Brahman is the only reality; the world is an illusion or a false appearance, the individual Self is identical with Brahman. This principle of illusion is known as *maya*. Through this illusion, the Self believes that it is an individual. This individuality experiences plurality of names and forms *(namarūpa)*. The *Adi Grantha* accepts the view that the illusion of *maya* takes the individual away from God and thus leads him towards transmigration. When the influence of *māyā* vanishes, the *Jiva* realises the false appearance of the world. The three *gunas* are created through *maya*. God is said to have two forms—the first as immanent in the world i.e. coming into contact with *maya*, the second as *trigunatīt*, i.e. di-ssociated from *māyā*. The first form is the Sarguṇa and the second is Nirguna."[23]

21. बुत कूं पूज हिन्दू मुए, तुरक मुए सिर न्याई ।
ओ ले जारे, ओ ले गाड़े, तेरी गत दोहूँ नहीं पाई ॥
A.G., p. 654

22. पाथर परमेसर कहैं, बड़ा अन्देसा मोह ।
पारस से भेंट्या नहीं, कैसे पलटै लोह ॥
G.G.S., p. 88

23. Dr. S.S. Kohli : *A Critical Study of Adi Granth*, Pp. 339-40.

Garib Das gives a similar view about *maya* in the hymn quoted below :

> The body is *māyā*, all the pleasures are *maya*,
> All the world-play is *maya* which leads to delusion and disease.[24]

The Saint

The Saint is glorified in similar words by the *Adi Grantha* and Garib Das. The Saint is the holiest of the holy. Without his association, the mind cannot be purified. The greatness of the Saint is beyond words.

> Even Vedas know not the greatness of the Saints,
> They describe them as far as they had heard of them.
> The greatness of the Saints is beyond the three *gunas*.
> The greatness of the Saints pervadeth every place.
> There is no end to the glory of the Saints,
> The glory of the Saints is ever endless,
> The glory of the Saints is highest of the high,
> The glory of the Saints is greatest of the great,
> The glory of the Saints appertaineth to them alone;
> Saith Nanak, my brethren, there is no difference
> Between God and His Saints.[25]

Garib Das also says :

> The glory of the Saints cannot be described,
> The sixty-eight places of pilgrimage are at their feet.
> The glory of the Saints is endless,
> They meet the Perfect Being and Creator;

24. काया माया जाणियो, माया के सब भोग ।
माया की बाजी खड़ी, वहुबिध सांसा शोक ।।
G.G.S., p. 85

25. साध की महमा वेद न जानै, जेता सुणै तेता बिखयाणै ।
साध की उपमा तेह गुण ते दूर, साध की उपमा रही भरपूर ।।
साध की शोभा का नहिं अन्त, साध की शोभा सदा बेअन्त ।।
साध की शोभा उच ते ऊँची, साध की शोभा मुच ते मूची ।।
साध की शोभा साध बनाई, नानक साध प्रभ भेद न आई ।।
A.G., Sukhmani.

> The glory of the Saints is beyond speech,
> They have saved Narad and Prahlada;
> Undescribable is the glory of the Saints
> They saved the drowning elephant from the alligator.[26]

God shines forth on the brow of the Saint and all impurity is removed from the hearts of those who meet him. The whole creation yearns after the dust of the feet of the righteous men.

Love or Devotion

From the *Adi Grantha* and the Saints associated with it, Garib Das imbibes the spirit of true devotion or love, which he calls by various names: *ishak*, *priti. prem*, *pyar*. Love means an undying, passionate, deep love for God. It makes a human soul perfect, immortal, blissful, free from all changing moods, ever calm and restful in Him. The devotee has only one desire : to taste love's sweetness more and more so that he may share in God's great game. He cares nothing for what the world may say or think about him. This intense devotion is symbolised by those poets and saints who died for love. The *Adi Grantha* says:

> He in whose mind He instils His love
> Through the true word; quite naturally,
> He knows the pain of this love; what can others know?
> He unites, He inspires the meeting;
> He bestows His own love.
> He knows the value of Love on whom He showerest
> His grace.[27]

26. सन्त की महमा कही न जाय, अडसठ तीरथ चरणों पाय ।
सन्त की महमा अपरम्पार, पूरण ब्रह्म मिले करतार ॥
सन्त की महमा अगम अगाध, नारद से उधरे प्रल्हाद ।
सन्त की महमा अगम अगाध, बूडत राखे गज से ग्राह ॥
G.G.S., p. 673

27. जिसनो प्रेमु मनि बसाए, साचै सबद सहजि सुभाए ।
एहा वेदन सोई जाणै, अवर को जाणनकारी जीव ॥
आपै मेले, आप मिलाए, आपण प्यार आपै लाए ।
प्रेम की सार सोई जाणै, जिसनै नजर तुम्हारी जीव ॥
A.G., p. 1016

Garib Das refers to the love of Mansur as the ideal love:

Be a lover like Mansur,
The intoxicated Saint who shouted *Anal-Haqq*.
His head had been cut off,
Yet he bathed his face with blood;
He will not give up his love for God
For the sake of love he suffered on the cross.[28]

Intense love which merges the human soul in the Spirit of God is the love preached by the saints of the *Adi Grantha* as well as by Garib Das. Their expression of *birha* (longing) and *vairagya* associated with love is the same.

Hukam (Will of God)

The concept of *Hukam* is paiticuliar to the *Adi Grantha*, particularly the writings of the Sikh Gurus.[29] The Will of God is the law that works behind the universe and behind everyone's life. By the Will of God we come and by the Will of God we go. The *Adi Grantha* declares :

By His Will he comes, by His Will he goes,
He who realises His Will realises Truth.[30]

Garib Das conceives of ***Hukam*** exactly in the same way. He says :

Knowledge is the horse with a fine saddle.
By His Will it came, by His Will it will go.
The soul is the rider of this horse.[31]

28. मंसूर कूँ देख मासूक यों हूजिए, अनलही हक्क बोलै दिवाना।
सीस कूँ काट है रुधर मुख धोवता, इश्क नहीं छाँडि सूली चढाना ।।
G.G.S., p. 437

29. हुकमै आवै हुकमै जाए, आगे पाछे हुकम समाए ।
A.G., p. 151

30. हुकमै आवै हुकमै जावै, बूझै हुकम सो साँच समावै
A.G., p. 1025

31. ज्ञान हमारा घुडला कहिए, जीन अजब गुलजारा ।
हुकमै आए हुकम पढाए, हंस भए अस्वारा ।।
G.G.S., p. 358

While the social and political ethics taught by the *Adi Grantha* is different from that of a passive saint like Garib Das, the religious ethics of Garib Das is the same as that preached by the saints of the *Adi Grantha.* He preaches abstemious habits of eating and sleeping, telling the truth, being honest, sincere, calm, patient and tolerant. *Adi Grantha* has some verses against cruelty to animals. There are some verses to show that neither vegetarianism nor meat-eating can be a means to salvation. But Garib Das preaches vegetarianism very aggressively and condemns all those, Hindus and Muslims, who eat meat in any form.

Like the saints of the *Adi Grantha*, Garib Das also condemns all ritualistic religious practices and even the formal wearing of the sacred thread, the sectarian signs and the coloured robes as marks of holiness. He is strongly of the view that holiness should be reflected in a man's actions and not in his garb. Hinduism had suffered much from these sectaian garbs which divided the *Sanyasins* into ten sects, the Yogis into twelve divisions, the Vaishnavas into many schools and the Shaivas into many classes.

Karma and Transmigration

The *Adi Grantha* goes very deep into the theory of *Karma* and Transmigration. Fundamentally, the doctrine is as old in Indian religious literature as the Upanishads. Garib Das also shares the basic belief that everyone reaps what he sows. Those who commit evil have to suffer the cycle of eighty-four *lakh* births and deaths. But all evil effeets of *Karma* can be destroyed by the grace of God. The *Adi Grantha* says : "Every *jiva* desires, thinks and acts. Every action has its associations in the past, present and future. Every action is like a seed sown in the body which is a field of action."[32]

Similar views are expressed by Garib Das also when he says :

> Everyone reaps the fruits of his deeds,
> Even the deeds of father and son may be different ;

32. *The Adi Granth*, Sri Rag M.V.

Hiranyakashyapa was punished, while Prahlada was blessed.[33]

Ego

The views of Garib Das about human ego are exactly like those of the *Adi Grantha.* The latter says :

As long as man is absorbed in egoism,
He does not realize Truth.
When egoism departs, he attains the Supreme state.[34]

Garib Das also condemns egoism in the following words:

He who says I, I, or me and mine
Is like an ass and he-goat;
Those who forget worship of God are like dogs.[35]

Grace

As in the *Adi Grantha*, so in Garib Das emphasis is laid on grace. The grace of God is very essential for Bhakti. The *Adi Grantha* says :

It is only by Grace that the supreme state is attained ;
This is the wonder wonders.
You are the Doer, You do every thing,
What can a mere mortal do.[36]

Garib Das follows :

Within this body is the shop divine,

33. अपनी करनी पाय है, कहा पिता कहा पूत ।
हिरणाकुश तो हरि छले, प्रल्हाद भक्ति अनुभूत ।।
G.G.S., 152-54

34. हौं हौं करत नहीं सच पाइए, होमइ जाय परम पद पाई ।
A.G., Gandi I

35. हौं हौं करे सो गधा है, मैं मैं करे सो बोक वे ।
बन्दा बिसरा बन्दगी, तो श्वान हैं सब लोक वे ।।
G.G.S., p. 458

36. करम होवे तन परम पद पाइए, कथे अकथ कहानी ।
तू करता किया सब तेरा, क्या को करे पिरानी ।।
A.G., Asa Mohall I

By His grace man can reach it,
And receive the gifts He gives.[37]

Mysticism

All medieval saints were fundamentally great mystics. But all the saints did not belong to the same school of mysticism. Indian mysticism of this period can be divided broadly into three groups :

(1) Monistic Mysticism (*Nirgun*)

(2) Theistic Mysticism like Krishna Cult and Rama Cult (*Saguna*)

(3) Occult Mysticism of the Siddha and Natha Yogis.

As in the *Adi Grantha*, Garib Das disappoves of Theistic Mysticism and showsallegiance only to one Supreme Being. He denounces the Occult Mysticism of Natha Yogis in the same way as has been done in the *Adi Grantha*. In his compositions, *Krishna Stotra*, and *Siva Stotra*, he shows respect for Krishna and Siva, though he identifies Krishna and Siva with his one God.

In the *Adi Grantha*, the approach to *Nirguna* and *Saguna* ideals is stated as follows :

He is the *Nirguna* as well as the *Sarguna*
He who realise this truth is a Pandit.[38]

The Word of God is considered to be above the dispute of *Nirguna* and *Saguna*:

The Word of God is distinct from the *Nirguna* and the *Sarguna*,
He is Beyond words and matchless.
The *Nirguna* is the mind of the Brahmagyani,
Sarguna is his body which envelops him.

37. बजर पोल ड्योढी लगी, अन्दर अरस दुकान ।
मेहर दया से पैसई, सतगुरु देवै दान ॥
G.G.S., p. 29

38. निरगुण सरगुण आपै सौई, तत पिछाणै सो पण्डत होई ।
A.G., Majh 128.

He is the *Nirguna* which pervades the realm of sound,
He is the music behind the five elements,
God is in the world and the world is in God,
God still remains the Sovereign Yogi.[39]

It is not a matter of coincidence that Garib Das names one of his compositions as *Sukhmani Sampat* after the Sukhmani of Guru Arjan. It is also not a matter of coincidence that he uses the word Brahmagyani which occurs repeatedly in an *Ashtapadi* of the *Sukhmani.*

The Nirgun Bhaktas looked on God as the Supreme Light which in the *Adi Grantha* is expressed as *Jyoti* and *Nur.* God first emanated His Light out of which all beings were created. That act of creation makes every one equal in the eyes of God. To attain this Light is the aim of a Bhakta's life. The *Adi Grantha* says :

First of all God created Light
And from that Light all were created.
All of us are His creatures ; None is good none bad.[40]

The supreme state, *turiya-avastha*, of realising the Light of God is called Begampura (city without sorrow). According to the *Adi Grantha* :

There is a City without sorrows,
There is no pain, no disease, no one suffers there.
There are no tax gatherers, no one levies tribute,
There is no worry, no sin, no fear and no death.[41]

39. निरगुण सरगुण सें है न्यारा, शब्द अतीत अमोलं ।
निरगुण मन माया बह्म ज्ञानी, सरगुण काया खोलं ।।
निर्गुण कहूँ सही गुणवंता, शब्द समाना दरिया है ।
पांच तत्त्व तीनौं गुण तूरा, आपै सृष्टि संजोगी है ।
खालिक खलक खलक मैं खालिक, अविगति अदली जोगी है ।।
G.G.S., p. 330

40. अवलि अलह नूरू उपाइया, कुदरति के सब बन्दे ।
एक नूर ते सभ जग उपज्या, कउन भले को मन्दे ।।
A.G., p. 1349

41. बेगमपुर सहरि को नाँव, दुख अन्दोह नहीं ते थाँव ।
ना तसवीस, खिराज न माल, खौफ न खता तरस न जवाल ।।
A.G., p. 345

Garib Das also says :

Allah is self-existent in His Light,
See Him absorbed within Himself.
The Lord sits in heaven on His throne,
Sacrifice your head for a glimpse of Him.[42]

Again :

Concentrate your mind on the Liberator Lord,
His is Light, self-dependent and wonderful,
You can see it spread in this and the other world.[43]

And again :

The City of Light and the City without sorrow
Is the name of the supreme place.
The Satguru has revealed that supreme state of *Nirvana*
The lovers have concentrated their minds on Him
By giving up all self-hood they will go to His place.[44]

Thus we see that Garib not only identifies himself with the Bhakti ideal of the *Adi Grantha* but also borrows its ideas and expressions, sometime *verbatim*. The supreme state that is achieved by devotees is described as *Sunya, Anahada, Turiya, in* Garib Das' *Granth*. The names given to these mystical states are identical with those found in the *Adi Grantha*. It says :

42. अलाह नूर मौले मगन आप है जी, गलतान सुभान सही देख लीजै ।
बैठा अरस के तखत पर आप साँई, दीदार के वास्ते सीस दीजै ॥
G.G.S., p. 435

43. बन्दी छोड़ साहब का ध्यान धारो,
निरालम्ब निज नूर निज नेक है जी ।
जल थल में थीर गँभीर गैबी, देखो लोक परलोक में एक है जी ॥
G.G.S., p. 435

44. नूरनगर बेगमपुरा परपट्टन थान,
सतगुरु सैन लगाइया जो पद निरबानं ।
अनुरागी निहतत्त्व में ले सुरति समोई,
महल मरहमी जाँहिगे तन आपा खोई ॥
G.G.S., p. 594

The Guru has given the Nectar,
In the *dasam dvara* (tenth seat) He is revealed,
There *Anahada Sabad* (Unstruck Music) is ringing,
Naturally, my mind is absorbed in Him.[45]

Again :

Every one speaks of *Sunya* and says he has attained.
How can you hear the Unstruck Music of the *Sunya*?
How do they feel who are absorbed in *Sunya* ?
They are just like God Himself who created them.
They are never born and they never die.[46]

Garib Das follows :

Travel to the *Sunya Mandal*, the Unknown and wonderful,
Unfathomable and Unstruck Music is the abode of the Beloved.
There is the light of millions of suns and moons,
Enjoy the spiritual dance with Him.[47]

Again :

Within every heart there rings His music,
He sings His melodies in His Palace;
There is the sound of *mridanga* and conch,
And He sings without using His mouth;
O, Garib Das, overcome your lower mind,

45. अमृत रस सतगुरु चुआया, दसवें दुआर परगट हो आया ।
अनहद शब्द बजै धुन बानी, सहजै सहज समाई है ।।
A.G., Maru Sohle

46. सुन्नो सुन्न कहै सब कोई, अनहद दुन्या कहा ते होई ।
अनहद सुन्या रते से कैसे; जिस तों उपजे तिस ही जैसे ।।
ओ जन्मे ना मरे, ना आवै ना जाय ।।
A.G., Sidha Gosht

47. बन्दे देखि ले दरहाल वे ।
सुन्न मण्डल सैल कर ले, अजब गैबी ख्याल वे ।।
अगम अनाहद अदल है, फजली फजल महबूब वे ।
अजब रास बिलास बानी, चन्द सूर करोर वे ।
G.G.S., p. 455

And get absorbed in *Sunya*,
Which is beyond speech.[48]

Summing up the discussion, we can now conclude that Garib Das had closely studied the *Adi Grantha* and imbibed its inspiration, language and thoughts. When we say that he derived inspiration from the *Adi Grantha*, we mean not only the sayings of the Sikh Gurus, but also those of the Bhaktas of the *Adi Grantha* like Jaideva, Namdeva, Ravidas, Farid, Kabir, Sadhna, Pipa, Ramananda and others. He mentions their names and mentions the historical biographies of Kabir and Namdeva on which the *Adi Grantha* was the first and oldest document to throw light.

Yet we cannot say that he accepted everything he found in the *Adi Grantha*. The *Adi Grantha* definitely shows that the Gurus had interest in the political freedom of the country strongly in their minds. They condemned alien rule and the atrocities perpetuated by the Muslim rulers. By the time of Garib Das the conditions had become worse. Even though the greatest upheavels took place during the time of Garib Das, he remained silent about them.

48. घट घट में उचार बानी, मिहि महल में मारफत गावता है ।
ताल मृदंग जहां शंख सुर पूरिए, बिन मुख नाद बजावता है ।।
दास गरीब दिल दूसरा दूर कर, शब्द अतीत शून्य में समाधि ।।
Ibid.

CHAPTER VII

Language of Garib Das

Garib Das was a native of Hariyana. We naturally expect his native language to form the back-bone of his writings. The language of Hariyana has for centuries developed under the influence of its neighbouring langueges—Punjabi, Western Hindi and Rajasthani. The influence of Persian on it has been to the same extent as we find in Punjabi and Western Hindi.

Both the language and culture of this region have been neglected for centuries. "The language spoken by the people of these tracts is, with almost imperceptible modifications from village to village, one and the same. It is known as Bangru, Hariani or Jatu and in Haryana as Deswati or Desari. In Rohtak it is generally called Jatu while in Delhi it sometimes takes the name of Chamarva from the Chamārs who speak it. The Chamārs, however, speak it ungrammatically, making, for example, mistakes in gender."[1]

Except for a considerable amount of folk literature, the poets of this area have not produced any distinct literature which may be called purely Hariyanvi literature. They accepted the influences of many other neighbouring languages and the scribes who copied them in Punjabi script (*Gurmukhi*), gave it a Punjabi phonetical colouring and spellings, while those who wrote in Hindi script (*Devanagri*), made it look like pure Hindi. The same is true of Garib Das' poetry. We find the influence and usage of the following languages in his poetry : (1) Sanskrit, (2) Prakrit and Apabhramsha, (3) Punjabi, (4) Sadhu Bhasha or Sant Bhakha, (5) Western Hindi, (6) Persian and (7) Bangru (Hariyanvi).

The Influence of Sanskrit

Sanskrit language has been, as Dr. Suniti Kumar Chatterjee puts it, "a symbol of Indian Culture as it was completed, so to

1. *Punjab District Gazetteer* : *Rohtak District 1910*, Vol. III A, p. 97

say, by the Aryanisation throughout the greater part of Northern India of non-Aryan elements in life, in religion and philosophy, in historical tradition, in myth and legend and their incorporation within the body of a composite Hindu Culture."[2]

Even though Sanskrit was replaced as a literary language by Prakrit, Apabhraṁsha and the present provincial languages, the religious and philosophical terminology has been retained throughout history either in its original Sanskrit form or has undergone extremely minor changes. Many Sanskrit words which were easy to be spoken and understood have also been retained either in their original form or with slight phonetical variations.

Garib Das was not a Sanskrit scholar. But, according to Kellog, "Western Hindi and the neighbouring languages possessed so many Sanskrit words that it forms nine-tenths of the language."[3] This statement may be a little exaggerated but we do find that Sanskrit words have been used mainly to express categories of thought and ideas. Even though there are some verses in the poetry of Garib Das in which Sanskrit has been profusely used, yet they cannot be called Sanskrit verses as the conjunctions and verbs are not in pure Sanskrit form. The following verses are outstanding examples :

संख कल्प युग युग अटल, अजर अमर शिव शंभु ।[4]
निराकार निर्विषं काल जाल भय भंजनं, निर्लेपं निज निर्गुणं ।[5]

Two types of Sanskrit words can be traced in the writings of Garib Das : Tatsama and Tadbhava. "The word *Tatsama*, meaning 'the same as that' appropriately denotes all purely Sanskrit words i.e., all such as have entered Hindi (or Punjabi) with no alteration save the loss of the ancient affixes of the declension. The word *Tadbhava*, i.e., 'of the nature of that', denotes, on the other hand, all corrupt Sanskrit words, which, by the addition, loss, or change of certain letters, have come to appear in Hindi (or Punjabi) in a form more or less modified

2. Suniti Kumar Chatterji, *Indo Arvan and Hindi*, p. 65
3. Kellog, *Grammar of the Hindi Language*, p. 41
4. *Rattan Sagar*, p. 36
5. G.G.S., p. 1

and often greatly disguised. Tatsama words, as is evident from the above definition appear in every dialect under one and the same form. But inasmuch as pure Sanskrit words in Hindi, like most words of Latin and Greek origin in English, are especially appropriated to the expression of higher or scientific thought, it is evident that the proportion of these Tetsamas actually found in various dialects, must needs be very great in proportion to their literary cultivation."[6]

Tatsam Sanskrit words are used mostly where they have been permanently retained by our religious literature and spoken languages. Sanskrit words are more often used, (1) as names or attributes of God or (2) for the body and the mind or (3) for theological and mystical terms or (4) for miscellaneous other purposes.

1. Sanskrit terms used as attributes of God

निराकार, निर्लेप, निरञ्जन, गुणातीत, देव ।[7]

निर्गुण, निरालम्भ ।[8]

पीताम्बर, पट, सूक्ष्म, स्वरूप ।[9]

ब्रह्मा, विष्णु, ब्रह्मज्ञानी, अनादि, साधु, नाथ, नारद, अखण्ड, कश्मल ।[10]

जगन्नाथ, करुणानिधि, कृपानिधि, कमलनयन ।[11]

6. Kellog, *Grammar of the Hindi Language*, p. 42

7. निराकार, निर्लेप, निरंजन, गुणातीत तिहु देवा ।
R.S., p. 278.

8. निर्गुण निरालम्भ जाण्या है तोह ।
R.S., p. 175

9. पीताम्बर पट में है सूक्ष्म स्वरूप ।
Ibid

10. अहो ब्रह्मज्ञानी अमानी अनादं, कटैं कोटि कश्मल जपै सन्त साधं ।
तुही ब्रह्मा विष्णु तुही मारकण्डे, तुही नाथ नारद तुही है अखण्डे।।
R.S., p. 164

11. जगन्नाथं काटन दु:ख फंदनं, करुणामय कमलनयन कृपासिन्धं ।
R.S. p. 162

अविगति, राम, अविनाशी, अनन्त, इन्द्र, प्रतिहार । [12]

निश्चल, अचल, अगाध, निष्कामी, पूर्ण, परम, अकल, गुरु । [13]

2. Sanskrit terms about body and mind

शीश, तन । [14]

रसना, मुख, पिण्ड, प्राण, मन, चित्त, सुरति, निरति । [15]

माया, रस, गगनमण्डल, पारब्रह्म, शून्य, हंस ।[16]

12. अविगति राजाराम है, चकवै अविनाशी ।
ब्रह्मा विष्णु वजीर हैं, शिव करत खवासी ।।
इन्द्र कोटि अनन्त है, जाके प्रतिहारा ।
R.S., p. 363

13. निश्चल अचल अगाध, तू निर्गुण निष्कामी ।
पूरण ब्रह्म परम गुरु अकल अविनाशी ।।
R.S., p. 346

14. शीश तुम्हारा जायगा कर सतगुरु को दान ।
तन मन धन जगदीश का रति सुमेर समान ।।
R.S., p. 28

15. बिनही रसना सब गुण गावै ।
मुख जाका सेत सूहा, चिसम में गुलाब रूहा ।।
G.G.S., p. 527
जिन ये पिण्ड प्राण सिरजे हैं, सो दीनदयाल
G.G.S., p. 529
मन की माया मेर है, मन जीते जगजीत ।
मन ही मुक्ता हो गया, मन ही पड़दा भीत ।।
G.G.S., p. 79
चित्त चन्दन छिरकत, मलागिर बेग घसी ।
R.S., p. 312
सुरति निरति में पौन खंभा, कमल हिंडोले झूलिए ।
R.S., p. 311

16. माया का रस पीय कर, गए खट दल गारत गोर ।
R.S., p. 6
गगनमण्डल गादी जहाँ, पारब्रह्म अस्थान ।
शून्य शिखर के महल में हंस करे बिसराम ।।
R.S., p. 7

शील, सन्तोष, विवेक, काम, क्रोध, लोभ, दुःख, ।[17]

भक्त, मुक्त, ज्ञान, समाधि, तेजपुञ्ज, प्रकाश, ज्योति, अनाहृत नाद ।[18]

शून्य, शब्द, गायत्री, ध्वनि, ध्यान, दीव्य, दृष्टि, राग, द्वेष, ।[19]

द्वादश, अष्ट, मुक्ता, मणि, वनखण्ड, गिरि, पर्वत, रत्न ।[20]

Prakrit and Apabhramsha Words

"Sanskrit was followed", says Dr. Suniti Kumar Chatterjee, "by what may without being unscientific be described its younger

17. शील सन्तोष विवेक विचारो ।
G.G.S., p. 561

काम, क्रोध, मद, लोभ, दुःख दुँद भागनिया ।
G.G.S., p. 557

18. ज्ञान जोग अरु भक्ति लेह, शील सन्तोष समाधि ।
R.S. p. 47

तेजपुञ्ज, प्रकाश, ज्योति, झल अनाहृद नाद गुंजार ।
G.G.S., p. 505

19. सुन्न बेसुन्न में अगम है, पिण्ड ब्रह्माण्ड से न्यार ।
सबद समाना सबद में, अवगत आर न पार ॥
R.S., p. 9

गुझ गायत्री नाम है, बिन रसना ध्वनि ध्यान ।
R.S., p. 17

दीव्य दृष्टि देवा दयाल, सतगुरु संत सुजान ।
R.S., p. 26

20. द्वादश ऊपर बोलै सोय ।
G.G.S., p. 566

अष्ट कमल दल आरती ।
R.S., p. 29

मुक्ताहल की पीठ लगी सौदागरी ।
मणि मंहगी महबूब बिकै नंहि मोलि रे ।
G.G.S., p. 545

वनखण्ड जाय न बसती बासै, गिरि पर्वत नंहि चाहै ।
G.G.S., p. 529

रत्न अमोल कलाल पाया ।
G.G.S., p. 19.

forms, the old Prakrits and the modern Bhāṣās. Inspite of dialects which are as links in the chain, Indian speech was looked upon as one by most foreigners in old times, Sanskrit being the central pendant. In the Chinese lexicons, a good many vernacular Prakritic words are given as Sanskrit. They were Indian words related to Sanskrit, in fact its later development, and they had therefore their natural place in the train of Sanskrit. This was the feeling of the Indian people also. Prakrit and Sanskrit could never be disassociated from each other—neither of them could be conceived of as having an independent existence; they were very much inter-dependent."[21]

In 300 A.D., Bharata confused Apabhraṁsha with the language of the nomadic people and called it a barbaric dialect spoken by those who rear sheep, cattle, horses and camels, though he distinguished it from Dravadi. "Three centuries later Apabhraṁsha attained the status of a literary dialect. Thus Bhamaha regards Apabhraṁsha as the name of the dialect of poetry and that too of a particular form of literature Dandin thinks that poetic compositions in the dialect of Abhiras is Apabhraṁsha. This literary status of Apabhraṁsha is confirmed by the pride in the ability of composing in Apabhraṁsha found in the copper plates of Dharasena (600 A.D.)."[22]

"Later writers like Mammata, Vagbhata, Gunachandra and Hemachandra, the great grammarian, unanimously agree in regarding Apabhraṁsha as a literary dialect equal in status to Sanskrit and Prakrit. By the term Apabhraṁsh these writers seem to understand spoken language or 'provinctal language.' Linguistically, Apabhraṁsh is the name of a stage in the development of Indo-Aryan branch of the Indo-Iranian group of the Indo-European family of languages."[23]

The whole bulk of Prakrit and Apabhramsha has become so deeply absorbed in provincial languages that we find it to be part and parcel of provincial languages. The following will illustrate:

21. Dr. Suniti Kumar Chatterjee, *Indo-Aryan and Hindi*, p. 77
22. G.V. Tagre, *Historical Grammar of Apabhrams*, p. 2
23. *Ibid.*, p. 3

Sanskrit	Prakrit and Apabhramsa
आत्मा	आपा
अमृत	अमीय
अम्बा	अम्मा
उच्छल	उथल
कमल	कँवल
कृष्ण	कान्ह
पितृ	पिता, पियो
घृत	घी

कुंजी कच्छप अलल कू, किन समझाया ग्यान ।
आड़ा पड़दा है नहीं, हिरदे अन्दर ध्यान ।।

R.S., p. 39

दीठी अनदीठी करैं, जिनके हूँ मैं साथ ।
भगत परातम देय तू, पीड़ा लगै न गात ।।

Ibid., p. 51

Such Prakrit and Apabhramsha words are found in all the Punjabi and Hindi writings of Garib Das. They form the backbone of these provincial languages.

Punjabi in Garib Das' Poetry

There is an overwhelming use of Punjabi language in Garib Das' poetry. There are verses of pure Punjabi and his vocabulary of Punjabi appears to be as complete as that of the Punjabi Sufi poets. An example is given below :

मति देंदी बालिम बहेरनूं ।
संसारी दी गल कूँ चीन्हैं, नंहि बूझि शब्द जगहरेनूँ ।।
मुरद्यों सेती प्रीति लगावैं, नंहि जानै सतगुरु महरेनूं ।।
ऊँची थलिया खेती बोवै, भूलि गए निज डहरेनूँ ।।
योह संसार समझदा नाहीं, कहता शाम सबेरेनूं ।।
सेतछत्र सिर मुकट बिराजै, देखत ना उस चेहरेनूँ ।।
गरीबदास यो बखत जात है, रोवैंगे इस पहरेनूँ ।।

G.G.S., p. 656

His Kafis are written mainly in Punjabi. The Punjabi is mostly of the Lahore area with a mixture of popular words from other areas. The following Kāfī is another example of pure Punjabi language with a mixture of Lehndī words.

दम दा नहीं भरोसा वो, अब तू कर चलने दा सूलं ।
मुए पुरुष संग सती जरत है, पड़ी भरम दी झूल ।।
पीठ मुनक्का दाख लदी है, खर खाता बम्बूल ।
मैण्डी मन्दर बाग बगीचे, रहसी डाल न मूल ।।
जिन्दा पुरुष अचल अबिनासी, बिना पिण्ड अस्थूल ।
नैनों आगै झुक झुक आवै, रतन अमोली फूल ।।
गरीबदास ये अलल ध्यान है, सुरत हिण्डोले झूल ।

Words as *rehsi*, *vo*, *karhi* show a slender mixture of *lehandi*. Post-positions like *da*, *de*, *seti* are pure Punjabi. Apart from a few words which are common to Hindi and Punjabi all the rest are Punjabi, viz, *dam*, *bharosa*, *calne*, *sūl*, *mue*, *dakh*, *munekha*, *hiñdol*, *jhūl*, *mūl bagīce*, *bambūl*. Words like *thah*, *theh*, *dhundh*, *dhar*, *bahañde*, *pracande*, are used in the following verse :

घनघोर नदी जाके थाह न थेहा, मूढ नरा धुंध धार बंहदे ।
पातरी फूहरी चूहरी चित्त है, देख अदेख लावें परचंदे ।।
G.G.S., p. 412.

Unfortunately, the ignorant copyists have changed many Punjabi words into Hindi while writing them in Hindi script. The phonetics of many words can be conveyed only through Punjabi script. Throughout the Granth of Garib Das we note that Hariyanvi and Punjabi words have been sanskritised and changed into Eastern Hindi. Even the *khadi boli* words of Western Hindi have suffered such a change. A few more verses of pure Punjabi language are given below :

मति देंदी बालिम गूंगैनूं ।
जा बालिम दी बलि बलि जांवां, ध्यान लगावै अंगेंनूं ।।
छाड्या मूल फूल क्या तोंरै, कहा चढावै सूंबेनूं ।।
दूध गऊदा बछै बिटाल्या, कहा चावै चूंघेंनूं ।।
याह तन देही विनशि जात है, बहुरि आनियौं भूंगेंनूं ।।
ये तन देही हाथ न आवै, कहा करैगा रूंगैनूं ।।
नघ नारायण भूलि रह्या है, कहा परखै मोंती मूंगेंनू ।।

गरीबदास यौं शाखा सूकै, बीज न बोंया डूंघेनूं ॥

G.G.S., p. 656

अपनां लाल सिभालि कुडिये, क्या करदी है ।
रतन अमोली नजरि न आया, पाहन सैं शिर मारि ॥
यौह पांहन परमेश्वर नाहीं, शिर सैं बोंझा डारि।
जप तप करनी काम न आवै, बिन सुमरन सिरजन हार ॥
कर्मकंड कलपत्र बीतै, नाहक तन मन जारि ।
अठसठि तीरथ हैं तन माहिं, गंग सहंस मुख धार ॥
ब्रह्मा विष्णु महेशर शेषा, जाप जपै ररंकार ।
अनंत कोटि जहाँ नौंबति बाजैं, अदल फजल दरबार ॥
चरखा अजब रँगीला वो, सोहं झंकारत है तार ।
खूंटे खालक खूब बनाए, पिण्डा है गुलजार ॥
साथ तीन सौ लगी पँखड़ियाँ, घड्या पुरुष करतार ।
परदी पिंडा रंग बिरंगे, कढ़ती फूल हजार ॥
जतकी जितनी खूब चढ़ाईं, तीजन देख बहार ।
प्रेम प्रभाती, चित्त की चरमख, सूत कतै चौतार ॥
तत के तकवे उलट समोवै, मोहकम कर लई मार ।
हथली बिच जो ग्यान फेरनी, कोई कातै कातनहार ॥
आतम दूल्हन कातन बैठी, फिरता अधर अधार ।
लाम्बा तार गगन स्यूँ खैंचे, सो पावै दीदार ॥
महमूदी खासा बुन लीजै, पहरै हँस हमार ।
गरीबदास वै बहुर न आवै, उतरै भौजल पार ॥

Ibid

मैंडी जिंदडिये वो जग मैं जीवन है दिन दोय ।
जिनि कादर यौह महल बनाया, जाकी कदरि न पाई ।
मन मैं मक्का दिल बिचि काबा, महजदि काहे जाई ॥
मस्तक जांनि मसीति भुलानें, किसकू वंग सुनाई ।
सिदक सबूरी साबति रहनां, खडी पडी नहीं खाई ॥
माटी ईंट राज चिनि आया, कूकैं बंग मुलांनां ।
रबका सिरज्या नेश किया है, मारि लिया हिंलवाना ॥
पेर बांधि रूंखौं कै टाँगे, काढि लिया दिलम्याना ।
येता कुफर न करि बे काजी, देखत है रहमाना ॥
एक बूंद का सकल पसारा, क्या तुरका क्या हिंदू ।
सूर गऊ मैं एकै रब है, समझत नाहीं भौंदू ॥

जिभ्या स्वाद सरेकूँ भूले, खाते गोसत गूँदू ।
जोति सरूपी हाथि न आया, उदर बधाया दूँदू ॥
या तन अंदरि तसवी है रे, जपौ सुहंगम बानी ।
मौला मूल अर्श मैं बैठ्या, देखत है दिलदानी ॥
सब घट देखौ नूर नबीका, गला कौन का भांनी ।
दास गरीब कहै बे काजी, छानौं दूधर पानी ॥

G.G.S., Pp. 664-65

Persian and Arabic in Garib Das

The Persian and Arabic influence on Garib Das' poetry is tremendous. Garib Das does not believe in the lasting purity of any language. During his time, Persianised Urdu had become an important influence in the court and in general literature. This influence decreases as we go eastwards to Bengal and increases as we go westward to Punjab and Kashmir. To Garib Das, this influence seems to have come from the close proximity of his place to Delhi and from his association with Sufi saints and literature. Garib Das mentions the study of Persian, Arabic and Hindwani (which at that time was deemed to be Punjabi and not Hindi).[24] This shows that he was quite conscious of the study and influence of these languages.

We get no evidence from either the Granth of Garib Das or from any outside source that he was a scholar of Persian or Arabic. But he has used Persian and Arabic words of common usage in far greater abundance than the literary traditions of the time permitted. Very few of the Persian and Arabic words are used in their pure and original form. Most of them have been corrupted by the common usage and popular speech. The Indian way of pronouncing and writing Persian and Arabic words is almost the same throughout Northern India. Some of these words became part and parcel of Punjabi and Hindi languages. The following are outstanding examples of Persian words used by Garib Das:

24. अरबी, तुरकी, फारसी, हिन्दवानी पद यार ।

G.G.S., p. 92

बंदे जान साहिब सार वे ।
पिदर मादर आप कादर, नहीं कुल परिवार वे ।
आब खाक न बाद आतस, ना जिमीं असमान वे ।
अर्स ऊपर महल मालिक, दर झिलमिला नूर वे ।
बांदी गुलाम गरीब तेरा, देखते सुख चैन वे ।

R.S., Pp. 262-263

दरीखाने दम दुलीचा, चिसम कर दर स्वास वे ।
काय कुलफ कूंची लगी, खोलै सोइ सत् पीर वे ।।

R.S., p. 226

फजल तालब इश्क गालिब, बिरह बंग वियोग वे ।
नेमी निमाजी दगाबाजी, दूर कर यौह शोग वे ।।
काबा अर्स बिन कुर्स है, बंगी दर्द दिल बंग वे ।
मक्का मनी सै बगल है, पहुँचै कोई तहां मर्द वे ।।
मर्द हाजी होत हैं, जहाँ नहीं कायर काम वे ।
तत्त तसबी फेरिये, जहाँ साफ सीना नाम वे ।।
जीवता ही मर मुलाने, नाम नंका गोर वे ।
खूनी खुशालं फिरत है, निकसी जहाँ किताब वे ।।
कीते गुनाह गनीम तैं, अब जवाब करि किस भान्ति वे ।
गूदा गुलाम खात है, वै कटे जीव अनाथ वे ।।
कटे जीव अनाथ करदं, सरै बदला दीन वे ।
गरीबदास हक्क हाजी तजो गोस्त जीव वे ।।

R.S., p. 267

गुलसफा की गली मैं निफस कूं गाड दे,
मार विचार का तीर तुक्का ।
शीश कूं काट करि हाथ महबूब ले,
इश्क कूं छाड़ कर कहां लुक्या ।।
मनसूर कूं देख माशूक यों हूजिये ।

R.S., p. 234

महम्मद नबी कूं न पाया है राह ।
अरस पंथ बाँका है अगमी अगाह ।।
सरे की सरीकत तज्या है न दीन ।
उलटा अपूठा पर्‍या है जमीन ।।
दोजख भिस्त का जु देख्या है अंत ।
या बीच जमराय तोड़े है दंत ।।

सतोगुन का सामा जमईत जमाल ।
देखैं तमासा सभ कुदरत कमाल ॥

R.S., p. 173

Sadhu Bhasha or Sant Bhakha

The saints of India broke provincial barriers and tried to write in a simple language which could be understood all over North India. They avoided the use of difficult words and petronised the words of Prakrit origin, which with slight variations had pervaded all north Indian languages. It also came to be known as Hindusthani on a secular level. But as a lot of religious literature has been produced in this language it is generally called *Sant Bhakha* or *Sadhu Bhasha*. It is distinguished from provincial languages by its simplicity and universality. It avoids those words of the dislects which are not properly understood beyond their own regions. We give below examples of some verses which are written completely in *Sadhu Bhasha* :

राम सुमर राम सुमर, राम सुमर हंसा ।
भक्ति जान ग्यान ध्यान, छाड़ो कुल बंसा ॥
मुक्ति लोक पाय मोख, नाम जो उचारै ।
सुरति सिंध कोटि चन्द, झलकैं पल माहीं ॥
कोटि भानु साच मान, रूंम रूंम पेख्या ॥
अमृत रस अमी खीर, खुरदनी खुस्याली ।
प्याले मस्ताक पाक, लालन सिर लाली ॥

R.S., p. 323

विषै हलाहल खाय, जगत सभ धूता हो ।
ज्यूं हेड़ी कै संग, शिकारी कूता हो ॥
कउवा तजै न बीठ, हंस कैसे होई हो ।
अन्ध गुरू का चेल, खेल सब खोई हो ॥
बैठ्या मंझ मंजार, मूष्टे खाई हो ।
बाहर किसा आचार, बूडि पंडिताई हो ॥

R.S., p. 307

आज हमारे आए सन्त सुजान, तन मन धन वारूँ गी प्राण ।
चरण कमल रज धारूँ शीस, मानो आप मिले जगदीस ॥
सन्तों की महमा कही न जाय, अठसढ़ तीरथ चरणों पाय ।

सन्तों की महमा अपरम पार, पूरण ब्रह्म मिले करतार ।।
सन्तो की महमा अगम अगाध, नारद सें उधरे प्रल्हाद ।
ध्रू भेंटे नारद निरबान, अमरापुर में रचे बिमान ।।
सन्तों की महमा अगम अगाध, बूडन ते राखा गज ग्राह ।
सन्तों की महमा निह्चल थीर, द्रुपद सुता के बढ़ गए चीर ।।
सन्तों की महमा अधिक सुमेर, भीलनी के झूठे खाए बेर ।
सन्तों की महमा निह्चल अंक, बाल्मीक का बाज्या संख ।।
सन्तों की महमा अमन अमान, देखी गणिका चढी बिमान ।
सन्तो की महमा पद गरगाप, तिरलोचन के परतिया आप ।।
पुन्दर पुरी नाम निरबान, देवल फेर छिवा दै छान ।
काशीपुरी कबीर कमाल, गैवी बालद आई रिसाल ।।
दिया भण्डारा जन रैदास, कनक जनेऊ पद परकास ।
सन्तों की महमा कही न जाय, पीपा कूद पडे दरियाय ।।
दास गरीब सन्तन कूं, सेव चौरासी मिट गई सुखदेव ।।

R.S., Pp. 187-88

ये देख मिही क्या मोटी रे, नार जानो सब ही खोटी रे ।
ये मन माया की जाली रे, ये निरगुण सरगुण ताली रे ।।
चल सुख सागर ले जाऊँ रे, मै आगै देस दिखाऊँ रे ।
कर सुख सागर अस्नाना रे, चल देखो देस दिवाना रे ।।
चल देखो देस हमारा रे, जहाँ कोट पदम उजियारा रे ।
चल देखो देस हमारा रे, जहाँ तात सबद झँकारा रे ।।
चल देखो देस हमारा रे, जहाँ अनत फूल गुलजारा रे ।
चल देखो देस हमारा रे, जहाँ भाटी चुवै कलारा रे ।।
जहाँ बाजै अनहद तूरा रे, चल देखो अजब जहूरा रे ।
चल सिन्धे सिन्धु मिलाऊँ रे, भवसागर बहुर न आऊँ रे ।।

G.G.S., Pp. 86-87

Western Hindi

The influence of Hindi on the writings of Garib Das is fairly extensive. As Garib Das stayed close to Delhi and was well versed in the religious Hindi literature of the period, we find that the influence of Hindi on his poetry is tremendous. The compilers and copyists of his writings have all been biased in favour of Hindi and while copying and compiling they have taken full liberty of turning Punjabi and Hariyanvi words into words of high Hindi. We note that Garib Das shows a strong preference for Western Hindi as against Eastern Hindi. Western Hindi includes Braj, Kanaouji and Khari Boli while Eastern Hindi include Avadhi, Bhojpuri, Maghdi and Maithli. The post-positions used by Garib Das are mostly of Western Hindi such as *kau, ko, kun, nai.* So also are the personal pronouns : *tu, tai, tune, tera, tero, tujh se* etc. We give below two examples of Western Hindi which have an overwhelming number of Bra words :

मूल कंवल कूँ दृढ़ कर बांधौं, रक्त वर्ण रंग लागै ।
चित्र पंखड़ी बसै गणेशा, किलियं शब्द विहागै ।।
स्वाद चक्र ब्रह्मा का बासा, अष्ट फंखरी मेलं ।
ऊँ जाप जपै निशि बासर, ज्ञान बुद्धि का खेलं ।।
काल चक्र आवत दम हेरै, नहीं ज्ञान परकाशा ।
त्रिकुटि कँवल तौ दो दल वरनौं, परम हंस परवाना ।।

R.S., p. 145

ऐसा मूल ज्ञान गौहराऊं, आदि अन्त का भेद लखाऊं ।
दरसै परसै हिल मिल खेलै, आप तरै औरन कूँ बेलै ।
बिकट पंथ अब सुनो हमारा, दो पर्वत के मध्य है धारा ।
तिल प्रवान जहां लगी किवारी, हलके जाहीं सुधा अम्बारी ।
तिल प्रवान में है त्रिवैणी, पल पल परबी है सुखचैनी ।
गंगा जमुना मध्य सरस्वती, जुगल मस्त जहां खेलें कुश्ती ।

R.S., p. 150

Hariyanvi : Bangru or Jatu

The language of Hariyana is a mixture of many languages. It has been strongly influenced by Punjabi from the West, by Western Hindi from the east and by Rajasthani from the south. It is, as a matter of fact, a crude synthesis of all these languages. Different scholars have different views about it. We will sum up the views of all and then give some examples of Hariyānvi language from the works of Garib Das.

"The language is a dialect of Western Hindi modified on the one hand by the disturbing influence of Punjabi in the north and on the other by Ahirwāti dialect of Gurgaon in the south which is classed by Grierson as a form of Mewāti dialect of Rajasthan. South of Jhajjar the dialect rapidly passes into Ahirwāti, the distinguishing note of which is the substitution of *o* for final *a*. If the Ahir wishes to say he has had a good crop of *bajra* he will say, '*baro achcho bajro huyo*.'... The Jattu is a difficult language to understand and acquire. It is spoken very broad and with a drawl. Good is not merely *achcha* but *aachcha*. The oblique plurals of nouns end in *ān* and not with *on* ; the verb substansive is *sūn* not *hūn* ; the past participle is *marya* and not *mara* and the future *marnala* and not *marnewala*. *Ni* or *nai* is at once the sign of the agent case and of the dative accusative, *ko* being an imported termination, while *te* or *tai* is the proper form for the ablative *se*.[25]

While Grierson considers the language of the whole of Hariyānā region as Bangru or Jātu, Dr. Nanak Chand Sharma, in his *Origin and Evolution of Hariyanvi Language*, divides Hariyānvi into three dialects : Bangru to the north, Kaindri Hariyānvi in the Rohtak District, and Ahirwāti in the south in Mahendragarh District.

Grierson says : "That portion of the tract which consists of the east of the district of Hissar and the country immediately adjoining it is known to natives as Harianā. The rest is known as Bāngar or Khādar. Then again the north eastern portion of the Dadri Nizmat of Jind State and the adjoining portions of the state of Dujānā are also parts of Harianā and the Bāngrū spoken here is called Hariāni. In the Nizamat of Jind, although this is certainly true Bāngar country, the local form of speech is also known as Hariāni. Natives profess to distinguish between Hariāni and Bāngrū and say that the former and not Bāngrū is heard in the Jāt villages of Karnal."[26]

Dr. Nanak Chand Sharma and Dr. Shankar Lal Yadav (in his *Hariyana Pradesh Ka Lok Sahitya*) have pointed out only the similarity of Haryānvi with Punjābi and Braj Bhāsha as well as their distinguishing features. As Dr. Shankar Lal's book was written earlier and has been accepted by Dr. Nanak Chand in

25. *The Punjab District Gazetteer*, *Rohtak District*, 1910 Vol. III, p. 98
26. Grierson, *Linguistic Survey*, Vol XI, Part I, p. 66

his thesis, we are quoting some opinious from the former's book. Dr. Shankar Lal admits that Haryānvi has accepted the largest amount of Punjabi influence. We give below the distinguishing features of Haryānvi as compared to Punjabi and Western Hindi:

1. In both Haryānvi and Punjābi, the musculine 'ā' becomes 'i' when changed into feminine gender : *chora* becomes *chori*, *ghoda* becomes *ghodi*.
2. The adjective also changes according to the gender : *kala ghoda* becomes *kali ghodi*.
3. The *dh* sound of Hindi is not found in Punjabi and Haryānvi
4. The 'v' of Sanskrit and Hindi becomes 'b' in Haryānvi, as in *bair*, *birodh*, *bat*, *bari*, *barge*, *beena*, *birla*.
5. The 'y' of Sanskrit and Hindi becomes '*j*' in Haryānvi, as it does in Punjabi : *judh*, *jatra*, *jamraj*
6. The 's' of Sanskrit and Hindi becomes '*ch*' in Haryānvi : *tulchi* for *tulsi* : *chudama* for *sudama*, *chama* for *kshama*.
7. The 'v' of Hindi becomes '*m*' in Haryanvi : *ravan* becomes *raman*, *suhavno* becomes *suhamno*
8. The change into 'ṇ' : *kahna* becomes *kahṇa*, *gahna* becomes *gahṇa*, *rani* becomes *raṇi*, *jivan* becomes *jivaṇ*
9. In Braj we say *mo* or *mohe*, but in Haryānvi we say *mujhe* or *mannai* ;
10. In Braj we say *to*, but in Haryanvi we say *tain*, *tū*
11. In Braj we say *toro* or *tumharo*, but in Haryānvi we say *tera* or *thara*.
12. In Braj we say *karat*, *parat*, *jat*, *khat*, but in Haryānvi we say *karta*, *parta*, *khata*, *jata*.
13. *Haun* and *mo* of Braj become *mo*, *mero* in Haryanvi and *hamaro* becomes *mharo*
14. *Hūn* and *han* of Hindi become *sūn* and *san* in Haryanvi

We give below some exemples of Haryanvi language as found in Garib Das' poetry:

क्रिया सैं कारज नहीं सरता, भक्ति भाव सैं दूखे ।
घीव बसंदर देदे पांडे, होम बहुत से फूके ॥

होम हनोज किये निशिवासर, जीव हिते बहु दगदे ।
ऊत भूत की पूजा खाई, भोजन बहु विधि बगदे ॥
देवी के तुम दास कहावो, मशानी मन माला ।
चण्डी का तुम चाव रखत हो, इत होसी मूँह काला ॥
दुर्गा कै ले मुरगा दौरें, चण्डी कै ले बकरा ।
बहुत खफीफ शरै में होंगे, छाती दीजै लकरा ॥
सेढ शीतला गद्दहा मांगै, याह कौन अविद्या पांडे ।
आगे की तो आगै होगी, इत ही जमकूं डांडे ॥

G.G.S., p. 354

अजब तमाशा संतौं दीठा, सतगुरु दृष्टि उघारी ।
क्षेत्रपाल काल होय लाग्या, भूत भये ब्रह्मचारी ॥
ये ब्रह्मचारी करैं अग्यारी, मुरदे ऊपर खांही ।
तेंरामी का तार न काढ्या, कारज जीमन तांही ॥
जा दिन हंसा करैं पियाना, कौन धाम कूं जाई ।
जिस काया में रहता हंसा, सो तो ठोक जराई ॥
ठोक जराई छार उडाई, किस की मुक्ति करोगे ।
कौंन भर्मणा भूले पाण्डे, काके पिण्ड भरोगे ॥

Ibid

कदि ब्रह्माकुँ छापे लीन्हें, द्वारामती नरेशा ।
कदि पत्थरकूँ पान खुवाये, जटा बधाये केशा ॥
शेष गणेश गंग कदि न्हाये, कदि गायत्री लापी ।
धूंमी घालि दिये कदि घामें, पीठ कौन दिन तापी ॥
कदि नारदमुनि नाद बजाया, शंखा भालरि पीटी ।
होम आचार कौन दिन कीन्हें, चंदन चरच्या घींटी ॥

G.G.S., p. 355

बन में मन मन ही में बन है, कहो कहां डेरा लीजै ।
अजरावर घर करो पियाना, यहां तो छिन छिन चोला छीजै ॥
जा दिन कहां पत्थर की पूजा, कौंन बजावै टालं ॥

G.G.S., p. 359

आठौं का तो अटका फोरूँ, छैका छींका बांधूं ।
पांचो कूं तो चाक चढाऊं, कूवटै रस्सी साधूं ॥
दोया कूं तो दक्खन भेजूं, एक रखूं रखवाला ।

तीनौं कूँ तो सूली द्यौंगा, जम का मुँह करि काला ॥
पांचौ कूँ तो पाट पढाऊं, पचीसौं प्रमोधूँ ।
ऐसा रमूं शब्द कै सेफै, नौ खण्ड रांमत सोंधूँ ॥
सातौं का तो संपट मूंदूँ , ग्यारह गंग न्हवाऊँ ।
बारह कूं तो बिरहा द्यौंगा, तेराह तंत सुनाऊं ॥
चौदाह की तो चद्दरि खोसूं , पन्दराह कुँ प्रवाना ।
सोलाह की तो सुलह करूँगा, सतराह कुँ सैलाना ।
ठारा की तो ठेक लगाऊं, उन्नीसों धडवाई ।
बीसौं का तो बनज करूँगा, पूँजी राखि सवाई ॥
इक्कीसां कूं अकलि पढाऊं, बाईसा कूँ बेलूँ ।
तेईसा कुँ तांन सुनाऊँ, नौखंड रामत खेलूँ ॥

G.G.S., p. 338

योह मन जम का रूप, मनै है धर्मराय ध्यानी ।
मनहीं आवै जाय, मनै भुगतै चहूँ खानी ॥
मनै रिच प्रपंच, मनै मन खाय लिया है ।
मनहीं दूतर भूत, मनै मन लागि जिया है ॥

G.G.S., p. 378

याह दुनिया संसार सरीकति जाहिगी ।
न्हिचै बिसवे बीस सु जौंरा खायगी ॥
साची बात परेर न पूरा पाइया ।
देखो अंध गंवार कहां डहकाइया ॥
पांहन सैं नघ फोरि खुसी फिर तैं खरा ।
इस तैं आगै और कहा होगा बुरा ॥
खोया लाल रतन जतन जान्या नहीं ।
सतगुरु अरथ विचारि शब्द मान्या नहीं ।
कोटि पाप शिर ओटि जगत संगि जात है ।
खाली रह्या खलील लग्या क्या हाथि है ॥
दंत नहीं जदि खीर दीया था खांन कूँ ।
राख्या जठरा मांहि तुम्हारे प्राण कुँ ॥
मल मुत्र कै बीचि विश्वंभर राखिया ।
ऐसी जठरा मांहि हंस भला किया ॥
जूँनी संकट काढि जु बंधि छुटाईयां ।
आया जग कै मांहि सु पीर पूजाईया ॥

बाजैं ढोल बिलल गुललड गावहीं ।
नाचै चंद चुडेल धनी नहीं घ्यावहीं ॥
न्हिचै नूर जहूर धनी की दाति है ।
यौह बालक बिलकंत समझि कुछि भिरांति है ।

G.G.S., p. 445

यौह सौदा सति भाय करौ प्रभातिरे ।
तन मन रतन अमोल बटाऊ साथरे ॥
बिछरि जांहिगे मीत मात सुनि लीजिये ।
बौहरि न मेला होय कहौ क्या कीजिये ॥
सील संतोष विवेक दया के धाम है ।
ज्ञान रतन गुलजार संगाती राम है ॥
धर्म धजा फरकंत फरहरैं लोक रे ।
ता मध्य अजपा नाम सु सौदा रोक रे ॥
चले बनजुवा ऊठि हूँड गढ छाडि रे ।
हरिहां महबूब कहता दास गरीब लगे जम डांड रे ॥

G.G.S., p. 449.

सम्मन नै कदि ब्राह्मण पूजे, कदि सेऊ लाई सेवा ।
रंका बंका कदि रज मंडे, चीन्हें निर्गुण देवा ॥
मोरध्वज कदि मुद्रा पहरी, हरिचन्द हाट उगाही ।
अंगद नें कदि आगम लीन्हा, तिथी बार बतलाई ॥
कपिल मुनी कदि माला फेरि, रामानन्द रण झूझे ।
दुर्वासा कदि खासा पहर्या, पांचौ इन्द्री लूझे ॥
तुलसीदास ल्हैस कदि बांधी, फरीद न फरसी घाली ।
टीला किस दिन टाल बजाई, घर घर भोजन खाये ॥
गरीबदास कदि राज मण्डल करि, जग मैं दीनी फेरी ।

G.G.S., p. 356.

ये तो बातां कहन सुनन की नाहीं ।
करि पाड़ने की हैं ।
यौह मन माया का जाल बिछ्या है ।
कर्म चबीना हंस चुगै हैं ।
पारधी शर सांधे खड़ा है ।
तेरी पर कुट हैं ।
जैतूं फंध्या तो यहां ही रहैगा ।

युगन युगन कम चबीना चबाईयेगा ।
एक एक दाणें का लेखा है ।
जे जे दाणें तूं चाबैगा ।
जेती बेर तेरी गुद्दी की राह जुबान काढियेगी ।
मोहम्मद और माधो कूं पूछि देखो ।
एक एक दाणा चाब्या था ।
सो आज हूँ नहीं छूटे ।

G.G.S., p. 383.

इस काया में नीझर झरते, औंडे दरिया कूप ।
शीशी शंख फिरैं सुर पीवै, प्याले अजब अनूप ।।
इस काया मैं रास मंडल है, बाजै अनहद तूर ।
सोहं हंसा सिंघि मिलें हैं, झिलमिल नूर जहूर ।।
आपा मेटि भेट साहिबस्यौं, बौहरि न आवन होई ।।

G.G.S., p. 583.

CHAPTER VIII

Poetry of Garib Das

Medieval Saints expressed themselves through such poetry as was at once popular and literary in style and expression. Kabir, Nanak and Namadev set the tradition of writing devotional songs in a certain style which is closely followed by Garib Das.

While Garib Das has imitated his predecessors in style, he shows great flow and abundance in his output. He takes up a theme and writes on it in a smooth running style to the point of exhausting it. While all medieval poets and saints were fond of repetition to drive home their message, Garib Das surpasses them all in repetition of an idea or a theme.

In the opinion of Dr. Mohan Singh, Garib Das "may be considered as the last of the Hindu Rajayogis and Bhakta poets who had as great a mastery of popular poetic language and style as Ghulam Farid had, but whose range of thought and whose knowledge of other Indian languages was greater than that of any other Indian poet of medieval India, the only poet who comes near to him being Shah Qayam Din Chisti of Kari Gaon in Bombay, a descendant of Baba Farid and successor to his *gaddi* in the 16th century."[1]

Accepting openly the influence of all earlier great figures and also the influence of contemporary folk literature, Garib Das made his poetry simple, forceful and appealing to the masses and the religious devotees. His aim was not to produce artistic poetry but to write religious songs which could bring moral and spiritual awakening. There is an amalgamation of languages and thought to bring them closer to each other and to break down linguistic and religious barriers. Thus Garib Das achieves a variety of poetic expressions rarely seen in the common run of poets of the time.

Prosody in almost all medieval Indian poetry in north India was based mainly on Sanskrit prosody called *Pingala Chhanda*

1. Dr. Mohan Singh, *An Introduction to Punjabi Literature*, p. 152.

Shastra (attributed to the Sage Pingala) which consists of *Sutras* distributed over eight books. The *Agni Purana* also gives a complete system of prosody founded apparently on Pingala's prosody. A verse is a combination of various *padas* which are regulated either by the number of syllables (*aksharas*) or by the number of syllabic instants (*matras*) in each line. A syllable is as much of a word as can be pronounced at once, that is, a vowel with or without one or more consonants. A syllable is *laghu* (short) or *guru* (long), according as its vowel is short or long. A short vowel becomes long when it is followed by an *anusvara* or a *visarga*. The last syllable of a *pada* is either long or short according to the exigence of metre, whatever be its natural length.

In metres regulated by the number of syllabic instants one instant is allotted a short vowel and two a long one. For the purpose of scanning metres regulated by the number of syllables, writers on prosody have devised eight *ganas*, each consisting of three syllables, and distinguished from one another by particular syllables being short or long. Expressed in symbols, the symbol 1 denoting a short syllable and 5 a long one, the different *ganas* may be represented as follows :

Magan	555
Ragan	515
Tagan	551
Yagan	155
Sagan	115
Bhagan	511
Naman	111
Jagan	151

Garib Das shows considerable knowledge of Indian prosody as he uses different types of metres in his poems. His diction is always apt in all his metres. The following are the examples of metres used by Garib Das:

Aril also called *Adil*

Each *aril* has four lines. There is one type of *aril* which has 16 *matras*, each line ending either in *bhagan* or *yagan*. This type is rarely used by Garib Das. There is another type of *aril* having

21 *matras* with a pause after 10 or 11 *matras*. It is also known as *Chandrain.* Out of the four lines of the verse the first rhymes with the second while the third rhymes with the fourth.

याह दुनिया संसार, सरीकत जायगी, निश्चय बिसवे बीस सु जौरा खायगी ।
साची बात परेर न पूरा पाइया, देखो अंध गंवार कहां डहकाइया ।।

R.S., p. 245

There are also *arils* with all the four lines rhyming with one another. (*R.S.*, Pp. 251, 252, 253).

Doha or *Dohra* or *Slokas*

Like Kabir's *Bijak*, most of the Granth of Garib Das is in the form of couplets which are sometime called *slokas* and sometime *sakhis*. Westcott describes them as "rhyming couplets bearing witness to the Truth." The rhyme of many couplets is very fine, with the result that important teachings given in this form are easily remembered. In Sanskrit, a *sloka* is not a verse form. It is only a "hymn of praise written in verse". The popular *doha* has 24 *matras* with *visrama* (break) at 13 and 11. Different writers vary the form of their *dohas* by changing the number of *laghu* and *guru* combinations.

Garib Das makes the *dohas*, which are also called *sakhis*, the chief vehicle of his thoughts. We give below examples of the various forms of *dohas* composed by him. It should be noted that while counting the *matras*, the word Garib, occurring in the beginning of the first line of the couplet, should not be counted in the syllabic instants. The following are the main types of *dohas* in Garib Das:

Doha of 25 *matras, visrama* at 14+11

ऐसा अबिगत राम है, अगम अगोचर नूर ।
सुन्न सनेही आदि है, सकल लोक भरपूर ।।

R.S., p. 11

Doha with 23 *matras, visrama* at 13+10

तीन लोक तखत किया, कीच रही ना बाकी ।
अबल बली वरयाम है, चाँद सूरज साखी ।।

R.S., p. 97

Doha with 25 *matras, visrama* at 11+14

कहा कहूं जगदीश, सकल जानराय बिनानी ।
दुरयोधन कू कुमति दई, दुरबासा बानी ।।

R.S., p. 104

Doha with 22 *matras* with *visrama* at 10+12

षट दरसन सब भेख, होत गृही घर बासे ।
अपनी नारी छाड़, सकल वेश्या दर जासे ।।

R.S., p. 47

Doha with 25 *maatras, visrama* at 13+12

ज तेरे उपजे नहीं, तो सबद साख सुन लेह ।
साखी भूत सँगीत है, जासै लावो नेह ।।

R.S. p. 132

Rekhtas

According to Kahan Singh, the Persian writers described the *Prakrit* and *Apabhramsa* poems as *Rekhtas.* Later on a verse having a mixture of Hindi and Persian words came to be known as *Rekhta*[2]. Giving the historical background of *Rekhtas,* Dr. Suniti Kumar Chatterjee says : "Hindustani speakers from North India took the lesson from the Deccan Muslims and followed their example from the end of the 17th century in striving consciously to write literature in Persianised Delhi Hindusthani, the 'speech of the exalted court', which they, too, began to write in the Persian character. Wali is the first known poet of Delhi Hindusthani in the Persianised form; and he had lived in the South. The language as yet was not so much Persianised as in later times. Persian words were comparatively few, being just 'scattered' (*rekhte*) in the line, and hence the language was called *Rekhta,* the earliest form of the present day Urdu Hindusthani poetical speech. Some of Kabir's verses composed in the 15th century, nay, even those of Baba Farid, 12th-13th century, may be described as *Rekhta:* and Baba Farid *merits* the sobriquet of *Baba-i-Rextra* or the Father of the *Rekhta* speech more than Wali. Among the Muhammedans of North India, the *Rekhta* speech of Wali and others met a real want, and in no time it became popular. An Urdu form of Hindustani as a literary

2. **Kahan Singh, *Gurchand Diwakar*, p. 305.**

language thus took rise, and when Wali settled in Delhi about 1723 A.D. a school of Urdu poetry came into being."[3] Mehmood Sherani calls *Rekhta* a simple verse easily understandable in which there is a mixture of Persian and Hindi Music.[4]

So, poetry called *Rekhta* is what later on developed into Urdu poetry. In the earlier stages *Rekhta* was the type of poetry in which there was a free mixture of Persian with Hindi and Punjabi. The *Rekhtas* of Garib Das also have a mixture of Punjabi, Hindi and Persian words. He has written over 300 *Rekhtas*. The following are a few examples :

योह् गुरमुखी ज्ञान बजार ब्योहार है, सतगुरां बिन नहीं सधि मेला ।
दास गरीब पुष्प गंध झीन है, सबद अतीत अबिगत अकेला ।।

G.G.S. p. 421

पीर कबीर दुहु दीन दरबेस है, अलह् अलाह् अबिगत होय ।
आदि अन्त मध सत्य कबीर है, तखत खवास हज़ूरी होय ।।

G.G.S. p. 423

बे अकल बेरूह् बेदीन जानैं नहीं, साध के महल की बात बूझैं ।
घोर मसान मसीत मध जाय कर, मौन पाथर सही प्रीत पूजैं ।।

Ibid.

कुफर के निफस पर धर चल्या है, मिट गई मानी सब दगाबाजी ।
अरस की कुंज में जाय कलमा पढ़या, रब्ब रमजान चीन्हा अबाजी ।।

G.G.S p. 431

We find the following Persian words in the above lines : bazar, akela, pir, darves, allah, takhat, khvas, hazuri, beakal, beruh, bedin, kufar, nifas, daghabazi, kalma, ramzan. The Punjabi words are gurmukhi, satguran, soi, prit, rab. Other words are from Western Hindi.

Writing of the *Rekhtas* attained the height of popularity in the eighteenth century. There is such a blend of Persian and Arabic words with Indian languages of Prakrit origin that they have become an inseparable part of Punjabi and Hindi upto this day.

Tribhangi Chhanda

This is an important *chhanda* of the *Riti Kavya* poets.

3. Dr. Suniti Kumar Chatterjee, *Indo-Aryan and Hindi*, p. 189.
4. Mahmood Sherani, *Panjab me Urdu*, p. 14.

Generally it consists of four lines of 32 *matras* each, each line having a *visrama* at 8+8 and 8+8, or 10+8 and 8+6 and all rhyming in the middle. Garib Das' *Tribhangi Chhanda* is peculiar in construction. It has five lines, each of 9-12 *matras* ending with *re*. There are three middle rhymes in the first *visrama* of every line. Sometimes there is a middle rhyme in the fourth *visrama* also.

निज सबद न सूझै रे, जड़ जूनी लूझै रे, जो पाहन पूजै रे।
कोइ मरहम बूझैरे, वोह अमरत दूझै रे ॥

G.G.S, p. 317

Thus there are 60 *matras* in the *chhanda* with *visrama* at every 12 *matras*.

Sawayyas

Garib Das has made an extensive use of *Sawayyas*. It has 31 matras with *visrama* at 16+15 ending with *laghu*. They do not generally rhyme in the middle. It is a type of *Sawayya* which Garib Das calls *Gaind Ucchal Sawayya*. It resembles *Bir Sawayyas*. Here is an example :

पापी परभात नहीं भेंटै, मुख देखत पाप लगै जाका,
जननी नो मास त्रास देई, धिकार जनम तास मा का।
चौरासी कुण्ड पड़ै पापी, है जुगन जुगन कुंभी नाका,
गरभ छेदन भेदन पीर लागै, मिटता नहीं इच्छा टांका॥

G.G.S., Pp 417-418

वोह भजत हिरम्बर न्यारा है, नामा से संत करै रटना।
अढसढ तीरथ तिलक तिल में, सब धाम भया कासी पटना ॥
सूजा सैंना बाजीद बींधे, पीपा परबान पिछान्या है ।
वोह लोक अलोक गवन सैली, रैंदास अगमपुर जान्या है॥

G.G.S., p. 415

Baint (Persian *Bait*)

Bait is Persian name for a couplet which has a lyrical theme and conveys a complete idea. It is these *Baits* which later gave rise to couplets. In Punjabi literature, *Baints* have been written in abundance by such prominent poets as Guru Gobind Singh, Waris Shah and Hafiz. Waris Shah writes *Baints* of 40 *matras* with *visrama* at 20+20. Hafiz writes *Baints* of 28 *matras* with *visrama* at 16+12.

Garib Das has written *Baints* of 28 *matras* with *visrama* at 16+12:

मादर पिदर हैं संग तेरे, बिछड़ता नहीं पलक वे।
कायम कला कुरबान जां, खालक बसै है खलक वे।।

G.G.S, p. 456

There are also *Baints* of 26 *matras* with *visrama* at 14+12 *matras*:

अजर नैना अजर बैंना, अजर माला तिलक वे।
एक अजरी कहां गावै, अजर है सभ मुलक वे।।

G.G.S., p. 457

Garib Das has given the heading *Parsi Baint* to his *Baints*. It does not mean that he has written them in Persian. It only means that the *Baints* are in Persian prosody. There is of course a considerable use of words of Persian origin which had been absorbed in the common North Indian languages.

Jhulna

It is a type of *chhanda* which has many variations. One type resembles *Sawayyas* and is known as Manidhar Jhulna. It is considered as a metric *chhanda* by some and as a *gan chhand* by others. The *gan chhanda* generally has four lines with 8 *yagans* or 7 *sagans* and 1 *yagan*. The metric *chhanda* has 37 *matras* with *visrama* as follows : 10+10+10+7. Garib Das' *Jhulna* has 40 *matras* in a line with *visrama* on 20+20. There is a slight variation found in some *Jhulnas* which is probably due to the errors of copyists and editors. The following is an example of *Jhulna* with 40 matras:

अरस कुरस के बाग में कौन माली, जहां नूर जहूर के कंद हैं जी।
कहै दास गरीब संभाल भैया, देखो चाखते नहीं सो अंध हैं जी।।

G.G.S, p. 437

Ramaini

Ramaini according to some is a type of *chhanda*. According to others it is conventional religious poetry, like *padavali* and *sabad*. Each line of *Ramaini* has 32 *matras*, with a *visrama* on 16+16

इन पांचन मिल कीन्ह बंधाना, समझै नहीं जीव दिवाना।
इन पांचन मिल जीव अटकाए, जुगन जुग हम आन छुडाए।।
मूल रमैणी अरब करोड़ी, धरमराय की हम बंध तोडी।
चौदह अरब रमैणी रासा, सुन कर हंस न पावै त्रासा।।

G.G.S, p. 487

Besides poetry in *chhandas*, Garib Das wrote poetry in conventional forms of which the following are the chief :

1. *Sabad* or *Sabadi*. Explaining the term *Sabad*, Westcott writes: "In the writings of Kabir three thoughts seem to underlie such teachings : (i) All thought is expressed in language; (ii) Every letter of the alphabet, as a constituent part of language, has significance; and (iii) The plurality of letters and words now in use will appear as one, when the *maya* that deludes men in their present conditions shall have been overcome. The two lettered *Rama* seems to Kabir the nearest approach in this world to the unity of Truth or the letterless one. A distinguished Sanskrit scholar explained to me the Hindu conception of *Shabda* somewhat in this way: Man desires knowledge. Knowledge is obtainable by means of (*i*) Perception and (ii) Inference. These two channels are acknowledged by all and to them are added by some (iii) *Shabda*, sound (including the voice of the teacher) and (iv) *Upamana* or reasoning by analogy."[5]

The term *Sabad* or its diminutive *Sabdi*, in the religious literature of the time, simply means the word of God. A hymn of praise to God began to be called a *Sabad*. But more particularly those hymns that glorified the Name of God were called *Sabad*. Garib Das' *sabads* deal mostly with the planes of higher consciousness such as *surati nirati, anahad sabad* etc. For example :

जहां बाजै अनहद नाद, जहां ध्यान धरै कोई साध।
लाग्या गगन मंडल में डोरा, जहां नाचै हंस और मोरा।
देखी गगन मंडल में ज्योती, जहां बरसैं माणक मोती।

G.G.S, p. 671

2. *Padavali* : A *pada* is a song. The *padavalis* of Vidyapati, Chandidas and other Vaishnava poets are well known. From these *padavalis* emerged many types of songs known as *Vishnupada* or *Vishampada*. In Garib Das we find *Pada Hansavali*. According to Dr. Charan Singh, when a *padavali* has no particular name attached to it is called a *Sabad*. Here is an instance:

दम दा नहीं भरोसा बे, अब तू कर चलने दा सूल,
मुए पुरुस संग सती जरत है, पड़ी भरम की भूल।
पीठ मुनक्का दाख लदी है, खरहा खात बबूल,

5. Westcott, *Kabir And the Kabir Panth*, Pp. 49-50.

मैंडी मंदर बाग बगीचे, रहसी डाल न मूल।
जिन्दा पुरुष अचल अबिनासी, बिना .पिंड अस्थूल,
नैना आगे झुक झुक आवैं, रतन अमोली फूल।
गरीबदास योह अचल ध्यान है, सुरत हिंडोले झूल ॥

R.S., p. 385

3. *Nasihatnama :* It is another conventional composition. We have a *Nasihatnama* attributed to Guru Nanak but not accepted by the compiler of *Adi Grantha* as authentic. *Nasihatnama* is a kind of instruction to the disciple. *Nasihatnamas* were written mainly by Sufi poets. Garib Das also writes his *Nasihatnama* in the language of the Sufis and calls it *Baint Parsi.* The following will illustrate:

दुहूं दीन की दया को, लेय गए हैं चोर।
गरीबदास हरि भक्ति बिन, तांते भए कठोर ॥
राम रहीम एक है भाई, दोय कहै सो दोजख जाई।
अलह् अलेख एक करि बूझो, देवल धाम घोर मत पूजो ॥

G.G.S, p. 453

4. *Arati :* It is a devotional song sung with a lamp and a dance before the idol. It could be tuned to various *Ragas.* In one or two places, Garib Das describes *Arati* as a *Raga.* The Nirgun School of Bhakti poets did not believe in idol worship, but they composed *Aratis* in praise of the Infinite God. We have the *Arati* of Guru Nanak which he sang at Jagannath Puri. We have the following *Aratis* by Garib Das :

Shiv ki Arati	G.G.S, p. 342
Anna Dev ki Arati Badi	G.G.S, p. 343
Adi Maya ki Aarati	G.G.S, p. 346
Sandhya Arati	R.S., p. 379

The above headings show that the word Arati means songs sung in praise of God. The word *Sandhya Arati* makes it clear still further because *Arati* is generally sung along with evening prayers. The following excerpts illustrate the character of his *Artis:*

नूर की आरति नूर कै छाजै, नूर के ताल पखावज बाजैं।
नूर के गायन नूर कूं गावैं, नूर सुनैं ते बहुर न आवैं ॥
नूर की बानी बोल नूर, झिलमिल नूर रह्या भरपूर।
नूर कबीरा नूर ही भावै, नूर के कहै परमपद पावै ॥

R.S., p. 278

आपै आरति आपै साजै, आपै किंकर आपै बाजै ।
आपै ताल झांझ झंकारा, आप नचै आप देखनहारा ।।
आपै दीपक आपै बाती, आपैं पुष्प आप ही पाती ।
कहै कबीर ऐसी आरति गाऊं, आपा मद्धै आप समाऊं ।।

R.S., p. 272

The above quoted passages show that music and dance is associated with the *Arati* worship. Instead of worshipping the idol, Garib Das worships the *Nur* (Light). In tune with the song there is the dance of nature (*apai nache*) and the jingling sound of the dance (*tal jhanjh jhankara*). *Arati* is associated with the self merging within the Over-self (*ape madhai apa samaun*).

5. *Mulamantra* and *Gayatri:* In Hindu theology, *Mulamantra* and the *Gayatri* form the core of formal religion. The *Mulamantra* differs from one Hindu sect to another while the *Gayatri* is common to all. In the *Adi Grantha,* the introductory *Sloka* is called the *Mulamantra*. Garib Das gives his own *Mulamantra* and *Surya Gayatri*. Both are much longer than *Mulamantra* and *Gayatri* normally are. Both are devotional songs addressed to the one Supreme God. The following are the first two verses of *Mulamantra*:

निरंजन निरंजन निराकार भज रे, ताता न सीरा राता न पीरा ।
धरो ध्यान धीरा रह्या आप थिर रे,
अडोलं अबोलं अछेदं अभंदं, परे से परे रे कहो कौन है रे ।
अगम अथाह दरिया गया तू बिसर रे ।।

R.S., p. 133

It is the praise of God as *Niranjana* (Spotless), *Nirankara* (Unmanifest), Steadfast, Immovable, Infinite and Supreme. This *Mulamantra* is not in praise of any particular god or deity. The *Surya Gayatri* is written in the same strain:

उगमत सूरं बरसत नूरं बाजत तूरं, सकल लोक भरपूरं काल कंटक दूरं ।
सत सुकृत श्री सूरज बाला, जप तप संयम का रखवाला ।।
हाथ खड़ग गल पोहप माला, कानों कुंडल रूप बिसाला ।।
रिध सिध दीजी कर पिरतपाला, मोख मुक्ति के तुम्हीं द्याला ।
हम पर सूरज कर पिरतपाला, दास गरीब चितावन वाला ।।

R.S., p. 133

The original *Gayatri* in the *Ṛgveda* is an invocation to Savitri, the God of Light. Garib Das' *Gayatri* is an invocation to the Supreme Sun, the Almighty God. He is the Light, the giver of *Mukti* (salvation) and the bestower of spiritual powers.

6. *Bhaktamala.* The famous biographies of Bhaktas are known as *Bhaktamalas.* Garib Das has written his own *Bhaktamala* which has a great historical importance. The Bhaktas have been treated with great reverence and respect. Garib Das has discussed the important life stories of almost all the well known saints of the period. He has also written about the Muslim Sufi saints. He has given more space in his *Bhaktamala* to the life of his Guru, Bhakta Kabir. He gives a vivid portrayal of the lives of these saints in a dramatic way. This portion of his work reflects his ability to write epic poetry. He brings in action and dialogue within the framework of his poetry without any distraction. The flow of his narrative is as natural, spontaneous and impressive as the poetry of Tulsi Das in *Ramacharitamanas.* Here is an example:

नामा कहै सुनो मात पिताय, हरी बीठला दूध पिया जू धाय ।
माता पिता देखैं नामा का नेह, हरी बीठला दूध कैसे पीये ।।
दूध कटोरा लिया माता जु हाथ, चाल्या पिता नामदेव जु की साथ ।
दूध पीवो नै गोविंद गोपाल, माता पिता भरम तोड़ो नै जाल ।।
पाहन सै परमेसर होय, मात पिता खड़े देखैं जु दोय ।
दो कर पकड़्या कटोरा कसीस, दूध पीवै हरि बीठल ईस ।।
माता पिता का जु मेट्या संदेह, पिया दूध बीठल जु नामा स्नेह ।।

R.S., p. 165

7. *Goshthis.* Debates and discussions amongst the heads of the great religious movements was the order of the day. The winner of the debate generally won over the opponent and his disciple to his own creed. Many saints have recorded their historical *Goshthis.* But the followers of many saints started writing imaginary *Goshthis* about their Masters. We have many *Goshthis* written about Gorakh Nath but most of them are legendry. We have a number of *Goshthis* attributed to Kabir and Kamal but they all appear to be later-day compositions. We have the *Sidh Gosht* of Guru Nanak in the *Adi Grantha* which is considered to be historical by scholars. Garib Das has written three *Goshthis*: (1) *Ramanand and Kabir ki Goshta,* (2) *Kabir te Sikandar di Goshta* and (3) *Vaishnav Dharam Das and Kabir ki Goshta.*

These *Goshthis* are based on some historical traditions which Garib Das had before him. But the historical events are always made legendry by including supernatural events. We have the dialogue between Emperor Sikander Lodhi and Kabir when, on the report of the Qazis, the latter was persecuted. In the *Goshthi* between Kabir and Dharam Das, Kabir tries to prove that Rama and Krishna were not God as the Vaishnavas believe and that in the creation of God there are many Ramas and Krishnas:

धरमदास : सुन जिदे मम ज्ञान को बैष्णव रूप हमार ।
अठसढ तीरथ हम किए, चीन्हा सिरजनहार ।
कबीर : बोले जिंदा बैन, कहां से सालिग आए ।
को अठसढ को धाम, मुझे ततकाल बताए ॥
राम कृष्ण कहां रहैं, नगर वो कौन कहावै ।
ये जड़वत हैं देव, तात क्यों घंट बजावै ॥
सुनैं गनैं नहीं बात, धात पत्थर के स्वामी ।
कहां भरमै धरमदास, चीन्ह निजपद निष्कामी ॥
आवत जात न कोय, अलख अविनासी सांई ।
रहत सकल सरबंग, बोल है तुझ मुझ मांही ॥
बोलत घट घट ब्रह्म, धरम आदौं नहीं जाण्या ।
चिदानंद को चीन्ह, डारि पत्थर पाषाण ॥
राम कृष्ण कोटिक गए, धनी एक का एक ।
जिद कहै धरमदास सैं, बूझौ ज्ञान बिबेक ॥

G.G.S., p. 220

8. *Puranic Compositions :* Just as *Goshthis* became conventional compositions, imitation *Puranas* under various names also became conventional compositions. These *Puranas* had nothing to do with the classical *Puranas*. Their theme is purely based on Nirgun traditions of thought. Garib Das has written three such *Puranas:* (1) *Adi Purana*, (2) *Ganesh Purana*, (3) *Karam Kanda Mokha Purana*. *Adi Purana* has been written in excellent *dohas* and *chaupais*. The theme is the Origin of Creation, a theme common to the classical *Puranas*. But here God and Creation are described in a different way:

दोहा—नमो नमो सतपुरुष कूं, नमस्कार गुरू कीन्ह ।
सुर नर मुनि जन सोधवा, सन्तों सरबस दीन्ह ॥

चौपाई—ओंकार बीज उतपत्ती, उपजै ब्रह्मा सत के नाती।
दण्ड कमण्डल ब्रह्मा लाए, जुग छत्तीस कमल भरमाए।।

G.G.S. p. 271.

Ganesh Puran is also written in *chaupais, Sakhis* and *Ramainis.* The theme resembeles that of *Adi Puranas:*

परम शक्ति संगीतं, रिधि सिधि दाता सोई।
अबिगति गुणह् अतीतं, सत्य पुरुष निरमोही।।

G.G.S, p. 300

Karam Kand Mokha Puran is remarkable for its variety of metrical forms. Here the poet follows the tradition of the *Riti Kavya* poetry of *Brajbhasa* and his language is also close to *Brajabhasa.* We find *Ekachari Chhanda* also known as *Shashi Chhanda* and also *Ardha Bhuyang Prayat Chhanda:*

सतगुरम्,
सिसवरम्,
परसरम्,
केसरम्।

G.G.S., p. 306

त्रिशूलमालम्,
अगर खोलम्,
अरस पुष्पम्,
ध्यान धूपम्,

G.G.S., p. 307

9. *Bodha Grantha:* It is another conventional composition which may be called poetic exposition of various themes. The following compositions of this type are attributed to Kabir: *Bhopal Bodha, Garur Bodha, Madad Bodha, Musa Bodha, Santokh Bodha, Sikander Bodha.* Garib Das has written the following compositions of this type: *Bilas Bodha, Sukhsagar Bodha, Vigyan Bihangam Bodha, Hirambar Bodha, Muhammad Bodha, Kafir Bodha. Bilas Bodha* is a criticism of the life of pleasures. Even the pleasures of heaven are deprecated. Pleasures always lead to pain. Examples are given from history and mythology. The poetry of *Bilas Bodha* is quite romantic. The pleasures of *Indraloka* and other godly mansions are described as futile. The rhymes are disorderly. In some places poetry runs like prose poems of today. This

poetry is like the earliest prose which emerged from poetry:

तब इन्द्र आन कर, मारकंडे गुसाईं के चरणों पड़े।
चलो बन्दानवाज, इन्द्रपुरी लीजै।
मारकंडे गुसाई बोले, रे रे इन्द्र तू क्या कहै है,
हमारे इन्द्रपुरी किस काम की है।
हम निहकामी है, हम निरइच्छा हैं॥

G.G.S., p. 385

Vigyan Bihangam Bodha: The subject matter and poetry of *Vigyan Bihangam Bodha* is slightly different, but it resembles that of *Hirambar Bodha.* The whole poetry of these portions is in *Chaupais* and the theme is the Name and Meditation of God:

पाकम पाक है निज नाम, निर्गुण सत्य निरालम्ब राम।
साहब सत्य सुभानं नूर, जल थल है सकलं भरपूर॥

G.G.S., p. 394

Muhammad Bodh and *Kafir Bodh* give Garib Das' views about Islam and *Kafirs* (infidels). Addressing the Qazi, Garib Das says:

काजी कौन कतेब तुम्हारी।
ना तू काजी, ना तू मुल्ला, झूठा है व्योपारी॥

G.G.S., p. 396

A *kafir* according to the Koran is a heretic, an idolator, and a disbeliever in God. During the period of Garib Das, orthodox and fanatic Muslims used this word for Hindus. But Garib Das gives a more ethical definition of *Kafir:*

वे काफिर जो बड़-बड़ बोलैं, काफिर कहो घाट जो तोलैं।
वे काफिर रिण हत्या राखैं, वे काफिर परदारा ताकैं॥

G.G.S., p. 397

He who talks too much, weighs less, does not return his debts and looks on other women with an evil eye is a *kafir.* The poetry of this portion is extremely simple in which every line tries to give a definition of *kafir* which includes all evil minded people, both Hindus and Muslims.

10. *Sukhmani Sampat.* This composition appears to have been inspired by Guru Arjun's *sampat.* The poetry is in *Ghakala*

Chhanda. In poetic form it resembles the *Solhe* of *Adi Grantha.* It has four lines, 63 *matras, visrama* at 16+16+16+15. Sometimes the fourth *visrama* is of 14 *matras:*

हुई चढ़ाई गढ़ पर भाई, जाय मुहल्ला जीता है।
चढ़े उजीर अमीर भिड़नकूं, प्रेम पियाला पीता है।।

G.G.S., p. 332

Punjabi words are predominant in this composition.

Other conventional poems which Garib Das has written are *Satvara, Thithi, Stotras* and *Arjnama.* In all his conventional poetry Garib Das has not strictly followed the principles or the rules of a particular composition. He has used them all as a means to give exposition of his thoughts which differed from the Hindus and Muslims of orthodox type.

Ragas in Garib Das

"Raga has been defined by Matanga as a combination of notes, illustrated by melodic movements (*varna*), which is capable of producing pleasant sensations. The depth, height or compass of a *Raga* thus depends upon the discernment and depth of feeling of the artist and his capacity to select and arrange the notes in a mode that can evoke and hold a mood at its highest pitch."[6] O.C. Ganguly says: "A *Raga* is generally mistranslated as a tune, air or key. It is in fact a peculiar conception, having no other parallel in any other system of music. Literally, a *Raga* is something that colours or tinges the mind with some definite feeling, a wave of passion or emotion. In a special sense a *Raga* is a tonal composition of musical notes (*svaras*) having a sequence, form or structure of peculiar significance."[7]

Garib Das has shown immense interest in the *Ragas.* With the exception of a small portion of his writings, the major portion are strung to the *Ragas.* We find that Garib Das has written his poetry in the following Ragas:

Asavari	Kehra
Todi Hindolni	Kafi
Sarang Bilawal	Binod

6. Goswami: *The Story of Indian Music,* p. 55
7. O.C. Gangoly: *Ragas and Raginis,* p. 1.

Nat Prabhati	Mangal
Hori	Malar
Bajaj	Ramkali
Sindhu	Nehpal
Chaure	Bihagda
Maru	Dip
Bhairav	Mali Gaudi
Jaijaiwanti	
Kalyan	
Gaudi	

Ragas have had an interesting origin. *Malkauns* is said to have originated from the Malwas. It first came to be known as *Malawa Kosi* and is now vulgarised into Malkaus. Similarly *Gujari* has originated from the Gurjari tribe. Says Goswami: "The present *Raga Gujari* owes its origin to Gujjara tribe, originally white Huns, who entered India near about the 5th century. Certain regions, towns and villages also have contributed to embroider the fabric of Indian Music. Thus we find that *Bangala,* a melody referred to by Matanga, is derived from the region of Bengal or an Austro-Negroid tribe of the same name. So was the *Sindhu* contributed by the *Sindhu Desa,* the modern Sindh. *Sorath,* a vulgrisation of *Saurastri,* is a gift of Saurastra. *Gaudi* is derived from *Gauda Desa,* a part of Bengal as it was then known. So also *Purbi,* another of our current *Ragas,* is the shortened form of *Purvika Raga,* emerging from the Eastern region. *Kalyan Raga* must have originated in the city of Kalyani where the Western Chalukya dynasty ruled."[8] O.C. Gangoly, writing about the origin of the *Ragas,* says : "*Bhairava* and *Bhairavi,* (probably associated generally with Bhairava clans) became the medium of singing solemn hymns to Siva. *Kedara* (a name given to Siva), *Sankrabharana* (the ornament of Sankara), are apparently namas given by devout Siva worshippers. *Kanada* came to be associated with the cult of Krishna (*Kanara,* the Hindi-Prakrit form of Krishna). The more significant examples of melody associated with Vaishnava worship is *Natta Narayana* (the Dance of Krishna)."[9]

8. Goswami, *The Story of Indian Music,* p. 56.
9. O.C. Gangoly, *Ragas and Raginis,* p. 72.

"Many *Ragas* of Non-Aryan origin have been sanskritised later on. The Dravidian *vella-ulli* became *Velavali* or *Bilawal.* The Dravidian *Tuddi* became *Todika,* later *Todi. Asavari* and *Dhanasika,* which are meaningless as Sanskrit terms, probably conceal within their modern forms, their original non-Aryan names."[10]

Garib Das has written many *Kafis.* There is a considerable controversy among Punjabi scholars whether *Kafi* is a *chhanda* or a *Raga.* Garib Das' Granth points out clearly that *Kafi* is a *Raga* (or rather a *Ragini*). The title of the hymns on page 653 is *Atha Raga Kafi.*

In the *Adi Grantha, Kafi* is associated as a *Ragini* with other *Ragas* like *Asa* and *Suhi.* The headlines in the *Adi Grantha* indicate that *Kafi* is not a *Chhanda* but is an associated *Ragini.* "*Kafi,* as the word signifies," writes Goswami, "is not a Sanskrit word. All we know is that *Kafi* is a type of composition sung in a particular way by the Sufi poets of Sindh where it is still almost an institution."[11] Dr. S.S. Kohli in his Introduction to *Chonvian Kafian* suggests that *Kafi* is derived from *Kaifi* which means "intoxicating". All compositions about the intoxication of *Nama* are *Kafis.*

But as we have already stated, Garib Das pointedly calls it a Ragini. Earlier saints, mostly Sufis who were associated with the literature and thought of Sindh had written *Kafis.* By the time of Garib Das, *Kafis* had become very popular all over north India. Garib Das' *Kafis* have close resemblance with the *Kafis* of Punjab's Sufi poets.

Many poets accepted one particular system of *Ragas* indicated, by the *Ragmala* of their choice. Of the principal schools of *Ragas,* three are well known, those of Hanuman, Siva and Bharata. Garib Das does not appear to be particularly attached to any school. He has made a free and wide choice of *Ragas* from various schools. Whether these songs can be sung in these *Ragas* is a point which has not been verified by anyone.

There is also no indication in Garib Das' Granth as to the relation of the *Ragas* and *Raginis.* Garib Das has not commented

10. *Ibid,* p. 75.
11. Goswami, *The Story of Indian Music,* p. 79.

on any *Ragas* as the Gurus have done in the *Adi Grantha.* But it has to be admitted that the poetry of Garib Das is very musical. The lyrical strain of the songs dominates. Every poem, even when it is not classified under a *Raga,* is written with the main object of being sung in *Kirtan.* Great importance is given to *Hari Kirtan,* which is considered a means of salvation. Singing the glory of God as a means to attaining salvation is considered the highest Bhakti in the Nirgun Bhakti Movement.

Imagery and Pictorial Qualities

Like all poets of high order the imagery and idea-pictures drawn by Garib Das are remarkable: "What difference is there between a Pandit and a Pariah. Both of them are like outwardly different vessels of water in which the same moon is shining." He describes the *mulla* going up the minaret and giving the call to prayer, and points out that the real mosque is within the mind.[12]

His flights of imagination and depth of thought are wonderful. He describes the spiritual experience through the imagery of a heavenly brewery from which flows the wine of wisdom extracted from the flower of meditation and carried in *surahi* (pitcher) of the mind:

रस मौले के महल में, गगन झरोखा जोर ।
पीवे सूरे सन्तजन, कूर चले मुख मोड़ ।।
इस मौले के महल में, मण्डल अरस झरन्त ।
जहां कलाली हाट है, चोखा फूल चवन्त ।।
फूल चवें चिन्तामणी, कलस बिना इक कुम्भ ।
सुरति सुराही फिरत है, देख्या अती अचम्भ ।।

G.G.S., p. 29

The tendency of Garib Das is to describe the innery mystery of life in terms of outer objects and experiences. His images are homely, rural and those found in everyday life of the village community.

12. को पंडित किस को कहो चूहडा, एकै बोलनहारा ।
ज्यों मटकी मैं झिलकै चंदा, है मांही पर न्यारा ।।

G.G.S., p. 653

मस्तक जान मसीत प्यारे, जा चढ़ मुल्ला बांग पुकारे ।

G.G.S., p. 463

Nature in Garib Das' Poetry

All medieval saints of India were great lovers of Nature. In Nature and even in the commonest of creatures, they saw the light of God. They valued not only the life of human beings but also of the most insignificant animals. To them even a blade of grass was living and alive with the presence of God:

ऐसा तत्व विसार्या भाई, जरे मरे तिस काल न खाई।
कादर है कुदरत के मांही, रब्ब रूह कुछ परदा नांही ।।
कादर कुदरत मे बसै, कुदरत कादर मांहि ।
गरीबदास पाषाण जल, नाहक पूजन जांहि ।।

G.G.S., p. 454

The Creator lives in Nature, and Nature is a living part of the Creator. Instead of worshiping stones in the form of idols, or water in the form of *tirathas,* it is, according to Garib Das, better to worship God in Nature and Nature in God.

Nature is described even in a romantic and poetic way as inspirer of nobler feelings. Garib Das identifies his feelings with the rain-loaded clouds and his soul begins to pant like the *papiha* thirsting for the rain clouds:

आया सावन महमंता, जहां गरजि गरजि बरसन्ता।
जहां दामनि खिमै अनन्ता, जहां गरजत हैं घनघोरा।
सुनि करत पपीहा शोरा, जहां बोले दादुर मोरा ।।

G.G.S. p. 539

Holi is described in all its colourful beauty in an enchanting manner. One feels *Holi* being played in a very realistic manner, though according to Garib Das the participants in his spiritual *Holi* are Farid, Kabir, Bajid, Dhanna, Sadana, Namadeva and Ravidas:

उड़त गुलाल बिसाल बिसम्भर, रिमझिम रिमझिम रंग ।
अगर अबीर कबीर खवासा, जम जौरा जित जंग ।।
सुन्न बेधई सबद सनेही, अवगति गति कुरबान ।
केसर की पिचकारी छूटै, शिव ब्रह्मा खेलै है आन ।।

G.G.S., p. 639

Garib Das has great feeling and compassion for animals. He feels that their life is as precious as that of human beings. All birds and animals should be treated as creatures of God who have every right to live and enjoy their lives. He mentions various animals and birds like, hen, goat, sparrow, partridge, cow, swine:

मुरगी, बकरी, चिड़ी, बटेरी, सूर, गऊ में एकै सेरी ।
रूम रूम में देवस्थाना, दूध दही और घिरत समाना ।।

G.G.S., p. 451

लवा बटेर तीतर हतैं हेर कै, खा गए भून कर मुरग चिड़िया ।
पकड़ हिलावन ततबीर टीके किए, अजौं नर भिसत के भरम पड़िया ।।

G.G.S. p. 426

For Garib Das, all animals and birds carry within them the precious life of God. Every part of their body is a *devasthana* to him. Kindness to animals is compassion for life and humanity. It was on the basis of this compassion that he remained a strict vegetarian.

Rasas in Garib Das' Poetry

Rasa is described by Dr. Ananda Coomarswamy as "aesthetic emotion". What is the essential element in poetry, asks Coomarswamy. He himself answers: "According to some authors this consists in style or figures or in suggestion. But the greater writers refute these views and are agreed that the one essential element in poetry is what they term *rasa* or flavour. With this term, which is equivalent of beauty or aesthetic emotion in the stricter sense of the philosopher, must be considered the derivative adjective *rasavanta*, having *rasa,* and the derivative substantive *rasika,* one who enjoys *rasa,* a connoisseur or lover."

Here are a few examples of the various *rasas* depicted by Garib Das in his poetry:

Srinagara Rasa (the Erotic):

नैनों काजर बाहि कर, खाय लिए हैं हंस ।
हाथों मेहंदी लाय कर, डोब दिए कुल बंस ।।
उलटी मांग भराय कर, मञ्जन करिहै गात ।
मीठी बोले मगन हो, लावै बोह बिध घात ।।

G.G.S., p. 104

Vibhatsa Rasa (the Terrible):

रुद्र भरे जहां कुण्ड हैं, कुम्भी जिन का नाम।
द्वारा है मुख लोध का, बड़ा भयंकर धाम ।।
सौ सौ योजन कुण्ड हैं, गीध गती बहू भीड़ ।
कोटों जीव उजाड़िए, कहीं न आया थीर ।।

G.G.S., p. 267

Adbhuta Rasa (the Wonderful):

बंगला अजब बण्या है खूब, जहां पारब्रह्म महबूब ।
आगै नौलख पातर नाचै, ब्रह्मानन्द रिझावै ।
तेजपुंज की सुन्दर नारी, अनहद मंगल गावै ।।

R.S., p. 318

Shanta Rasa (the Peaceful):

ऐसा सतगुरु हम मिल्या, सिन्ध सुरति की सैन ।
उर अन्तर परकासिया, अजब सुनाए बैन ।।
ऐसा सतगुरु हम मिल्या, बेपरवाह अबन्ध ।
परमहंस पूरण पुरुष, रोम रोम रविचंद ।।

R.S., p. 2-3

Karuna Rasa (the Pathetic):

ज्यूं कुन्जी कुरलात है, अण्डे पावै पोख ।
ऐसे बिरहण ध्यान धर, इस बिरहा के लोक ।।
मैं जोगण जग ढूंढिया, नौखण्ड रामत कीन्ह ।
दरस बिना दुख बहुत है, जैंसे जल बिन मीन ।।

G.G.S., p. 12

Satire and Irony

The following are outstanding examples of the use of satire and irony in Garib Das' poetry:

काजी मुल्ला चोर हैं, सरह सरीत जवाब ।
जुगन जुगन छूटैं नहीं, खाए जिन्हे कबाब ।।
काजी तसबी पहर कै, गुसल किया कै बार ।
अन्दरून साबत नहीं, दरगह पड़सी मार ।।
मुल्ला मूरत रब्ब दी, गल काटत नहीं शंक ।
छुरा देर औजूद मैं, भनसी तोड़ी अंख ।।

G.G.S., p. 91

चंडी लंडी बकरे खाणी, ज्वालामुखी जुहारम् ।
कर ततबीर करद गल काटै, बूड़े भवजल धारम् ।।
गीतापाठ पूराणम् ध्यानम्, घड़ी महूरत साधी ।
जो तिथ बार लगन सब लिखते, जमपुर गुरजा खाधी ।।

G.G.S., p. 507

चग मलीदे खाय कर, मनवा भया है डाग वे ।
ऊपर ऊपर हंस बाना, मध्य कव्वा काग वे ।।
गूदड़ लगाई अजब चींधी, अरन बरन बिरंग वे ।
फिरै बनखंड भेड़िया ज्यूं, नहीं सतगुरू संग वे ।।
भगे बिनंगे फिरत हैं, कच कोल कोरा काढ वे ।
भांग पोसत गरक गोसत, नांहि दीखें हाड़ वे ।।
खाखी खता में पड़त है, भसमी लगाए भसम वे ।
भूले फिरैं जग भाण्ड हैं, दर नांहि जोड़े चसम वे ।।
मुदरा बिलोरी कान में, मसतक सिंदूरी तिलक वे ।
पाडे जंगल के रोज हैं, जो नांहि चीन्हया अलख वे ।।
मोटा मुतंगा बांध कर, कीन्हीं बजर कोपीन वे ।
मनवा बाहर भाग्या फिरै, टुक भेख लहजा लीन वे ।।

G.G.S., p. 458

Alamkaras in Garib Das' poetry

The following alankaras are found in Garib Das's poetry:

1. *Sabdalamkara*

अलख आप अलह साहिब, कुरस कुञ्ज जहूर वे ।
कुलफ कुञ्जी खोल खालक, दम्म में दीदार वे ।।

R.S., p. 263-64

2. *Gharoli Alamkara*

गुण कलील जाणै नहीं, चीचड मुख नहीं दूध ।
लख चौरासी यों बधी, सुर का बेला सूध ।।
रुधर पिवत निसबासरम्, नहीं दूध की धार ।
अरस कुरस नहीं जात हैं, खीर समन्दर न्यार ।।

G.G.S., p. 84

3. *Drishtanta Alamkara*

ज्यूं बादल जल नीर है, दीखे नहीं अदेख
काया मध कुरबान है, अबहड़ आदि अलेख ॥
घिरत दूध में रम रह्या, यों अबहड़ तन बीच ।
घट घट पूरण ब्रह्म है, क्या उत्तम क्या नीच ॥

G.G.S., p. 126

4. *Slesha Alamkara*

अथाह अलील, अजून अमून अजीत ।
अपार अधार, उचार विचार सुजीत ॥

G.G.S., p. 339

Thus the poetry of Garib Das has achieved artistic excellence of all types. It is full of *alamkaras* and is a distinct contribution to the language and literature of our country.

CHAPTER IX

Conclusion

The poetry of Garib Das, as our study shows, occupies a fairly prominent place in the history of medieval literature and is no doubt an outstanding contribution to the eighteenth century religious literature of the Punjab and Hariyana. It has enriched both Punjabi and Western Hindi literature.

The first and most important contribution of Garib Das to Indian thought is his universalism. Like his predecessors he thinks of mankind not as Hindus or Muslims, *Kafirs* or *Mlecchas,* but as a human brotherhood. There is one and the same God everywhere and he judges the sins and virtues of all men and women impartially. No creed has exclusive access to God and no prophet is final or the only one to realize God. The divisions of race, nationality and caste are artificial divisions made by society, and it is the duty of all truth-loving saints to remove these differences. Although creeds divide man from man, the love of God and the love of virtues unites all men.

In the eighteenth century, when terrible conflicts were going on between Mughals and Pathans, between Hindus and Muslims and between Sikhs and Muslims and Maharathas and Muslims in the political field and between Yogis, Sanyasis, Jains, Buddhists, Shaivas and Vaishnavas, Sunnis and Shias in the religious sphere, Garib Das was a great integrating influence, though the sphere of his influence was limited. The Saint did not lose heart in his mission although the religious, cultural and political conflicts around him were violent. He fearlessly asserted his stand on the fatherhood of God and the brotherhood of men. He strongly condemned hatred, bitterness and pride on religious grounds. An inspired saint-poet, he continued to exert his moral and spiritual influence on society as a whole. He restlessly preached unity and cultural understanding between the divergent creeds like Hinduism and Islam and unity and equality between the rich and the poor, the high and the low.

The thoughts of Garib Das, like those of Kabir, can be called a healthy synthesis of the progressive elements of Hinduism and Islam. After making a deep study of both, they criticised unhealthy elements in Hinduism and Islam and tried to find a common meeting ground for both. Thus they found ready followers among both Hindus and Muslims. The orthodox sections of both Islam and Hinduism resented this new approach but these great saints disregarded their orthodoxy and gave progressive inspiration to Indian thought and religion.

Although Garib Das had a distinct philosophy of life, he did not write any philosophical treatise. His approach to the problems of life was that of a mystic poet who gives spiritual but practical solutions of the moral degradation that had over-taken society. His effort was to show a practical way for the attainment of the highest spiritual state.

We find that Garib Das is a very clear and independent thinker. He accepted the best that was in his predecessors, and although he impresses us with his spiritual debt to Kabir, he differed almost as much from Kabir as Kabir differed from Ramanand. Although like Kabir he rejected the authority of *Vedas* and *Kutabs,* he accepted Hindu traditions and cultural influences much more than Kabir ever did. While the influence of Kabir spread beyond his provincial sphere to the Hindus and Muslims and later on to Sikhs, Garib Das' influence was mainly confined to a group of disciples in Hariyana and Punjab. Kabir's influence was accepted by Muslims as well as Hindus but Garib Das exercised practically no influence on Muslim society of his days except a few individuals.

Like all medieval mystics Garib Das was a cosmopolitan. He stood for what has been described by Prof. R.D. Ranade and Prof. W.B. Patwardhan as the spiritual democracy of the Bhakti School. "The gates of Bhakti school were ever open. Whoever entered was hailed as a brother, nay more, was honoured as a saint. He was addressed as a *Santa*. The very atmosphere was sacred and holy. The breath of heaven played freely, and all were equal there. Love, true, genuine, pure love, admits not of high and low, rich and poor; all are one and equal. All separatist tendencies vanished; the haughty isolation of pride, of heredity, of tradition melted away, and all men, women, weak, frail, lame and blind were calling on the same strength, seeking the same line, hoping the same hope, dreaming the same dream, and seeing the same vision."[1]

Garib Das points out that God can be realised in any walk of life. The tailor, the barber, the maid servant, the gardener, the sweeper, the potter, the goldsmith, even the prostitute could realize God in their different stations of life. It was not at all necessary to renounce the householder's life and go to the forests in search of God. In the poetry of Garib Das we find a unique reconciliation of worldly and spiritual life.

A signal contribution of Garib Das is his enrichment of the Punjabi as well as Western Hindi languages. He spent all his life near Delhi where Punjabi and Western Hindi meet. He enriched each of these languages separately and brought them close to each other in a healthy synthesis of simple *Sant Bhakha*. The partisans of Sanskrit were still very powerful and the contempt for the saimple language of the people was still rampant. But saints like Garib Das never wrote for name and fame among the learned Pundits. They wrote for diffusion of light among the common people and even among women and the *Sudras*. The yscorned the scorn of the learned and championed the voiceless millions. They had to fight for upholding the language and literature of the people and this fight was continued into our own times. The view of the learned during these days was that Punjabi and Hindi were the languages of the illiterate and the vulgar. Those versed in Sanskrit had nothing to do with it. Garib Das like other mystic saints of the sixteenth, seventeenth and eighteenth centuries fought against these tendencies and championed the language of the people. Garib Das strongly held the view that the word of God is holy in each and every language.

Following closely the literary traditions of Kabir, Dadu and Nanak, Garib Das has contributed much more in bulk than any Punjabi or Hindi poet of his times. His linguistic and literary importance has been neglected because he belonged to a region the thought and literature of which has unfortunately been neglected by Punjabi and Hindi literary critics. Another reason for this was that uptil recently the writings of Garib Das were not easily

1. R.D. Ranade, *Indian Mysticism*, p. 209.

available either in Hindi or in Punjabi. Only a small circle of Garib Dasis kept the printed volumes strictly to themselves. They still do not show the manuscript copies of the writings of Garib Das and the errors of copyists and printers cannot be easily eradicated.

The question that now arises is: Why did not the mission and writings of Garib Das become popular? The reasons are many. Firstly, in the struggle between orthodox and liberal forces, the orthodox forces were ultimately victorious. The mission of Namadeva, Ravidas, Kabir and Ramanand weakened so much that they have left now only a handful of followers. Research scholars have only recently started taking linguistic interest in the writings of medieval saints. Sufi literature is studied with great interest but Sufism is waning. Similarly Kabirism and Namadevism have practically subsided. Garib Das' popularity has suffered the same fate. Garib Panthis have built a narrow sectarian superstructure about the Panth and its present form and features are such that very few people can accept it. There is lack of inspired men in the Panth and they have failed to move forward with the times. Garib Das' ideas were so liberal that they could be adjusted to the social needs of all times. But the active link with society is lost as the work of propagation of this faith is undertaken mostly by anchorites.

Linguistic and literary studies of the writings of Garib Das are bound to have a regenerating influence on the future if they are properly presented to the younger generation. The study of the writings of Garib Das should be taken up as seriously as those of Kabir and Nanak. Their linguistic and cultural importance is very great. It is what may be termed the representative poetry of the Hariyana region in which Punjabi, Braj, Persian or Khadi Boli have mingled together into a truly national language.

Garib Das is a revivalist of the Kabirpanth. Like Dadu he did it in his own way. He was proud of being called upon to carry the message of Kabir. The writings of Garib Das should be considered an important phase in the evolution and development of Kabirpanth. The sectarian followers of Garib Das have narrowed the scope of the ideas of Garib Das. Their methods of propagation and preaching have limited the knowledge of his writings to a few of his devotees, mostly Hindus. With the creation of Hariyana as an independent State, it is earnestly hoped that the study of the writings of Garib Das will be taken up seriously as he is the most outstanding national poet of Hariyana.

BIBLIOGRAPHY

Ajra Nand Garib Dasi, Granth Sahib Arthat Bani Sri Garib Das Ji, Printed in Arya Sudharak Press, Baroda in 1924.

A.C. Woolner, Introduction to Parakrit.

Adi Grantha.

Ananda Coomaraswamy, The Dance of Shiva.

Aldous Huxley, The Perennial Philosophy.

Ardha Magadhi Dictionary.

A.C. Bouquet, Comparative Religion : Hinduism.

Annie Besant, 1. The Wisdom of Upanishads,
2. An Introduction to Yoga.

Babu Ram Saxena, Samanya Bhasha Vigyan (H).

Bhagat Ram, Garib Acharya Ji Maharaj Ka Jiwan Charitra.

Bhai Randhir Singh, 1. Gurmat Karam Philosophy,
2. Anhad Sabad.

Bhai Mani Singh, Sikhan Ki Bhaktmal.

Bhai Sher Singh, Atam Darshan.

Bhadur Mal, A Study of Indian culture.

Bhaktmal (Nabha Das)

Banarsi Das Jain, Phonology of Panjab.

Cultural Heritage of India, Vols. III, IV, V, VI.

Chetan Das, Granth Sahib Arthat Sri Garib Das Ji Ki Bani. (Second Edition)

C. Dey Lewis, Poetic Image.

Charan Singh, Gurmat Sangeet Nirnaya.

C. Rajagopalacharya, Bhagavad Gita & Upanishads for the Lay Reader.

Duncan Greenless, The Gospel of Guru Granth Sahib.

Dhirendra Verma, Braja Bhasha.

Dharmendra Brahmachari Shastri, Sant Kavi Darya.

Encyclopaedia of Religion and Ethics.

Evelyn Underhill, Introduction to One Hundred Poems of Kabir.

F.E. Keay. Kabir and His Followers.

G.A. Natesan, Namadeva.

Ganesha Singh, Bharat Mat Darpan.

Gokal Chand Narang, 1. Transformation of Sikhism,
2. Real Hinduism.

Goswami, The Story of Indian Music.
Graham Bailey, Panjabi Grammar.
G.V. Tagara, Historical Grammar of Apabhramsa.
Grierson, Bharat ka Bhasha Sarvekshana, Vol. I. (Hindi).
Grierson, Linguistic Survey of India, Volume IX.
G.B. Singh, Gurmukhi Lipi da Janam te Vikas.
Gopal Singh Dardi, Panjabi Sahit da Itihas.
Hazara Singh, Gyan Marag.
Hindi Panjabi Kosh, Language Department, Patiala.
Hindi Sabda Sagar, Nagari Pracharini Sabha, Kashi.
Hazari Parshad Dvivedi, 1. Kabir, 2. Nath Sampradaya.
Hem Chand Suri, Prakrit Grammar.
H. Barekar, Kabir and the Kabir Panth.
Hardyal, Hints for Self-culture.
Jodh Singh, Gurmat Nirnaya.
John Dawson, A Classical Dictionary of Hindu Mythology and Religion.
J.C. Chatterji, Kashmir Shaivism, Part 1.
J.N. Farquhar, 1. An Outline of the Religious Literature of India. 2. Modern Religious Movements in India.
J.N. Sarkar, The Religious Quest of India.
J.E. Carpenter, Comparative Religion.
Kaka Ram, Apabhramsa Grammar.
Kahan Singh, 1. Mahan Kosh, 2. Gurchand Divakar, 3. Gur Shabad Alankar.
Kartar Singh, Life of Guru Gobind Singh.
Kapaldev Singh, Brij Bhasha Banam Khari Boli.
Khazan Singh, History of Sikh Philosophy.
Khushwant Singh, History of the Sikhs, Vol. I.
Kshiti Mohan Sen. Medieval Mysticism of India.
Max Muller, Six Systems of Indian Philosophy.
M.A. Macauliffe, The Sikh Religion, 6 Vols.
Madhvacharya, Paryanirnaya.
Mahmood Sharani, Panjab Me Urdu.
Mangal Das, Garib Das Ji Ki Bani.
Mohan Singh, 1. Gorakh Nath & Medieval Hindu Mysticism, 2. Kabir : His Biography, 3. An Introduction to Panjabi, 4. History of Panjabi Literature, 5. Kabir and the Bhakti Movement.

Mckenzie, Hindu Ethics.
M.P. Pandit, Sadhana in Sri Aurobindo's Yoga.
Naryanananda, The Gist of Religions.
Nicol Macnicol, The Living Religions of the Indian People.
O.C. Gangoly, Ragas and Raginis.
Paras Ram Chaturvedi, Uttari Bharat ki Sant Parampara.
Pitambar Dutt Barthwal, The Nigrun School of Hindi Poetry.
Paul David Devanandan, The Concept of Maya.
Prabhakar Machwe, Nirgun Sant Kavya
Prem Narain Tandon, Sur ki Bhasha.
Prem Parkash Singh, Panjabi Boli da Nikas Te Vikas.
P. Kielhorn, A Grammar of Sanskrit Language.
Partap Singh, Gurmat Philosophy.
Ram Chandra Shukla, Hindi Sahitya ka Itihas.
Ram Kumar Verma, Hindi Sahitya ka Alochanatmak Itihas.
Ram Naresh Tripathi, Khari Boli ka Sankshep Parichaya.
R.G. Bhandarkar, Vaishnavism, Saivaism & Minor Religious Systems.
Rabindra Nath Tagore, Poems of Kabir.
Reynolds A. Nicholson, Rumi, Poet and Mystic.
R.C. Majumadar and others, The Advanced History of India.
Robert Hume, Treasure House of Living Religions.
R. Flint, Theism.
Siddha Nath Tiwari, Nirgun Kavya Darshan.
Sher Singh, 1. Philosophy of Sikhism, 2. Gurmat Darshan.
Shyam Sundar Das, Kabir Granthavali.
S.S. Kohli, 1. A Critical Study of Adi Granth, 2. Panjabi Sahit da Itihas, 3. Chonvian Kafian (Manuscript), 4. Outlines of Sikh Thought, 5. Panjabi Sahit, Vastu te Vichar.
S.N. Dasgupta, 1. Hindu Mysticism, 2. Yoga as Philosophy and Religion.
S.N. Kellogg, A Grammar of Hindi Language.
Suniti Kumar Chaterji, Indo-Aryan and Hindi.
Sikh Review.
Sandilya Sutra.
Shri Ram Sharma, The Crescent in India.
Shabadarath Sharomani.
Sukhasagar.
Shankar Lal Yadav, Hariyana Pradesh ka Lok Sahitya.

Sri Aurobindo, The Future of Poetry.
Sircar, Grammar of Prakrit Language.
Shivprasad Aggarwal, Bhasha Vigyan aur Hindi.
Sham Singh Dara, The Teachings of Nanak.
Swami Satyananda, Lives of Saints.
Syed Muhammad Latif, A History of the Panjab.
S. Radhakrishnan, Indian Philosophy.
Tara Chand, Influence of Islam on Indian Culture.
Tara Singh Nirotam, Gurmat Nirnai Sagar.
Trilochan Singh, 1. Bhakti and Gurmat, 2. A Brief Life Sketch of Guru Gobind Singh.
Teja Singh and Ganda Singh, History of the Sikhs.
Trilochan Singh, Sacred Writings of the Sikhs.
T.L. Vasvani, A Prophet of the People.
V.B. Arun, A Comparature Phonology of Hindi and Panjabi.
Vivekananda, Complete Works, Vol. III.
Viveka Cudmani.
W.S. Deming, Ramdas and Ramdasis.
W. Crook, Religion and Folklore in Northern India.
Westcott, Kabir and Kabir Panth.

INDEX